Michael W. Apple

The Micro-Politics of the School

The Micro-Politics of the School

Towards a theory of school organization

STEPHEN J. BALL

Methuen   London and New York

For Trinidad

First published in 1987 by
Methuen & Co. Ltd
11 New Fetter Lane, London EC4P 4EE

Published in the USA by
Methuen & Co.
in association with Methuen, Inc.
29 West 35th Street, New York NY 10001

Printed in Great Britain

British Library Cataloguing in Publication Data
  Ball, Stephen, 1950–
  The micro-politics of the school: towards
  a theory of school organization.
  1. High schools—Administration
  I. Title
  373.12   LB2822

ISBN 0–416–00102–5
ISBN 0–416–00112–2 Pbk

Library of Congress Cataloging in Publication Data
  Ball, Stephen J.
  The micro-politics of the school.
  Bibliography: p. 284
  Includes index.
  1. School management and organization—Great Britain.
  2. Organizational behavior.
  3. Teacher–principal relationships.
  I. Title.
  LB2901.B274   1987   371.2'00941   86–25008

ISBN 0–416–00102–5
ISBN 0–416–00112–2 (pbk.)

Contents

Acknowledgements   vii

Introduction   viii

1   Orthodoxy and alternative   1
2   The politics of change: some case studies   28
3   Age and gender: rancorous change   60
4   The politics of leadership   80
5   Headship: opposition and control   120
6   Doing headship: leadership succession and
    the dilemmas of headship   149
7   The politics of career   166
8   Women's careers and the politics of gender   191
9   Resources and relationships   212
10 Inside/out: the school in political context   247

Notes   281

Appendix   282

Bibliography   284

Index   299

Acknowledgements

A large number of people have helped and supported me in different ways in the research for and writing of this book. Margaret Ralph, Alison Reeves, Janet Rider and Trinidad Ball transcribed tapes and typed drafts and disks. John Evans, Tony Knight, Ivor Goodson, Brian Davies, Carole Kay, Martyn Hammersley, John Scarth, Tony Becher, Stephen Walker, John Burke, Hilary Radnor, Colin Nash, Martin Skelton, Mike Davies, George Riseborough, Carole Dyhouse, Sandra Acker, Phil Frier and Sara Delamont read and criticized draft chapters and provided me with numerous bright ideas – not all of which I was wise enough to take advantage of. Bob Burgess persevered through the whole manuscript in draft and offered invaluable advice. However, without the material help and loving support of Trinidad, my wife, the project would never have been completed.

I would also want to thank all the teachers who gave their time to allow me to interview them and my MA students at Sussex and King's, who kept me close to the reality of the school through their discussion and written work. The Education Area, University of Sussex, provided a small grant to support part of the fieldwork, for which I am grateful.

Introduction

Probably my most important task in introducing this book is to make clear what it is not rather than what it is. It is not a case study report of a single school, nor is the analysis based upon data from a single research project. It is not intended to be an exhaustive or definitive account of school organization. None of the issues raised or concepts put forward is closed or complete. Furthermore, I have not attempted any kind of systematic refutation of existing theories: my criticisms are asserted rather than demonstrated. The analysis is put forward as an alternative, drawing on what seems useful from previous work, but coherent in its own terms. Above all, the book is a starting point, a first attempt, rather than a free standing, fully finished study. I have tended to be exhaustive and inclusive rather than overly-precise and exclusive: a wide range of diverse issues is covered.

The theory of school organization offered here is data-led: it is grounded in research materials; it is inductive. The categories and concepts employed emerged from the scanning and analysis of data. They were tested, elaborated and developed by further collection and interrogation of data. That is to say, analytical insights and interpretative hunches were ploughed back into and used to organize and direct the continuing process of data collection and literature search.

There are two primary types of data and they served different purposes in the development of the analysis. First, a variety of case studies are referred to and employed in the text. These draw upon my own work (on Beachside Comprehensive in 1981 and Casterbridge High in 1984 and 1985) or published research – for example, Riseborough (1981) on Phoenix Comprehensive, Richardson (1973b) on Nailsea Comprehensive, Woods (1979) on Lowfield Secondary Modern – or research done by my graduate students at Sussex University and King's College (e.g. Hanna, 1978; Price, 1979; Meadows, 1981). These case studies illustrate particular issues in some depth, in a particular context; for example, falling rolls, the effects of the arrival of a new headteacher or the impact of amalgamation (see Appendix). Second, interview data are deployed. These interviews were conducted by me over a period of three years in a variety of different types of schools, in different parts of the country (sixty-five interviews in all; ten headteachers were interviewed, several on more than one occasion). The sample was an opportunistic one and I made use of existing contacts to draw on people who would be willing to discuss the micro-politics of their institution. In a number of cases it was possible to cluster interviews in one school. On most occasions the intention was to get respondents to reflect generally upon the micro-politics of their school – the headteacher's style: the key, influential actors; how decisions were made; who tended to support and oppose the headteacher; the conduct of meetings; the distribution of resources; how promotions were made; and so on – and I asked for examples of micro-political activity. Thus I attempted to tap the respondents' 'folk knowledge' of their school and obtain first-order insights into the workings and effects of micro-political processes in schools, and also to obtain second-order commentary by encouraging teachers to offer their own analyses of the political structures and processes in which they were involved. These data are presented in the text primarily for purposes of illustration rather than proof. In a preliminary analysis of this kind I can make no grandiose claims for the representativeness or exhaustiveness of the data.

This approach, combining different sorts and sources of data, and data from different schools (and, on occasion, different school systems) is an unusual one, but it is based on an attempt to achieve both depth (through the case studies) and breadth (through the interviewing). Throughout, the aim was to identify common themes, issues and categories and to find or develop concepts which could encompass and begin to explain these. In the first chapter some of the most fundamental of these concepts – conflict, goal diversity, ideology, power, participation and control – are adumbrated. But it is important to be clear: these concepts were not starting points in the study, *they arose as significant in the process of data analysis*. The inevitable result of this process of induction is an unevenness in both coverage and elaboration; on occasion my discussion outruns or over-interprets a limited data base, but the issues and patterns evident in the data dictated the structure and the course of the analysis. Even so, the interrelationship of issues meant that some arbitrary divisions had to be imposed; some areas of discussion are clearly relevant at more than one point in the text. Some readers may prefer to begin the book at Chapter 2 and return to Chapter 1 after having digested the substantive material.

I experimented with several methods of coding the data presented in the text so as to give greater detail about the particular schools referred to, but eventually I decided against using any coding system. (The essence of the analysis suggest that school characteristics like size, catchment and structure are secondary to the micro-political factors identified (the head's style, patterns of influence, group coalitions, etc.) – not irrelevant but secondary. The complications arising from the inclusion of those details seemed unnecessary, but I recognize that some readers will see their omission as a flaw (see Appendix). It will become obvious that the study is *secondary biased*: data from primary schools is included, but the framework of the analysis is drawn from secondary-school material. Also the majority of the material is English and Welsh, but some American and Australian data are cited.

It is also worth pointing out that much more data (first- and second-hand) was collected and analysed than it was possible to include. Furthermore, there were several issues which emerged from the consideration of data which could not be integrated into the analysis (e.g. the deputy-head role and intradepartmental relationships).

Finally, all of the chapters in the study have been exposed to comment and criticism by a number of the respondents who are reported directly or indirectly in the text. They were asked to examine both the use made of their contribution and to comment on the analysis in which their contribution had played a part. Even so, I would want to reiterate the exploratory nature of this analysis. Many of the areas of discussion, concepts and ideas presented need further careful development and research. Some have been superficially glossed over. In one sense the material presented here is intended as an agenda for further research. Some of the areas that I have begun to explore have been virtually untouched by previous studies of schools. They concern, in some respects, as Hoyle points out, 'an organisational underworld' (1982, p. 87), which it is difficult to gain access to. Issues are touched upon which many teachers would prefer to deny or ignore, quite understandably. Hoyle also suggests that 'There may be good reason for the academic neglect of micro-politics. It is perhaps considered slightly unrespectable, or too self-indulgent' (p. 88). Yet to deny the relevance of micro-politics is in effect to condemn organizational research to be for ever ineffectual and out of step with the immediate realities of life in organizations.

Note

In some of the data quoted in the text and in some of the quotations from published material the male generic is used to refer to teachers. I would want to disassociate myself from such usage.

1
Orthodoxy and alternative

Over the last twenty years there has been a massive growth in writing and research in British sociology of education. In a whole variety of substantive areas considerable advance has been achieved in our understanding – theoretical and empirical – of educational processes. However, the sociology of school organization is one area where little or no progress has been made. Theories and concepts have changed and developed very little since the 1960s. Neither organizational theorists nor educational researchers have had much of use or import to contribute.

It is my contention that organizational analyses – I include both work in the organizational theory and the 'sociology of organizations' traditions (Albrow, 1973; King, 1984) – have had little of any significance to tell us about the way in which schools are actually run on a day-to-day basis. Indeed, a great deal of the writing in this field has actually tended to bypass and obscure the realities of organizational life in schools. To a great extent organizational theorists have remained locked, explicitly or implicitly, within the stultifying parameters of systems theory and have tended to neglect description in favour of prescription or to move uncertainly between the two. They prefer the abstract tidiness of conceptual debate to the concrete messiness of empirical research inside schools. Sociologists of education, using case studies of schools, have tended to concentrate their attention, with some success, on what might be called the technical aspects of schooling – grouping practices, pastoral care, the curriculum – or have focused on conflict between pupils and teachers in the classroom (Hargreaves, 1967; Lacey, 1970; Sharp and Green, 1975; Edwards and Furlong, 1976; King, 1978; Woods, 1979; Ball, 1981a; Turner, 1983; Burgess, 1983; Delamont, 1983; Evans, 1985; Griffin, 1985). Although a number of these writers, Woods and Burgess in particular, provide some very useful and insightful sidelights on school organization (Burgess on the role of headteachers, Woods on staffrooms), as Davies puts it:

> in such work we find the stultifying pressure of the focus of educational research upon variation in pupil achievement insufficiently embedded in a multi-level organizational and administrative framework. This has left us with attention at the organizational level by default and the door wide open for system and 'ought' theorists of every hue. (1981, p. 54)

Furthermore, sociologists of education in Britain interested in school processes, teachers' work or curriculum innovation have seemed reluctant to take account of the work done by sociologists of organization in other substantive fields. The work of Salaman, Clegg and Dunkerley and Silverman have had little impact on research on schools.

King is one of the few commentators who seems satisfied with the current state of affairs. He believes that 'we now have a body of theoretical and research studies, covering substantive matters as grouping practices, the distribution of authority and school size, which are the makings of a decent sociology of school organizations' (1984, p. 61). However, his view of school organization is almost exclusively pupil-centred and also theoretically parsimonious (e.g. the unreflexive use of the concept of 'authority'). He can offer little insight into teachers' experience of work in schools, and almost nothing in the way of relevant conceptual development.

In this book I shall be concentrating wholly upon organizational aspects of the school. What is meant by 'organizational' in this context is grounded in the empirical chapters which follow, but my major focus is upon the *control* of work and the determination of policy. My definition of an organization follows Barr-Greenfield (1975). Like him I reject the notion of 'a single abstraction called organization' but begin rather with 'the varied perceptions by individuals of what they can, should, or must do in dealing with others within the circumstances in which they find themselves' (Barr-Greenfield, 1975, p. 65). I intend to provide a set of analyses based closely upon the experiences of teachers as they are involved in the day-to-day running of schools. I shall offer some exploratory but I hope pertinent insights into the ways that schools are managed, changed, organized and defended that will both articulate the views and perspectives of teachers and contribute to the development of a coherent theory for describing and explaining schools as organizations. I believe this to be an important and worthwhile exercise, not simply as an end in itself or as a necessary tidying up of some loose ends in the sociology of education. An understanding of the way that schools change (or stay the same) and therefore of the practical limits and possibilities of educational development, must take account of intra-organizational processes. This is particularly crucial in examining developments which are related to the achievement of more equal, more just, as well as more effective education.

The sociological analysis of educational change in recent years has, for the most part, been focused either on the all-embracing effects and implications of structural movement (be it cultural or economic in origin) or on the responses, adaptations and strategies of individual actors. Indeed, the past fifteen years have been dominated in the sociology of education by the continually regurgitated motifs of macro versus micro, structure versus action, free will versus determinism, teachers versus the mode of production. In important ways this has led to both an under-emphasis on and a misrepresentation of other major arenas of analysis in sociological study – the work group and the organization – what might be called the meso-level. The first has been left to social-psychologists, the second to the tender mercies of organizational theory.

As suggested already, organizational theorists have failed to offer any sensible and comprehensive analysis of schools. Their work has tended to be fundamentally handicapped by a reliance upon theoretical models and empirical insights gleaned from and developed almost exclusively in relation to studies of industrial and business concerns or large-scale bureaucracies. The emphasis upon systems analysis in attempts to make sense of the working of schools has produced nothing more than a set of abstract descriptions which are conceptually arid and lack meaning and validity for teachers. In Britain Wilson (1962), Sugarman (1967), Turner (1968), Hoyle (1975, 1982) and King (1983) are typical examples of this genre.

In particular, British organizational theorists seemed to have been attracted to Parsons's (1951) pattern variables analysis, which involves the identification of particular aspects of the school organization with the appropriate functional prerequisite (goal attainment, adaptation, integration and pattern maintenance). Such an approach, as is the case with other versions of system theory, 'starts with a view of society and social life as inherently ordered and searches for shared agreements and convictions through an analysis of apparently mutually interlocked and adjusting systems and structures' (Salaman and Thompson, 1973). Furthermore, 'The systems notion posits an organizational force or framework which encompasses and gives order to people and events within it. The system – unseen behind everyday affairs – is real; it *is* the organization' (Barr-Greenfield, 1975, p. 65). As has been pointed out *ad nauseum*, systems theories provide only a limited and naive account of the possibilities of change and have no real capability for explaining or describing intra-organizational conflict or contradiction. Conflict is not necessarily totally ignored in this work but is regarded, within the logic of the paradigm, as aberrant and pathological. The emphasis is upon remediating or managing conflict, treating it as though it were a disease invading and crippling the body of the organization. Hannan says of Richardson's (1973b) study, 'Conflict or disagreement is interpreted as deviation from the task prompted by emotional reaction rather than the oppositon of those who define the task of the school differently' (Hannan, 1980, p. 6). The reason for this kind of conceptualization is only partly a matter of theory; it also lies in the historical relationship between the development of systems theories and the development of administrative control in organizations.

In a profession of administration based upon organizational science, the task of the administrator is to bring people and organizations together in a fruitful and satisfying union. In so doing, the work of the administrator carries the justification of the larger social order ... since he works to link day-to-day activity in organizations to that social order. (Barr-Greenfield, 1975, p. 60)

This type of relationship between 'organizational science' and administration is currently being reforged in Britain via the increasingly widespread provision of training in school management by university and polytechnic departments of education. The dominant theories in 'organizational science' thus come to reflect the particular interests and needs of administrators. They are top-dog theories; they contain a view of the organization looking down from the position of those 'in control'. They are inherently biased and distorted by this partiality. Furthermore, as the requirements and effects of training and consultancy bite, there is the tendency to slip casually from analysis to prescription. This is noted by Silverman as the tendency, when trying to explain the organization:

> to glide, imperceptibly, from the description of a *possible* model and definition of its various parts, to statements concerning the conditions and relationships necessary and existing *if* a certain system is to be stable and then assertions about phenomena and their relations as they actually exist. (1970, p.71)

In this way theories of organization actually become ideologies, legitimations for certain forms of organization. They deploy arguments in terms of rationality and efficiency to provide control. The limits that they impose upon the conception of organizations actually close down the possibility of considering alternative forms of organization. This is nowhere more clearly evident than in the current application of management theories to schools. They are widely accepted by administrators and teachers as the 'one best way' of organizing and running schools. As a result of this acceptance a whole variety of non-compatible concepts are set aside and condemned. Such theories marginalize empirical studies of school practice and dismiss the 'folk-knowledge' of teachers as irrelevant (these are the two bases for my own analysis). They are as significant for what they exclude as for what they include:

> a work is tied to ideology not so much by what it says as by what it does not say. It is in the significant *silences* of a text, in its gaps and absences, that the presence of ideology can be most positively felt. (Eagleton, 1976, pp. 34–5)

In the longer term the prescriptive approach to organizational research has been particularly strong in the United States, and understandably so for it articulates very well with a long-standing concern in that country with measuring and improving educational efficiency. This relationship is apparent from the very earliest stages of the development of organizational theory when Frederick 'Speedy' Taylor's work on scientific management was imported into schools. In particular, in the years between 1911 and 1925 educational administrators responded in a variety of ways to the demands for more efficient operation of the schools:

> Before the mania ran its course various 'efficiency' procedures were applied to classroom learning and to teachers, to the program of studies, to the organization of schools, to administrative functions, and to entire school systems. Most of the actions before 1916 were connected in some way by educators to the magic words 'scientific management'. (Callahan, 1962, p.95)

History repeats itself.

I am by no means the first to point out the disappointing achievements of the organizational analysis of schools. Bidwell bemoans the fact that 'Few students or organizations have turned their attention to schools, and few students of schools have been sensitive to their organizational attributes' (1965, p. 971). Abrahamson is appalled to find that 'There is no coherent sociological theory of the school as an organization and there is not even any systematized conceptual apparatus which could be used as a natural working basis' (1974, p.297). And Davies suggests: 'The arrival of a decent sociology of school organization has now been so long delayed that we must begin to suspect either that it has come already without our noticing it, or that there is something wrong with the news delivery system' (1981, p.47). Such complaints, however, only serve to highlight the problem. We need to go beyond the analysis of the failure of the existing attempts to develop an alternative sociology of school organization. What follows is an attempt at a wholesale escape from the dominant paradigm of 'organizational theory' rather than a piecemeal critique of its weaknesses. I will be offering new starting points, concepts and axioms and trying to rethink those aspects of school organization currently embedded in the taken-for-granted assumptions of systems-related theories. However, I regard none of the issues addressed here as closed: this is only a beginning.

Towards an alternative view

There are two basic problems with existing attempts to map out a coherent sociology of school organization. First there has been a continuing failure to recognize the peculiar nature of schools as organizations. Second, as noted already, there is a drastic lack of basic research into organizational aspects of school life. Clearly, these two problems are interrelated in a number of ways. As I have suggested, much analytical work on school organization has been founded upon the assumption that schools can be fitted, more or less unproblematically, into a conceptual apparatus derived from studies of factories or formal bureaucracies. This a priori approach has tended to bypass the need for thorough and open-ended studies of schools themselves. As a result much of the writing on schools as organizations has been based upon 'what we all know about school' as, more or less, informed outsiders. The views and experiences of the actors involved have been rarely sought and taken into account. It has failed to come to grips with all that we do *not* know about schools. This is recognized by Bell when he suggests that 'individuals often discover that they work in schools which are, organizationally, more complex, less stable, and less understandable than they have previously assumed and than the sociology of education literature might suggest' (1980, p.186). The future of the organizational analysis of schools, I intend to demonstrate in this book, lies in the area of what we do not know about schools, in particular in an understanding of the *micro-politics of school life*: what Hoyle calls the 'dark side of organizational life' (1982, p.87).

My objective here is to sketch out a schema for the analysis of school organization which is derived from and grounded in data. In the remaining chapters of the book I hope to elaborate this schema by the presentation and discussion of the evidence collected from schools. Thus some of the arguments adumbrated and concepts introduced in this section will be taken up and explored more fully later.

The analysis of data has highlighted a set of concepts, presented in Table 1.1, that can be counterposed to those of 'organizational science'. They provide a major difference in emphasis and axiomatic primacy. (They are not mutually exclusive.)

Table 1.1   Key concepts

Micro-political perspective (explicit adherence)	Organizational science (explicit or implicit adherence)
Power	Authority
Goal diversity	Goal coherence
Ideological disputation	Ideological neutrality
Conflict	Consensus
Interests	Motivation
Political activity	Decision-making
Control	Consent

In the sections below, under the headings of control, goal diversity, ideology and conflict, I initiate discussion of the concepts listed in the lefthand column of Table 1.1. Contrasts are drawn with those concepts listed in the right-hand column of Table 1.1.

Control

One of the problems involved in attempting to fit schools into existing categories of organizational type is that schools contain within them diverse and contradictory strategies of *control*. Collins (1975), following conventional practice, discusses the matters of structure and control in relation to three 'types' of organization: hierarchic organizations (essentially production, commercial or bureaucratic), membership-controlled organizations (e.g. political parties and trades unions) and professional communities. He suggests that teaching may be considered as a profession 'offering mostly organizational and ritual skills; these are important for members of society to learn to the degree that teachers have been able to advance their interests in making school important parts of careers' (Collins, 1975, p. 345). It is important, however, not to confuse a discussion of teaching as a profession with the consideration of schools as organizations. Realistically, schools, of virtually all varieties, contain elements of all three of Collins's types of organizations. In this respect they contain confusing messages both for the analyst and for their members (pupils and teachers and other school workers). At different times, in different sectors or in relation to different activities schools may be considered as hierarchic or membership-controlled or professional organizations. An analysis which relies on one of these typifications to the exclusion of the others risks distortion. In particular, schools occupy an uneasy middle ground between hierarchical work-organizations and member-controlled organizations (with individual schools differing from one another according to emphasis) and for that matter between product producing systems and public service institutions. The ordinary member (teacher) retains at least some control over the organization and the conduct of their work in it.

My argument here is not simply that as professional practitioners teachers retain a last-ditch control of their own activities in the privacy of their classroom. I am using control in a more general sense to refer to the organization as a whole. At times schools *are* run as though they were participative and democratic: there are staff meetings, committees and discussion days in which teachers are invited to make policy decisions (although the existence of such meetings is by no means a clear indicator of democratic participation; see Ch. 9). At other times they are bureaucratic and oligarchic, decisions being made with little or no teacher involvement or consultation, by the head and/or senior management team. Consider the following example described by Burgess (1983) taken from his study of Bishop McGregor Comprehensive School. Burgess presents a clear-cut analysis of the role and self-conception of the school's headteacher, Mr Goddard:

> For Goddard, being the head meant taking the lead: 'I became convinced that the more a head was about the more he led. I was a field officer, not a staff officer. I led from the front and it worked for me'. Mr Goddard therefore defined the role of the head as manager, co-ordinator, decision-maker, organizer and teacher. To him, the head was the main participant in the school. (p. 29)

What is suggested here is a strong, centralized, patrimonial leadership, with a high level of involvement in decision-making at all levels by the headteacher. (Headship and leadership are considered in some detail in Chs 4, 5 and 6). It is worth reminding ourselves that schools differ from many other organizations in as much as the leader will virtually inevitably have risen from the ranks. Very few captains of industry will have begun their careers on the shop floor in a similar way. This certainly allows the headteacher to make claims about task leadership that would be unavailable in other types of organization. However, we may compare this thumbnail impression of Mr Goddard with Burgess's account of an open-forum meeting at Bishop McGregor which was used to discuss the format of the school's prize-giving ceremony:

> The headmaster opened the discussion by explaining that he wanted to see a prize-giving that rewarded academic achievement. . . . However, by sheer force of numbers the junior staff were able to discuss and design, with the support of each other, a new-style prize-giving with a distribution of prizes, a short period for an address and discussion followed by an evening 'disco' . . . a recommendation which was later implemented by the headmaster. In this context, junior teachers were able to advance their ideas about school organization, which in turn led to a redefinition of the head's view of prize-giving. (p. 71)

Here we have an instance that apparently runs counter to the head's view of his leadership role and which suggests the relevance of membership-control concepts. The junior staff are able to assert a majority view over the headteacher's strongly held preference. These two images of the school – that presented by the head and that represented in the open-forum meeting – offer contradictory impressions about the nature of control within the institution and the ways in which decisions are made. Burgess's discussion of the open-forum meeting does not suggest that this was a decision which the head considered to be unimportant and would therefore be willing to 'give away' for the sake of harmony among the junior staff. The problem is, for the analyst as well as the members, that these 'fields' of control do not, indeed cannot, remain distinct. They are subject to negotiation, renegotiation and dispute (Strauss, 1978). The boundaries of control are continually being redrawn and they are drawn differently in different schools. These boundaries are often the outcome of struggle between headteachers and their staff (see Chs 4, 5 and 6), heads of department and their members, pastoral-care specialists and subject specialists (see Chs 2 and 9). The boundaries also come under pressure from outside intervention (see Ch. 10). The changing pattern of control is not the product of abstract organizational systems; rather, it emerges from the confrontations and interactions between individuals and groups in the organization.

Any attempt to portray school organization which uses just one category control will inevitably lead to distortion. That is not to say that analytical existing categories are totally redundant; rather, they tend to miss and obscure important features of school organization. Baldridge (1971), in a similar exercise addressed to the analysis of university organization, clearly points to the limitations of the frequently used bureaucratic and collegial (professional) categories. He says:

> certainly it would not be fair to judge them as completely bankrupt models, for their sensitivity to certain critical issues is quite helpful. By themselves, however, they gloss over many essential aspects of the universities' structures and processes. (p. 14)

These are my views exactly. I do not intend to abandon completely the existing categories of analysis, but to employ them, where it is conceptually coherent to do so, in a more flexible and subordinate way.

Goal diversity

One of the major distortions imposed by the use of social systems analysis is the over-emphasis on organizational goals and goal attainment. A great deal of effort has been expended by theorists who have tried to develop methods for the identification of the goal(s) of particular organizations. Furthermore, this search is often conducted on the basis of an assumption of consensus among the organization's members – an assumption which has extremely limited validity in almost all types of organizations. Thus, Silverman argues that 'It seems doubtful whether it is legitimate to conceive of an organization as having a goal except where there is an ongoing consensus between the members of the organization about the purposes of their interaction' (1970, p.9). Schools, as with other educational institutions, are typically lacking in such consensus. Indeed, the *structure* of schools allows for and reproduces dissensus and goal diversity. The relative autonomy of sub-units within the organization – departments, houses, year groups, special units, the sixth form – produces what Bidwell calls 'structural looseness'; that is, 'a lack of co-ordination between the activities and the goals of actors in separate functional units and the existence of multiple and overlapping areas of interest and jurisdiction, and complex decision-making processes' (1965, p. 978). This lack of co-ordination and the occasional absence of any form of immediate control over the organization's sub-units is called by Weick (1976) 'loose-coupling'; by this is meant that *structure is disconnected from technical (work) activity, and activity is disconnected from its effects* (Meyer and Rowan, 1978, p. 79). This is considered to be a basic property of educational organizations. They have rarely contained procedures for the direct supervision and monitoring of teaching work or for the quality control of the outcomes of teaching (although informal mechanisms may be used by colleagues or superiors to make judgements about the classroom effectiveness of individuals or sub-units (see Ball, 1981, pp. 132–3), but this may be changing. Certainly in this respect educational organizations have diverged quite markedly from the classic models of the industrial organizations. Some writers, though, have also argued that the assumptions about close co-ordination and control made about these organizations are also often misleading (e.g. Cyert and March, 1963). The autonomy and diversity of departmental interests in industrial organizations have frequently been seriously underestimated.

Pursuing this view of discoordination further, Bell (1980) has suggested that the effects of an increasingly 'wild' and unpredictable social environment upon a 'loosely coupled' internal structure 'have created a situation in which the internal organization of the school has begun to resemble what has been called an *anarchic organization*' (1980, p. 187). He goes on to say:

> The anarchic organization is not, as its name might imply, a formless or unpredictable collection of individuals. Rather it is an organization with a structure of its own which is partly determined by external pressures and partly a product of the nature of the organization itself. It is anarchic in the sense that the relationship between goals, members and technology is not as clearly functional as conventional organization theory indicates that it will be. (p. 187)

This concept of the anarchic organization is drawn from the work of Cohen, March and Olsen (1972) and March and Olsen (1976) and does seem particularly appropriate to understanding the organizational processes of schools in the current economic and political situation (see Ch. 10 below). On the one hand, schools contain within them members committed to and striving to achieve very different goals (see Ball, 1981a, pp. 11–13, 163–92). The teachers' own school experiences, their teacher training, and more specifically their socialization within a subject subculture, and their political affiliations outside school all contribute to this goal diversity. On the other hand, schools are confronted with a whole set of often contradictory demands and expectations from outside audiences and agencies. All of this creates difficulties in arriving at statements of goals or priorities that have any value or permanence. Furthermore, the salience of such abstract statements for the actual practice of teachers is doubtful.

Ideology[1]

Not only is it necessary to pay particular attention to the control and structure of organizational matters in school but also it is important to take account of the peculiar *content* of policy-making and decision-making in school. For a great deal of that content is *ideological*. Whereas in many types of organization (there are other exceptions of course) it is possible to plot and analyse decision-making in abstract terms, many decisions taken in school organizations are value laden and cannot be reduced to the simplicities of a procedural map. Debate, lobbying and discussion are not infrequently conducted in terms of principles like equality, fairness and justice. Decision-making can be invested with passion, and sometimes violent disagreements emerge over what seem at first sight to be innocuous technical issues. (But, conversely, it would be misleading to suggest that organizational life in schools is simply or even primarily a matter of high ideals and personal beliefs.)

> Given, then, that the education goals are ambiguous and may well not occupy a focal position in school life, the way in which schools attempt to fulfil these goals is equally unclear. Even when the goals are expressed in the most general of terms related to the facilitating of learning, different educational and political ideologies may lead teachers to approach their tasks in a number of ways. (Bell, 1980, p.188)

In terms of their classroom practice, their classification of pupils and their relationships with pupils, it is possible to find enormous differences between subject departments within the same school and even between teachers in the same department. These differences often rest on ideological foundations. In the normal course of events such differences are obscured or submerged in the welter of routine activities and interaction. However, at times of crisis or change, or in moments of reflection (occasional days, staff or department meetings), straightforward points of contention over practice can quickly lay bare deep divisions in *teaching ideology*. Sharp and Green define a teaching ideology as follows:

> A connected set of systematically related beliefs and ideas about what are felt to be the essential features of teaching. A teaching ideology involves both cognitive and evaluative aspects, it will include general ideas and assumptions about the nature of knowledge and of human nature – the latter entailing beliefs about motivation, learning and educability. It will include some characterization of society and the role and functions of education in the wider social context. There will also be assumptions about the nature of the tasks teachers have to perform, the specific skills and techniques required together with ideas about how these might be acquired and developed. Finally, the ideology will include criteria to assess adequate performance, both of the material on whom teachers 'work', i.e. pupils, and for self-evaluation or the evaluation of others involved in educating. In short, a teaching ideology involves a broad definition of the task and a set of prescriptions for performing it, all held at a relatively high level of abstraction.
>
> The content of the ideology will be a function of a complex of interrelated factors of which the following might be the most important: the image of teaching which the teachers formed whilst they, themselves, were pupils; second, the cognitive orientations and ideological commitments built into the course of professional training they receive; and third, the complex of experiences which teachers have encountered when faced with the practical exigencies of doing the job. Moreover, the teaching ideology will be embedded in a broader network of social and political world views whose determination, in the individual actor, derive from the socialization experiences undergone. (1975, pp. 68–9)

The ideological diversity of schools is frequently contained by a deliberate policy of *loose-coupling*. Departments or other sub-units (e.g. the sixth form, the lower school; see Beynon, 1985) are left to their own devices. Official school policy is open to 'interpretation' or special arrangements are negotiated (see Ball, 1981b). Individual teachers may be given considerable leeway to pursue their own 'vision' of education (see Woods, 1981), especially if 'less able' pupils are involved. None the less, once the loose-coupled or anarchic character of schools and their ideological diversity are recognized then the ever-present potential for conflict must also be accepted. Apple (1982, p.15) underlines both the practical basis, contested nature and inconsistency of educational ideologies.

Clearly, not all decisions faced by headteachers or schools are ideological, but virtually all matters which relate to the organization and teaching of pupils, the structure of the curriculum, the relationships between teachers and pupils and the pattern of decision-making in the institution have strong ideological underpinnings. That is to say, they contain seeds of political and philosophical dissention and partisanship. Shapiro (1982, p. 524) argues that conflicts in education have quickly spilled over into more fundamental questions of the structure and processes of class society. In no other institutions are notions of heirachy and equality, democracy and coercion forced to co-exist in the same close proximity. These conflicts often call up elements of personal belief and commitment that go beyond technical opinion and beyond individual or group interest, although in many cases philosophies and self-interest develop together in close and interdependent relation. Bennett and Wilkie certainly see this to be the case in relation to the curriculum:

> the allocation of the schools' resources inherent in the divisions bearing on the time-table will reflect political decisions. Academic criteria will clearly play their part in the allocation of resources. Yet the fact that schools differ in their allocation of time and resources to the various subject areas indicates that there are other than academic criteria at work. (1973, p. 464)

Bennett and Wilkie's comments draw attention to the crucial relationship between political dispute and the allocation of resources, between philosophy and material interests. However, once recognized, it is all too easy to overplay the importance of the ideological aspects of school decision-making, to assume, for example, that all teachers have the same high levels of ideological involvement in their work. Blecher and White certainly found in their study of an organizational situation highly charged with ideological issues and ideological dispute that not all the participants were motivated or influenced by ideological commitments:

> We can make an initial distinction here between 'believers' of various kinds for whom ideological values were subjectively important and behaviourally influential; 'non-believers' who find public ideologies more or less irrelevant to their lives; and 'cynics' whose world-outlook comprehends the domain of public ideology but only to ridicule, reject, or manipulate it. (1979, p. 99)

Undoubtedly it is possible to identify similar differences in orientation in virtually any staffroom.

Particular issues or decisions highlight the fact that, in common with actors in other types of organization, teachers are engaged in pursuit of their own personal and group vested interests as well as or in relation to their ideological commitments. Resources (material and social), careers and reputations are at stake when policies are agreed and decisions taken. The danger is that purely abstract forms of analysis will not tap into these dimensions of organizational life, which are otherwise destined to remain hidden behind a theoretical sham of systemic niceties. Management theories in particular contain a strong psychologistic and behaviourist emphasis on motivation; the recognition of interests, in a sociological sense, is muted. Furthermore, members of the organization are viewed in terms of individual 'needs' rather than group affiliations and shared concerns or ideologies. Both value controversies, and the forging of alliances and coalitions are thus both written out of account. A pragmatic and critical organizational analysis of schools must begin by being rooted in and developed upon the experiences, views and interpretations of the individual actors who constitute 'the organization' and their real and practical concerns and interests. Heuristically, teachers' interests, individual and collective, can be identified as being of three basic types: vested interests, ideological interests and self-interests.

Vested interests refer to the material concerns of teachers as related to working conditions: rewards from work, career and promotion. Access to and control of resources in the school are central here: time (timetabled lessons or free periods), materials, capitation allowance and special monies and grants, personnel (the definition and control of appointments and the formation of specialist teams) and territory (particularly offices and dedicated teaching-rooms and suites). These vested interests will be a matter of contention between individuals and between groups (e.g. departments, pastoral-care staff, administrative and non-teaching staff), especially when resources are scarce and promotion prospects limited. Ideological interests refer to matters of value and philosophical commitment – views of practice and organization that are preferred or advanced in debate or discussion. These interests often relate practical issues to fundamental political or philosophical positions. Self-interest employs the term 'self' in a particular way to refer to the sense of self or identity claimed or aspired to by the teacher, the sort of teacher a person believes themselves to be or wants to be (e.g. subject specialist, educator, pastoralist, administrator). The satisfactions associated with this sense of self may be directly related to certain sorts of work, work with particular groups of pupils, or even the use of specific resources or settings (e.g. laboratories, sports facilities). In this way it is easy to see the close interrelationships between the different types of interests; in the analysis of particular events it is often difficult or impossible to separate one set of interests out or give priority to one set (although in argument and debate one or other set of interests may be strategically deployed as prime by participants). Interests are crucially at stake in organizational decision-making and, as we shall see, for some teachers, participation in or attempts to influence decision-making are determined and circumscribed by the relevance of their own individual interests, the understanding and control of their situation, what Lane calls the 'closure principle' (1959, p. 141). For others, participation in these aspects of organizational life is in itself an expression of identity; it provides its own rewards and in some cases its own career.

Conflict

As noted above, at the basis of this alternative view of schools as organizations lies a set of concepts (which I intend to ground empirically in the following chapters) which are fundamentally antithetical to the social-system tradition, which underlies so much of organizational theory. These concepts, which are outlined in various forms in the work of Cyert and March (1963), Baldridge (1971), Collins (1975) and March and Olsen (1976), break away from the managerial or ownership perspective (Pfeffer, 1978) of the social-system tradition to take account of the conflict in preference orderings, objectives, interests and ideologies among organizational participants which result in contest or struggle for the control of the organization. This *conflict perspective* unlerlies virtually all aspects of the analysis outlined in the remainder of this book. Baldridge succinctly presents the main tenets involved:

1. Conflict theorists emphasize the fragmentation of social systems into interest groups, each with its own particular goals.
2. Conflict theorists study the interaction of these different interest groups and especially the conflict processes by which one group tries to gain advantage over another.
3. Interest groups cluster around divergent values, and the study of conflicting interests is a key part of the analysis.
4. The study of change is a central feature of the conflict approach, for change is to be expected if the social system is fragmented by divergent values and conflicting interest groups. (1971, p. 14)

In practice these dimensions specify a set of concerns with what I have called *the micro-politics of the school*. Hoyle defined micropolitics as embracing 'those strategies by which individuals and groups in organizational contexts seek to use their resources of power and influence to further their interests' (1982, p.88). In a similar view, but with greater specificity, Pfeffer suggests that organizational politics 'involves those activities taken within organizations to acquire, develop, and use power and other resources to obtain one's preferred outcomes in a situation in which there is uncertainty or dissensus' (1981, p. 7). Both definitions are open and exhaustive and, as Pfeffer goes on to point out, 'it is clearly important to be able to distinguish between political activity and administrative action in general' (p. 8). My use of micro-politics is also open and inclusive, but I limit and specify the concept in relation to three key and interrelated areas of organizational activity: (1) the interests of actors (as specified above), (2) the maintenance of organizational control (explored in detail in Chs 4 and 5 in particular) and (3) conflict over policy – in general terms which I call the definition of the school.

I take schools, in common with virtually all other social organizations, to be *arenas of struggle*; to be riven with actual or potential conflict between members; to be poorly co-ordinated; to be ideologically diverse. I take it to be essential that if we are to understand the nature of schools as organizations, we must achieve some understanding of these conflicts.

> the existence of unresolved conflict is a conspicuous feature of organizations, it is exceedingly difficult to construct a useful positive theory of organizational decision-making if we insist on internal goal-consistency. (Cyert and March, 1963, p. 18)

> Organizations, then, can be seen as power struggles along several dimensions and as using a number of tactics and devices, according to availability and the personal predilections of the individuals involved (Collins, 1975, p. 295)

> conflict between groups in organizations is not just an inevitability of organizational life but may be seen as a process through which organizations grow and develop over time. (Boyd-Barrett, 1976, p.92)

> the process of formulation of school policy is best understood in terms of the ideologies and conflicts located in the structure of the school. (Hannan, 1980, p. 6)

However, having set an agenda for the study of micro-politics and institutional conflict in schools, I do not want to fall into the same trap as the social-systems theorists, of seeing conflict everywhere, where they saw consensus. Blumer aptly points out the dangers of this:

> To see all human interaction ... as organized in the form of some special type of interaction does violence to the variety of forms that one can see if he wants to look. . . . It is my experience that the interaction usually shifts back and forth from one form to another form depending on the situations. (1971,p.19)

Much of what goes on in schools, on a day-to-day basis is not marked by dispute or strife among the teachers. Everyday talk and interaction is centred upon the routine, mundane and, for the most part, uncontroversial running of the institution. School life is dominated by what is most pressing and most immediate; priorities are constructed on the basis of practical necessity, of 'survival' (Woods, 1979). In effect, routine organizational life is set within the 'negotiated order' (Strauss, 1978), a patterned construct of contrasts, understandings, agreements and 'rules' which provides the basis of concerted action (see also Ch. 9). In this way conflicts may remain normally implicit and subterranean, only occasionally bursting into full view (Lacey, 1977) as issues or events of particular significance (social dramas) occur. When the 'negotiated order is thus disturbed, renegotiation and reappraisal are called for, but "successful" renegotiation is not always easy or possible – negotiation is the product of staff conflict mediated through the power differentials located in the structure of the organization' (Hannan, 1980, p. 6). However, it must be recognized that where the grounds for conflict are specified, the conditions for the absence of conflict may also be determined. Clearly, there are some educational institutions where conflict is minimal or perhaps non-existent.

It should not be assumed, as system theorists seem to do, that conflict is always destructive. Baldridge also points to the possibility of positive aspects to conflict in the organization: 'Although a political interpretation is based on conflict theory, it does not mean that the university is torn apart by ceaseless conflict. Conflict can be and often is quite healthy; or it may revitalize an otherwise stagnant system' (1971, p.202). There is a second dimension to the question of the prevalence of conflict which concerns the view of the person to be employed in a micro-political approach to the study of school life. Essentially the question is, 'Are all teachers political animals?', or more generally, 'Are all people in organizations politically aware and involved?' The answer to both is obviously 'no', and that strongly suggests the need for considerable care in the interpretation of events and actions. It is all too easy to read motives into actions which may completely subvert the meanings and intentions of the actor – although it is also important to recognize that the attribution of meaning is a prime component of micro-political activity and is stock in trade for the political activist. The problems involved here are not solved by the simple 'no' response quoted above, together with a counsel of caution.

The issues raised here require further unpacking. A set of tensions or contradictions may be discerned, and I will say in advance that I have no clear-cut solutions to offer for these dilemmas:

1. May we view 'political' behaviour as skilled strategic action, OR is much of this kind of activity relatively unthinking and intuitive or simply pragmatic?

2. Should we see 'political' behaviour as related to the long-term pursuit of strategic advantage OR as short-term or fairly immediate responses to particular issues or situations as and when they arise?

3. When they act, are individuals aware of the concerns, problems and potential lesser gain to their 'allegiance groups' OR do people act most of the time in terms of their own best interests or according to personal beliefs and principles?

4. If people do act with conscious strategic intent, whether with long- or short-term aims, as individuals or members of a group, are they primarily concerned with matters of value–interest (commitment and belief) OR are they acting in terms of their own material interests and personal advantage?

To put this final dilemma another way, are social actors in the organization primarily in pursuit of their *self-interest* or are they much more concerned with personal development and the achievement of *self-realization*?

Another much more pragmatic response is to say that it depends on the situation, the issues and the specific inclinations of individual actors. Some people may be politically active in the organization on a regular basis; others may get involved when particular issues arise; others still may never dabble in this sort of pursuit. Baldridge (1971) provides one example of this empirical approach in his analysis of the micro-politics of New York University. He identifies four types of actors – officials, activists, attentives and apathetics – who were differently involved and orientated to the institutional politics of the university. The *officials* are committed by career, life-style and ideology to the task of running the organization (Baldridge, 1971, p. 177). They are politically involved, by definition. They sit on committees, they have decision-making responsibilities, they receive the pleas and arguments of others. Headteachers of schools would be in this position, or at least it would be difficult to imagine how they could survive without such involvement, although some would disclaim the term 'politics' as a description of their actions. Baldridge's second type, the *activists*, 'are a relatively small body of people intensely involved in the universities politics' (p.177). They were involved both formally in committee work and informally in clique formation and lobbying or other action intended to *influence* decision-making. The formal/informal distinction is one we shall be returning to a number of times (see Ch. 9) and the notion of influence is one that will be of use later. Hoyle usefully clarifies this term:

> Influence differs from authority in having a number of sources in the organization, in being embedded in the actual relationships between groups rather than located in any abstract legal source and it is not 'fixed' but is variable and operates through bargaining, manipulation, exchange and so forth. (1982, p.90)

Interestingly, activists reported more loyalty to the university than other groups and were less willing to leave for other jobs: 'it seems that the activists have a whole set of intense involvements with the university, of which political action is only one' (Baldridge, 1971, p. 181). It could be said that they have more to defend, a greater *vested interest* in the future of the institution. Gray makes the point that 'A vested-interest is simply an involvement in an organization which gives valued reward to an individual. When the reward is at risk the individual will make every effort to retain it' (1975, p. 256).

Baldridge's third type, the *attentives*, 'are sideline watchers interested in the activities of the formal system' (1971, p. 178). This is the group who tended to become actively involved only when 'hot issues' emerged. They were aware but not normally engaged. They constituted a potentially powerful bloc in the eyes of the university authorities. The final type, the *apathetics*, 'almost never serve on committees, rarely show up for faculty meetings, and in general could not care less' (p. 178). Baldridge points out that the members of this type varied considerably; they were marginal for a whole variety of different reasons. For some, ignorance or non-involvement may be strategic, what Lane calls 'conflict-avoidance ignorance' (1959, p. 113), which ensures continued faith in the organization, or 'privatizing ignorance', which protects the person for the political saturation of their private life. I shall be making some attempts to explore this sort of variation in interest and participation in the micro-politics of the school in the later chapters.

In what amounts to a pre-emptive defence of a micro-political analysis of school organization there is one further area of possible criticism that must be faced. That is the danger that a meso-level, or organizational level, examination of the institution will tend to overplay the importance of internal factors in explaining school practices and underplay the role of external, structural influences and determinations. That is the danger of what Woods calls 'macro-blindness': 'Deep involvement in the scene can blind to external constraints and the researcher might find himself expressing things in their own terms when more powerful forces operating on the action lie elsewhere' (1983, p. 271). However, there are similar dangers involved in weighting the equation of cause in the opposite direction. It may be said that by focusing on the minutiae of interpersonal conflict within the institution I am drawing attention to trivial and epiphenomenal factors in the process of educational change. Certainly, this is an accusation that has been levelled against my previous work and has been taken to be symptomatic of much of the recent work done in the sociology of education in this country, which is seen by some as:

> engaging in a form of inner emigration in the face of the funda-
> mental structural changes in British society currently being
> orchestrated by significant factions in the capitalist class through
> Thatcherism at the level of state politics. (Sharp, 1981, p. 282)

Ultimately this position rests on an assumption that nothing of any importance happens at the institutional level or that the realities of institutional life can be read off from a priori theory about general class relations in society. Such assumptions are theoretically dangerous and empirically naive; the implications of theory remain untested and ossified. If the criticisms are accepted, then we also have to accept that 'the study of individual schools can never be more than illustrative of a more fundamental order of structuring mechanisms which require macro-analysis' (Sharp, 1981, p. 282).

Yet it is all too easy to overestimate the degree and misconstrue the nature of penetration and influence of structural factors in the social dynamics of institutions. The issue is in fact an empirical one.

Let me offer an illustration of the problem. The example which may seem to be a rather distant parallel to draw with schools is the case of a medical unit set in the midst of the Cultural Revolution in the Republic of China. Blecher and White (1979) present a micro-political analysis of the unit based on the accounts of participants. Despite the profound disruptions and social changes going on in the wider society, Belcher and White conclude that:

> the substance of political contention was based on *intra-unit* issues rather than those stemming from provincial or national levels of the movement. Although they had conceptual and linguistic links with the wider issues of national movement, they were more fundamentally *a response to stresses and contradictions inherent in the socio-political structure of the unit before the Cultural Revolution*. They were neither imported nor imposed, though some of them did resonate with the wider issues. (p. 75, my emphasis)

The *issue-factions* in the unit were based on cross-cutting ties, friendships, cabals and cliques that *pre-existed* the political changes going on outside. The development of the unit, the decisions taken and the policies pursued were to be understood primarily in terms of the internal dynamics of institution micro-politics. The rhetorics, shifts in power and changes in policy outside the unit provided a linguistic and conceptual framework for internal debate rather than a set of structural determinations.

I am not suggesting here that studies of schools can be conducted which take no account of the environment or leave aside entirely the impact of outside intervention. Clearly, the political interface between schools and local and national government is of *increasing* importance. Nevertheless, I shall be arguing for the need to explore the different ways in which different organizations cope with and respond differently to greater intervention and pressure from outside. Chapter 10 is particularly concerned with this issue. The relationship between schools and their local authorities has changed significantly over the past ten years in a number of ways. Cuts in public spending on education combined with the situation of falling rolls in many areas has meant that local officers and advisers have become much more active in matters concerning the school curriculum and teachers' careers. A number of local authorities have introduced corporate management systems which have 'consequences which affect the relationships between councillors, LEA officials, teacher union leaders and eventually the powers of teachers, parents and pupils' (Miller, 1984, p. 8). The effects of the 1980 Education Act are also of importance in as much that they have brought about a significant shift in the relationship between schools and parents, and that between different schools in the same locality, they are now in effect in competition for clients. In addition, there is a great pressure on schools to introduce new courses and subjects which have immediate social and economic relevance in the wider society. Innovation and retrenchment are strange bed-fellows but real problems facing many teachers. In other words, many schools find themselves operating within an increasingly 'wild' environment; for some their very survival is at stake. Even so, it may be that some schools are better able to cope with changes of this kind than others.

Finally, in relation to conflict I want to clarify my use of the concept of power. Systems theorists, almost by definition, tend to eschew the concept of power in favour of authority. In doing so they assume legitimacy and consent and again pathologize conflict. Significantly, studies and accounts of headship in schools invariably begin with a pre-emptive definition of role in terms of authority; the articles of governance are frequently quoted. Again, my claim is that the assumption of authority is unhelpful and distorting. Power is a more active, penetrating and flexible concept in this context, but the concept of power employed here is a particular one. It does not involve reference to position or capacity as such but to perform-ance, achievement and struggle (see Ch. 4). Power is taken to be an outcome. This aligns with Hindess's analysis:

> The exercise of control, the realization of one's will or objectives, the securing of interests, or whatever, always involves the de-ployment of definite means of action in particular situations, that these means of action themselves depend on definite conditions and that their deployment may confront obstacles including the practices of others. (1982, p. 504)

This view of power emerges in the recognition of variations between schools in the exercise and possibility of the headteachers' power. It also takes account of contingencies, changes over time and the results of conflict, 'the struggles over divergent objectives really are struggles, not the playing-out of some preordained script'

(Hindess, 1982, p. 506). Clearly, the conditions and means of action in schools may tend to favour one side, but this does not ensure that outcomes are 'the simple products of initial conditions': 'they are produced in the course of struggle itself'. Thus in the following chapters we find that compromises, negotiations and trade-offs, as well as threats, pressure and underhand dealing, have their part to play in the achievement and maintenance of the headteacher's powers. Decision-making is not an abstract rational process which can be plotted on an organizational chart; it is a political process, it is the stuff of micro-political activity.

Theory and data

I have outlined above the conceptual framework within which the topics and issues presented in the remaining chapters are to be addressed. Many of the ideas and concepts introduced briefly and schematically will be explored and fleshed out in greater detail in relation to illustrations and examples drawn from specific cases. Despite the variety of types and sources of data upon which I shall be drawing, one straightforward premise provides the basis for the two-way relationship between theory and data. Furlong and Edwards make the very important point that:

> Whatever picture of social life the scientists present is the out-
> come of selective observation and interpretation, because his
> theory determines not only how the 'data' are explained but also
> what are to count as data in the first place. (1977, p. 122)

What are to count as data in this exploration of the school as an organization are the views, experiences, meanings and interpretations of the social actors involved. In this case those actors are almost exclusively teachers. I accept that this ignores the majority of those who participate in the social dramas of schooling – the pupils – and neglects the roles of secretaries, caretakers, ancillaries and others. I also accept that pupils and other school workers play a part in the micro-politics of school life. However, in order to achieve the depth of analysis which seems necessary in this area, I can do justice to only those who are most obviously and directly involved in the organizational aspects of school: the teachers.

When people meet in groups or collectivities, in different situations, they are engaged in a process whereby they 'indicate lines of action to each other and interpret the indications made by others' (Blumer, 1976, p. 16). The logical methodological consequences of this is that 'It is necessary to view the given sphere of life under study as a moving process in which the participants are defining and interpreting each other's acts' (p. 16). Those definitions and interpretations in turn provide the building blocks for the 'categories that we use to give conceptual order to the social makeup and social life of a human group' (p. 17). Thus the analysis attempted here is derived and developed through the ongoing interplay between the data, in the form of actors' accounts of their experiences and intentions, their indications and interpretations and the conceptual categories which are identified in data. Data are the starting point and continual reference point for the analysis. I am operating within Saunders's view that:

> A consideration of actors' definitions of their situation need not preclude attempts at sociological explanation that go beyond the level of the actors' consciousness; indeed this was precisely the point of Weber's insistence on theoretical adequacy *both* at the level of *meaning and* at the level of causality. (1981, p. 203)

Compared with the social-systems model with which this chapter began, there is a dual reversal of interest and assumption here. First, rather than beginning with a reified view of the organization as a structure separate from those who make it up, this approach gives priority to the social actors as the basic constituents of the organization. Second, and concomitantly, the principles which guide the analysis of organizational functioning are represented in the way in which those actors define, interpret and handle the situations with which they are confronted. Blumer argues strongly that such an approach to organizational life will yield insights which bear directly upon those concerns typically ignored or obscured by organizational theorists or systems analysts:

> problems such as morale, the functioning of bureaucracy, block- age in effective communication, corruption and ranges of bribery, 'exploiting the system', favoritism and cliquishness, the rise (and decline) of oligarchic control, the disintegration of the organiz- ation, or the infusion of new vigor into the organization. (1976, p. 18)

These are some of the matters which constitute the micro-politics of the school.

2

The politics of change: some case studies

There is in public affairs, no state so bad, provided it has age and stability on its side, that is not preferable to change and disturbance.

(Michel de Montaigne)

A consideration of the politics of change is an appropriate starting point for a micro-politics of the school on at least two grounds. First, as Lacey (1977) indicates, change or the possibility of change brings to the suface those subterranean conflicts and differences which are otherwise glossed over or obscured in the daily routines of school life. Second, Baldridge, already quoted, sees change as being of central importance in a conflict perspective. However, his logic runs in a different direction. He sees change as an inevitable consequence of conflict within a social system: 'The study of change is a central feature of the conflict approach, for change is to be expected if the social system is fragmented by divergent values and conflicting interest groups' (1971, p. 14). Silverman makes a similar point, but takes a broader view: 'A situation may ... be usefully examined from the vantage point of "competing systems of interpretation"' (1970, p. 138), and this will provide important clues as to how it arose, why it continues in its present form and what circumstances will make it change. Thus it follows that an exploration of change should tell us something about the sources and processes of micro-political conflict within the school and could also help us to isolate the factors that lead some schools to moments of change while others stay the same. Change within institutions may be seen as a pre-eminently political process inasmuch as it reveals what Duverger calls the two faces of power:

The notion that politics is both a conflict between individuals and groups for the acquisition of power, which the victors use to their advantage at the expense of the vanquished, and an attempt to establish a social order beneficial to all. (1972, p. 19)

While innovation (or change) is the substantive concern of this chapter, and the one which follows, the exploration of innovation processes also provides a vechicle for identifying the major protagonists in the micro-politics of the school.

The study of educational change, and more specifically the analysis of processes of innovation, has a relatively short intellectual history, which begins with the work of Paul Mort at Columbia University's Teachers College in the 1920s and 1930s. A brief account of the basic tenets at work in the main contributions to this history will serve to indicate the distinctiveness of the micropolitical perspective. Mort's concern was primarily with diffusion, and the level of analysis pursued led to a focus on differences between schools. Rogers and Shoemaker summarize the Columbia findings as follows:

1. The best single predictor of school innovativeness is educational cost per pupil.
2. A considerable time lag is required for the widespread adoption of new educational ideas. 'The average American school lags 25 years behind the best practice.'
3. The pattern of adoption of an educational idea over time approaches an S-shaped curve. At first only a few innovator schools adopt the idea, then the majority decide the new idea is desirable, and finally the adopter curve levels off as the last remaining schools adopt. (1971, p. 59)

There is a parallel between these diffusion studies and the research on the diffusion of innovation in agriculture and medicine. As with agriculture and medicine, educational change is identified with the benefits of progress and regarded uproblematically as a good thing. 'The American studies tend to take the worthwhileness of innovation for granted and ignore the content of the curriculum in an analysis of success and failure' (Hannan, 1980, p. 20). The values and concepts of diffusion research provide the basis for what House (1979) calls the 'technological perspective' of the innovation process. In the 1960s this perspective was established as the dominant way of conceptualizing innovation, through the research, development and diffusion model (RD & D). This view of change-processes typically had as its vehicle 'the curriculum project', a mass-produced centrally developed educational product that was both easily transferable and economical. The research and design work was left to the experts at the centre, who would, at the high point of this approach, be seeking to construct a 'teacher-proof' package. New ideas would flow directly from the 'curriculum laboratory' into the classroom. Among the assumptions embedded in this approach, as House (1979) points out, are a view of the teacher as an essentially passive recipient and a belief that researchers, developers, diffusers and teachers share a common value-system and are working towards the same goals. The differences between institutions and institutional settings have little importance in this kind of thinking. Energy is expended primarily on refining 'the product' and overcoming 'the resistance' of adopters. The concern with overcoming resistance establishes a link between the RD & D model and the other major intellectual tradition in American innovation research, that of planned change. This tradition has its origins in social psychology, and specifically the action-research work of Kurt Lewin's small-group studies which examined the processes involved in the 'unfreezing–moving–refreezing' of group standards (Lewin, 1947). Lewin stressed the stategic effects of intervention in bringing about change and he highlighted the role of the change-agent and the importance of group participation. Acceptance of innovation decisions was found to be positively related to the degree of participation in the decision by members of the collectivity (Lewin, 1943). Both aspects, the change-agent role and the participation of 'adopters' in decision-making, lead towards a more dynamic conception of change. A somewhat more complex view of individual psychology begins to emerge, but the analysis remains locked into 'the psychological'. Building on Lewin's work, Schein argues that:

> the change agent must assume that the members of the system will be committed to their present ways of operating and will, therefore, resist learning something new. As a consequence the *essence* of a planned change process is the *unlearning* of present ways of doing things. It is felt to be in this unlearning process that most of the difficulties of planned change arise. (1972, p. 75)

This approach was taken up most significantly by Havelock (1973) in his 'linkage model', which represents a synthesis of RD & D with aspects of social interaction and problem-solving. Havelock's change-agent is a consultant engaged in analysing the client's 'needs' and seeking out and offering 'solutions'. As part of this process Havelock recognizes the need to take on board some kind of organizational analysis, although as Bailey points out, 'his treatment of this subject is a rather naive, atheoretical homespun version of structural functionalism with a preference for systems imagery' (1982, p. 54). While, as Bailey goes on to note, Havelock's work indicates at least a shift away from the recalcitrant individualism of diffusionism, the basic commitment to a positivist, rationalist view of the change process remains unaltered. 'The problem' of innovation is still essentially viewed as 'the installation of a product' (Everhart, 1976–7). The role of consultant represents a more sophisticated response to resistance, but the concern is still with ways of bringing about change in the behaviour of the institutional actors without taking seriously the actor's own interpretations of change. The approach is both functionalist and behaviourist, moving between an abstract and reified conception of the organization and a reductionist view of individual actors as 'psychological dopes'. The implicit assumption of consensus and coherence in this approach to organizational change reduces the organization itself to a bland technical mechanism inhabited by atomistic, malleable psychologies. No account is taken here of divergent interests embedded in change. No recognition of ideological dispute, loss and gain, coalition building or co-ordinated opposition. To resist is to act irrationally. Essentially, change is here something that is done *to* people and *to* organizations. The micro-political perspective presents a directly opposed view of the process of change.

This alternative ultimately rests upon taking seriously the active interpretational responses of the actors in the organization and thus involves abandoning the positivist/materialist conception of innovation which is central to both the RD & D and planned-change traditions. This alternative conception also places innovation within the interactive/political arena of the organization:

Innovation arises in, and acquires legitimacy through, group definitions and an appropriate structure of relationships. It is, therefore, a *cultural* phenomenon. Like any other idea-system, it

is subject to the constraints of power distribution and the interactional opportunities which are available to the participating
members. Even if the innovation originated at a time and place
far removed from a specific institution, its realization inside that
institution will nevertheless be mediated through its patterns of
social interaction. (Esland, 1972, p. 103, my emphasis)

As suggested earlier, change in an organization is almost certain
to produce dissonance among individuals or groups within the
membership. 'The unwary seeker after a modest degree of self-
improvement has often found himself unwittingly the spearhead of
an institutional confrontation he did not aspire to' (Macdonald and
Walker, 1976, p. 46). The introduction of, or proposal to introduce,
changes in structure or working practices must be viewed in terms of
its relationship to the immediate interests and concerns of those
members likely to be affected, directly or indirectly. Innovations
are rarely neutral. They tend to advance or enhance the position of
certain groups and disadvantage or damage the position of others.
Innovations can threaten the self-interests of participants by undermining established identities, by deskilling and therefore reducing
job satisfaction. By introducing new working practices which replace established and cherished ways of working, they threaten
individual self-concepts. Vested interests may also be under threat:
innovations not infrequently involve the redistribution of resources, the restructuring of job allocations and redirection of lines
of information flow. The career prospects of individuals or groups
may be curtailed or fundamentally diverted. Innovation may also
require that those involved 'reverse previously held beliefs, to
develop new loyalties' (Esland, 1972, p. 102). That is to say,
ideological interests may come under threat: an innovation 'can
represent a fundamental denial of much that they have hitherto
believed in' (p. 107). In the light of this, it is not surprising that
innovation processes in schools frequently take the form of political
conflict between advocacy and opposition groups. Either in public
debate or through 'behind the scenes' maneouvres and lobbying,
factional groups will seek to advance or defend their interests, being
for or against the change. Negotiations and compromises may
produce amendments to initial proposals, certain groups or individuals may be exempted, trade-offs arranged, bargains arrived
at. Trade-offs may take a concrete form, involving say the redistri-

bution of scale points or changes in departmental capitation, or may be, as Macdonald and Walker (1976) suggest, trade-offs in meaning, whereby fundamental value conflicts are subsumed beneath a common rhetoric to which all parties are willing to subscribe. This they call 'curriculum negotiation'. The use of rhetoric may change considerably within an institution with little impact being made on practice. (This alerts us to the common separation between the arena of debate and the arena of implementation, which is discussed below.)

Let us explore a case in point. The proposal to introduce mixed-ability grouping at Beachside Comprehensive (Ball, 1981a) provides a case where changes in the organization of pupils for teaching purposes were seen to have significant implications for the teachers involved. Here we have a proposed change which was initiated within the school and subjected to open debate among the staff. The crucial decisions about acceptance or rejection of the mixed-ability system were made by votes taken in meetings of the whole staff. The process of debate and decision-making was a gradual and sequential one whereby experience at one level was being fed back into decisions being made about the next. Mixed-ability was introduced in the first year, then the second, then the third. This 'democratic' method is certainly not typical of the decision-making processes associated with the introduction of mixed-ability grouping. Reid *et al.* (1981) found that the *directive* approach, where the headteacher effectively made the decision, was by far the most common form of introduction in their sample of twenty-six schools. However, the significance of the headteacher in the innovation process at Beachside must not be underestimated either. He played a critical role throughout the period of initiation and debate. Indeed, the idea of the innovation originated with him and was closely associated with him throughout in the minds of the teachers. He explained:

> I had always been interested in unstreaming. I was in my previous school ten years ago. It was one of the things I had had in my mind that I wanted to do, but I did not want to do it straightaway; it was necessary first of all to gain parental confidence. It would have been an outrageous move at the time.

Several points can be noted here: the headteacher's awareness of the limits and possibilities of change; the gradualist conception of change; and his own personal support for mixed-ability. This latter was clearly recognized among the staff. The headteacher's commitment to the change undoubtedly tempered the debate and affected the response of the staff, but this was certainly not enough to ensure the acceptance of the innovation to win the vote. The head was also very much involved in the practical micro-politics of the debate. Before the open discussions began, the head engaged in 'gathering a team', appointing teachers who were in favour of or sympathetic to mixed-ability. Within the course of the debate it was the headteacher who framed the motions to be voted on. This was crucial, particularly in the second and third votes, inasmuch as the languages, mathematics and science departments were allowed by the wording of the motions to 'set' pupils for their lessons. If these motions had required all subjects to adopt mixed-ability grouping in the second and third years, as some pro-mixed-ability teachers were urging, it is doubtful whether the majorities in favour would have been achieved. Furthermore, with the possibility of 'setting', some of the teachers who initially opposed mixed-ability began to see advantages in the new system. Not only would they be able to 'set' within their own subjects, thereby achieving finer gradations of ability, but they could still enjoy the general advantages, especially improvements in social atmosphere, which were to be derived from having mixed-ability grouping in the other subjects. Finally, it is important to recognize the significance of the headteacher's response to the claims being made by some staff, that mixed-ability would damage the educational opportunities of 'the more able pupil'. The headteacher promoted one of the most vociferous opponents of mixed-ability to a Scale 4 post 'with responsibility for the most able pupils'. The cynical (or political) interpretation of this would be that the headteacher achieved two things by this move: (1) he demonstrated his concern for the 'most able' pupils by making the appointment; and (2) he bought off one of the key figures in the opposition to mixed-ability. Despite the crucial role played throughout by the headteacher, 'he manipulated things so it would happen' (head of English), the outcome of the debate must still be seen in terms of the advocacy and opposition of distinct groups among the staff, and the outcome always remained 'a close run thing'.

The various responses of the Beachside staff may be understood in terms of three separate interpretations which were represented by distinct *group perspectives* (Becker *et al.*, 1961, pp. 33–4). Becker defines a perspective as 'a coordinated set of ideas and actions a person uses in dealing with some problematic situation, to refer to a person's ordinary way of thinking about and feeling about an action in such a situation'. Although it is vital to recognize that, for *most* of the staff their perspectival response to mixed-ability represented a priority rather than an absolute commitment. The pro- and anti-mixed-ability factions did not dismiss the concerns of their opponents; although they may have derided them for the purposes of debate, they merely saw them to be of secondary importance. Thus the two extremes in the debate were represented, on the one hand, by the *idealist perspective* and, on the other, by the *academic perspective*. Those teachers who adhered to the idealist perspective advocated mixed-ability as a fairer and more egalitarian form of organization, more in line with 'what a comprehensive school should be'. These teachers regarded streaming as a source of premature labelling and discrimination, which prevented many children from achieving to the full extent of their capabilities. Those who adhered to the academic perspective felt that mixed-ability would damage the school's academic performance and thus alienate parents, hinder the prospects of the more able pupils and make impossible demands on certain subjects (usually their own) which were based on a linear learning progression of skills or concepts.

The middle ground in the debate was taken by those teachers who adhered to a *disciplinary perspective*. These teachers came to see mixed-ability as a way of eradicating the low-stream groups of alienated pupils that were so difficult to control and to teach, and as likely to improve the general social atmosphere of the school and the social relations between teachers and pupils. Within these three very different interpretations of mixed-ability it is possible to identify aspects of the *group and individual interests* discussed previously. We may ask the question, 'What is at stake in the mixed-ability debate?' Clearly, at one level there are two distinct and opposing educational ideologies at work. These may be viewed in simple terms as meritocratic (on the part of the academic perspective) and egalitarian (on the part of the idealist perspective). Here we have an opposition between contending definitions of the comprehensive school: one stresses equality of access; the other, equality of outcome. These contending definitions are associated with alternative conceptions of the purposes of schooling, of appropriate teacher-pupil relations of learning and of the pedagogical role of the teacher.

Hannan produces an almost identical analysis in his case study of an innovative 14–18 Upper School, Redmond College. He characterizes the opposed positions among the staff as 'open and closed' ideologies:

> the main conflicts came over proposed solutions to the problems experienced with the unmotivated and most troublesome students. The discussion of problems revealed a clash of ideologies, in that some staff interpreted the causes as not enough integration and autonomy for students and others blamed too much integration (of pastoral and curricular, of more and less able) and too much student autonomy (too much choice in the curriculum, too much status difference between staff and students). (Hannan, 1980, p. 119)

The blanket introduction of mixed-ability grouping in the first three years at Beachside could be regarded as a radical shift in the definition of the school towards the egalitarian position. However, as we have seen, the academics were able, to some extent at least, to defend and maintain their definition of the school. Many of the cherished values and beliefs of the academics *were* at risk in the debate. For such teachers, their subject and their commitment to it is a major aspect of their overall commitment to teaching and a primary basis for the satisfactions that they achieve from their work.

Here the ideological and value conflicts evident in the debate shade over into the broader 'self' interests of the teachers involved. The teachers 'preferred view' of themselves as academics or educators is at stake. Furthermore, personal work-satisfaction is also at risk. For the academic teachers the introduction of mixed-ability represented a real threat to their substantive *identities* (Ball, 1972). They maintained a strong personal commitment to forms of education at odds with those championed by the advocates of mixed-ability and had developed self-conceptions and satisfactions from their expertise with the most able pupils – this expertise being measured in terms of examination success. They were engaged in the reproduction of their own educational experiences with succeeding generations of academically able, aspiring and well-motivated pupils. This they sought to defend. By contrast, the idealist teachers were uncomfortable with what they saw as the élitism and unfairness of the existing system of grouping. They expressed personal commitments to comprehensive education which were founded on ideas about treating all children equally. For some their views about mixed-ability and about schooling generally were an extension of a broader set of political beliefs and commitments. In Nias's (1984) terms, they were actively engaged in attempting to create or affect a congruent work setting by advocating a particular definition of that setting with their sense of self at stake. As the head of English announced dramatically in one staff meeting: 'To me comprehensive means mixed-ability and if it does not, then this is not the sort of school that I would want to be concerned with.'

However, a further aspect of the debate, a sub-text to the argument and value conflict, is concerned with a broader and longer-term struggle for power and influence within the school. The 'self' interests and ideological interests of the contesting groups are reflected in and underpinned by a set of material vested interests. Careers, resources, time and influence over policy-making in the school are all contested for. To the extent that the pro-mixed-ability lobby gained at least partial acceptance of their views, among the staff as a whole they were in the ascendancy, the spoils of battle were theirs. Certainly the English department, and in particular the head of English, asserted their position as a major influence upon school policy. As an indicator of this, not long after the period of debate the head of English was promoted to senior teacher. Even so, the rearguard action of the anti-mixed-ability faction, in particular the languages department, had certainly avoided a debacle. The academic position may have come under pressure in the debate, but it had certainly not been completely routed. The compromises were significant. There remained a considerable degree of concern among the staff as a whole for the 'fate of the brighter child' and worries about the likely effects of mixed-ability on the school's examination results and thus on the school's image among parents and others in the community. The opposition faction were certainly able to point to disquiet in the media about the untoward effects of 'progressive' innovations like mixed-ability. The headteacher was certainly aware that the school was unlikely to gain widespread parental support for complete mixed-ability grouping. He said:

> We cannot take up the possibilities of mixed-ability at this stage because we would be doing a disservice to the kids and have their parents in uproar because they are not doing exams, we cannot

do that locally until the system of 16+ examinations changes nationally.

The pro-mixed-ability teachers were also cognizant of this backdrop to their decisions and actions. They recognized the need to retain the support of their 'public'. Again, put cynically, damage to the reputation of the school could also mean interference in their careers and damage to their future prospects. Thus the micro-politics of the school cannot be viewed as operating in total isolation from the social environment in which it is set. Conversely, however, one cannot simply read off the outcomes of micro-political conflicts and debates from the prevailing norms in the social and political environment. Silverman points out that when organizations are initially set up, 'their "meaning-structures" reflect those generally prevalent in roles of a similar nature in the broader society', but over time 'as interaction continues, these expectations become modified to a certain extent in each organization, although they are never completely separate from the prevailing meaning-structure of the society' (1970, p. 38). At certain times the environment is more amenable to experimentation and divergence than at others, but in the mid-1970s, when the Beachside case study was conducted, the period of apparent 'progressive consensus' in educational politics was beginning to come to an end. Silverman goes on to suggest that 'participants may see the environment as threatening or as creating an opportunity, and act accordingly' (p. 38). Here the teachers were fully aware of the limits to change set by the changing political context of the time, but they were also aware of the extent of freedom of manoeuvre that was possible without producing untoward reactions.

Thus, while it is important to look outwards from the process of debate to the environment, to view the micro-politics of change in a broader context, it is also important to move beyond the debate in another direction. For the outcomes of debate, in this case at least, were only one aspect of the whole process of innovation; the debate was limited to the issue of the adoption of mixed-ability *grouping*. Other changes, or expectations of change, concerning mixed-ability *teaching* were focused upon the classroom (or departmental meetings). Adapting a model used by Macdonald and Walker (1976, p. 45), the public arena of debate, the staffroom, can be separated from the private arena of practice, the classroom.

The arena of debate, the staff meeting or key committee, is characterized by the language of policy, by grand rhetoric and purposeful idealism. Here the competing definitions of the innovation are in public contest. This is the arena of adoption where significant, but not necessarily binding, framing decisions are made. Limits are set, public policy is fixed. Here contrasts are stark, arguments are simple and to the point. The stakes are high; as we have seen, reputations may be made and lost here. The good public speaker may impress more than the thoughtful practitioner. The bold statement and personal stand may carry the day. Routine co-operation between colleagues may be replaced by personal invective, accusations, defamatory statements and camouflaged abuse. Alliances are tested and the strengths or weaknesses of the team performance (Goffman, 1971) may be exposed. Here the factions must show their strength of will, individuals must be willing to back up each other's arguments and to counter the arguments of the opposition. The success of prior caucusing or lobbying may bear fruit. The dramatic or directive leadership of particular individuals (Goffman, 1971, pp. 103–4) may become apparent. The course of the debate itself may be subject to strategic intervention or devices employed by powerful or dominant individuals. Humour is often an effective weapon in such situations. Also the contrasting of unacceptable practices can be used to define and maintain a degree of professional consensus among those involved (Hargreaves, 1981).

By contrast, the arena of practice is the arena of implementation. Here the decisions made elsewhere must be accommodated. The simple arguments of the debate are invariably overwhelmed by the complexities and messy realities of classroom life. The language employed here is the everyday discourse of pragmatism. The high-flown rhetoric must be adapted to the immediate physical and material constraints of teaching and the problems of survival at the chalkface. The performers here are the lone teachers who must bring off their new definition of the situation under the harsh and critical gaze of pupils who were not consulted about change. Some teachers at least may lack the practical skills or the will to struggle with new meanings, new methods of working or new forms of social relationship. Implementation may provide an opportunity to re-assert established practices behind a façade of innovation. The cellular 'egg-crate' (Lortie, 1975), closed-door world of teaching can allow for the development of personal, creative, sometimes subversive responses to changes which originate elsewhere. We should not be surprised that committed academics may be unwilling to rethink and reorganize their classroom methods and further undermine their personal satisfactions in order to pursue educational goals in which they have only marginal interest. While the collegial climate of expectation may be that classroom practices should change, there are other powerful vocabularies which can be mobilized to demonstrate the foolishness, or impossibility, of change at this level.

Changes in policy should not be confused with changes in practice. In the micro-politics of the school it is most often the former which are at stake, although micro-political strategies may also be deployed to promote or defend the latter. At Beachside the implementation of mixed-ability as a teaching problem was left almost entirely to the individual departments to cope with. Each department was asked by the headteacher to produce a report outlining their intended responses, but there was no follow-up to the reports, and in several cases the teaching strategies actually employed bore no resemblance to original stated intentions (see Ball, 1981a, Ch. 7). In practice headteachers are generally loath to infringe in any direct way on those areas of subject expertise (pedagogy and curriculum) that are traditionally regarded as the province of 'the department'. In this case the relative autonomy allowed to the departments in responding to mixed-ability certainly permitted the factional differences revealed in the debate to be returned 'to the subterranean'. Any attempt to pursue a policy of mixed-ability teaching through public debate would undoubtedly have created a further polarization between the advocacy and opposition factions.

As should be clear from the foregoing description and analysis of the Beachside innovation, much of the debate and the divisions it highlighted can be related back to subject or departmental 'positions'. The advocacy of mixed-ability was spearheaded by the English department and supported and promoted by an alliance of English, history and geography teachers. The opposition was led initially by the languages and mathematics departments, although there was some shifting of ground here as the debate continued and experience of mixed-ability teaching was accumulated. So, too, the implementation of mixed-ability teaching could be understood in terms of differences between departments. What are indicated by these differences in interpretation of and response to mixed-ability are both the technical differences between the subjects in terms of the currently established conceptions of content, structure and method, and differences in the assumptions held by practitioners about the broader purposes of education, about how children learn and about the classroom responsibilities of the teacher. These complexes of epistemological, pedagogical and educational values and assumptions constitute, in each case, *a subject subculture*. The values and assumptions representative of any particular subculture, that is 'the prevailing kernel of self-evidency' (Schutz and Luckmann, 1974, p. 9), are the product of a lengthy and intense process of socialization into a subject. For many teachers this socialization originates when they are still pupils as they begin to specialize as arts, science or social-science students. They become separated from those in other areas of specialism and are immersed in the particular self-evidencies of their chosen intellectual sub-world.

> pupils and students with each increase in their educational life are
> ... sub-divided and educationally insulated from each other.
> They are equally bound to subject hierarchies and for similar
> reasons to staff; their identities and their future is shaped by the
> department. Their vertical and work-based relationships are
> strong, whilst their horizontal relationships will tend to be limited
> to non-task areas. (Bernstein, 1971, p. 62)

This process of specialization and socialization through and into a subject also 'means accepting a given selection, organization, pacing and timing of knowledge realized in the pedagogical frame' (Bernstein, 1971, p. 57). The 'taken for granted' reference scheme that constitutes a particular subject at a particular time is thus one basis of conflict between subjects. Entrenched views about the possible and the desirable for one group of teachers are confronted by contrasting views held by another group. This level of subcultural division and antagonism between (certain) subjects is further maintained and reinforced in most secondary schools by their strongly bounded departmental structure. The department gives organizational teeth to the intellectual 'ethnocentrism of disciplines'; that is, what Campbell calls 'the symptoms of tribalism or nationalism or ingroup partisanship in the internal and external relations of ... academic disciplines' (1968, p. 328). The department as the organizational vehicle of the subject is a major focus of the group interests of most teachers in the secondary school.

Conflicts over access to scarce resources – time, personnel, capitation, territory and pupils, or at least particular varieties of pupils – are enjoined between departments. Clearly, in one sense, such conflicts are always unequal. In the English education system certain subjects start out in such a contest with in-built advantages. The strongly entrenched status hierarchy among subjects, which is based upon a combination of exchange-values and academic orientation, handicaps those departments which represent practical or enactive subjects. The most powerful and most influential departments are commonly, but not invariably, the 'big four': maths, English, languages and science. The traditional status of these subjects is certainly a necessary condition for the influence that they wield in the school but not always a sufficient one. To make the most of their advantage these departments must ensure, both in terms of objective measures like examination results and through impression-management strategies, that they retain the confidence and goodwill of the headteacher and their colleagues. In some cases the impression of a set of coherent and agreed policies and practices being pursued with well co-ordinated efficiency within a department is difficult to maintain (these issues are explored in more detail in Ch. 9). As Seeman points out:

> When they are not closing the ranks to contest for resources at the inter-professional level, ideological factions *within* subjects often dispute amongst themselves. One finds different beliefs about the aims of education, the essential constituents of the subject and how best to teach it. (1972, p. 50; my emphasis)

The public leakage of internecine dispute within a department can damage the standing and influence of the department in public debate and private negotiation. 'It seems to be generally felt that public disagreement among the members of a team not only incapacitates them for united action but also embarrasses the reality sponsored by the team' (Goffman, 1971, p. 91). However, the subject affiliations of the teacher is not necessarily the only focus for the development of shared interests and values. Factional groupings can coalesce on other bases. One such basis of groupings within the comprehensive school is the contrasting public/grammar and elementary/secondary-modern traditions. Hargreaves suggests that 'Today the resonances are still to be felt in the staffrooms of comprehensive schools where two distinct if overlapping occupational cultures have been brought together in an uncomfortable alliance' (1980, p. 129). To a great degree the dominant pattern of comprehensive education, and the extent of change or lack of change from existing models of schooling, can be explained in terms of the tensions and conflicts between these two occupational cultures. However, even this dual model of separate traditions may be an oversimplification. In fact Hargreaves goes on to point out, and others have reinforced this view (Reynolds and Sullivan, 1981), that during the 1950s and 1960s two ideal-typical forms of secondary-modern school developed. One reflected the accepted stereotype of a 'child-minding institution', as for example described by Partridge (1968), employing 'coercive collectivist strategies'; that is, an emphasis on social control backed up by physical punishment, generating 'a somewhat rebellious, unqualifed delinquescent output' (Reynolds and Sullivan, 1981, p. 132). The others anticipated many of the curricular reforms and 'progressive' teaching methods of early comprehensive schools and employing 'incorporative collectivist' strategies:

In essence, the schools were attempting to fulfil their allotted role of attaining goals concerned with social control/instrumental development of talent/expressive development of qualities of humanity and citizenship by attempting to tie their pupils into an acceptance of adult society and adult standards by means of developing relationships with the teachers who represented the adult society. (Reynolds and Sullivan, 1981, p. 124)

In other words, the development of the comprehensive school system in this country has drawn upon a teaching force socialized into and committed to a number of quite distinct, often conflicting, educational traditions and occupational cultures. The tensions and organizational problems of social integration which arise from these distinctions are most evident where comprehensive schools have been formed by amalgamation. Again, what is at stake in these situations are the interests of competing groups of teachers. Contesting definitions of the school carry with them the aspirations, career chances and professional identities of their adherents. We now have a number of case studies of comprehensive schools which display the consequences.

Phoenix Comprehensive

Riseborough (1981) describes a situation at Phoenix Comprehensive where the arrival of a new headteacher, who saw himself as a 'social democrat and evolutionary', produced a major career upheaval for a group of 'old' secondary-modern staff. These 'old' staff found themselves labelled as 'bad' teachers in the eyes of the new head; they represented values and methods of working which were at odds with the head's aspirations for the 'new' school. A number of them were not appointed to posts of responsibility after comprehensivization, and despite their protected salaries they were faced with vertical and horizontal demotion and 'professional degradation'. According to Riseborough:

> The 'old' staff reacted antagonistically, isolating and alienating themselves from the head and his 'good' teachers still further. In this situation of isolation and alienation they developed inverted norms and values which the head perceived as even more deviant than before. (1981, p. 361)

The 'old' staff formed a major obstacle to changes that the headteacher sought to introduce into the new school. They were already antagonistic to many of the headteacher's ideas and beliefs, and their experience of being stigmatized as unworthy reinforced their opposition to innovation. As the teachers described it, their opposition was deliberate and planned. They articulated and advocated an alternative view of goals, organization, curriculum and teaching methods for the school. They were unwilling to consider the headteacher's conception of comprehensive education. Here are two teacher's views:

> Things got worse and worse. We were in rebellion. Every suggestion he made we jettisoned for the hell of it. We took issue with him on every change. It's stupid that there should have been a rumpus over so many trivial things but that's how things got. (Age 37)

> We had to get out of the staffroom and talk about the latest incident. We'd get our heads together. We'd plot. We're all facing similar problems and we'd talk about them. If I'd been alone I'd have gone mad. I can't offer him loyalty. There can be no agreement between us, we agree to differ. I don't mind in the least backstabbing now. Once you would never have got me to

have an interview like this because it was disloyal. I don't like to talk to him. When I see him I walk in the other direction or I don't see him, if you know what I mean. Everything he does and says now as far as I'm concerned is stillborn. We've reached a position where we can't discuss anything. We're poles apart. I can't accept anything this man puts forward. Comprehensives are rubbish. If it was announced that we were going back to what it was there would be no groans here. As far as I'm concerned it has been shown not to work. (Age 46)
(Quoted in Riseborough, 1981, p. 261)

Archetypically these comments are expressed in the language of micro-politics. While they were denied access to the formal positions of power under the new regime, the 'old' teachers could exert considerable pressure through their opposition to and non-co-operation with the headteacher's new ideas. Although Riseborough points out that 'the Head was publically unperturbed, seeing it as a short-term management problem' (p. 257). Policy directives were ignored or subverted and the 'old' staff continued with classroom work virtually unchanged from their secondary-modern days; they were able to deny the head 'control of themselves'. Public confrontations and conflicts were commonplace, staff discussions were often acrimonious and emotive. The 'old' staff were openly hostile to the head and his proposed changes. Their 'latent' secondary-modern-school identity provided a source of alternative self-conception and subcultural affiliation to set against the 'dominant coalition' of pro-change teachers (Child, 1972, pp. 101–2) who were recruited and promoted by the headteacher and who supported his view of the school:

It's not in my nature to bury the hatchet. At least not on his terms. Besides, I now like to see how far it is possible to push the establishment. I'm not willing to conform. I couldn't change my ideas now on how the school should be run. I've become old as a result of disputing things. But I feel better when I stake my claims. Whatever happens I've not lost. I'm still able to oppose. I don't enjoy opposition but having done it again I feel I am still in my prime, am not counted out yet. I'm not worried that the Head thinks he's won, he won a long time ago, but I'd hate him to think that not only has he won but he has beaten me as well. He'll never beat me. The bigger the thorn I am in his side, the happier I am. I know he'd like me to leave but I wouldn't like to give him the satisfaction. (Sam, ex Senior Master, Clique Spokesman, age 53)

They fought back and it's very sad to see what it has done to them. The person who is most sad is Sam. Now for Sam life is ruined. He has let everything get under his skin, because he is an emotional man. Literally one wonders what is going to happen to him. Some of us get really worried about him because sometimes he is almost on the edge of some kind of collapse. He is a man of principle but of too much emotion. I've seen him nearly in tears. Sam's a nice person. I hate to think the head can do this to a person. I wish he'd got the ability to get out of it, start afresh. Certainly to get away, because the head regards Sam as some kind of snapping dog at his heels, a dog he can always beat. He's changed quite visibly. The spring's gone out of him. Sam has now got the reputation of a rabid dog. It's eroded him. It's done terrible things to him. He's an all-time loser. It's a tragedy because of course Sam's not the only one. (Colleague of 'Old' Staff) (Quoted in Riseborough, 1981, p. 364)

The talk is of winning and losing, and the person and the personal are part of the conflict and 'the stake'. This is no cool rational process; it is a conflict between persons, groups and ideologies. It is a matter of confrontation, influence, or the lack of it, and emotions. It is micro-politics.

Victoria Road Comprehensive

There is considerable support for Riseborough's analysis in Beynon's (1985) account of Victoria Road Comprehensive. In this case, former secondary-modern teachers were assigned to work in a separate lower-school building, physically and culturally isolated from the political mainstream of the school. Of the lower-school staff of seventeen, ten were permanently based there whilst the others had the status of 'visitors' in that they travelled between sites. The majority were former secondary-modern teachers (or their college-trained successors) doing what was seen by those in authority as necessary, highly laudible but essentially low-status, 'junior' work. During comprehensivization in the late 1960s the grammar-school staff (and their university-trained graduate successors) had secured the positions of real influence in Victoria Road.

The lower-school 'residents' felt, as a result, deprived of authority and remote from both the main site and the inner workings of even their own subject departments. Again, the teachers involved responded with anger and frustration. They failed to recognize the superiority of the 'paper qualifications' of the grammar-school teachers and valued instead a concept of 'schoolmastery' based upon teaching skills and pupil control. Here there are contrasting definitions of the school and competing systems of legitimation: teaching skill set against subject knowledge. However, in contrast to the 'old' staff at Phoenix the lower-school teachers were not opposed to change; indeed, they were advocates of mixed-ability grouping and curriculum innovation. None the less, as at Phoenix they were excluded from formal decision-making and they responded in a similar way by exploiting unofficial channels. Again, we should note that their ideological support for changes, like mixed-ability, were not entirely divorced from vested and self-interests. The secondary-modern staff as a whole were held responsible for the pattern of mixed-ability (with some banding) that had emerged in the first three years of Victoria Road. They had energetically advocated it, seeing it as a means of horizontal promotion in that it enabled them to teach a cross-section of pupils and not be confined, as formerly, to the less able. This made possible covert curriculum innovation. They were fiercely critical of the domination of department machinery and syllabuses by 'absentee' heads of department who rarely set foot in the lower school. They felt excluded from decisions made over the allocation of budgets, resources, content and pedagogy. Many had entered into protracted and acrimonious arguments, got nowhere and had been forced into more devious manoeuvrings to get their way. Whilst they paid lip-service to official demands and syllabuses, they covertly introduced their own topics, materials and approaches.

The Victoria Road case also demonstrates the continuing significance of the secondary-modern/grammar-school divide. Beynon's case study was conducted twelve years after amalgamation, and he says:

> The formation of Victoria Road had been achieved through the amalgamation of a number of secondary moderns with the grammar school to form a comprehensive of over 2000 boys. A true understanding of the undercurrents and staff relations in Lower

school was only possible in relation to that event, which still impinged on the lives of teachers, many of whom had not been there at the time. (Beynon, 1985, p. 170–1)

Beynon's account also alerts us to the perpetuation of subcultural distinctions within the teaching profession based upon different routes of qualification. The mantle of the ex-secondary-modern staff was taken on by college-trained, BEd teachers while the dominant ex-grammar tradition was maintained and reinforced by their university-trained, PGCE, successors. The emphasis of the former continued to be on 'schoolmastery' (the male generic being deliberate here), while the latter were subject and academic orientated. It may be that the lower-school teachers at Victoria Road can be identified with the 'incorporative collectivist' position, and the 'old' staff at Phoenix with the 'coercive collectivist'. We can certainly find evidence of this division in a third example, my own case study of an amalgamated school (Ball, 1985).

Casterbridge High School

At Casterbridge High three schools were amalgamated to form a comprehensive: two secondary moderns and a boys grammar. The differences in ethos and values and the resultant antipathies between the staffs of the two secondary moderns were as decisive here as those between the secondary-modern teachers and the grammar-school staff. The spoils of the amalgamation were shared between the senior staffs of one of the secondary moderns (Shottsford Road), a proto-comprehensive school in the 'collectivist incorporative' mould, and of the grammar school. The staff of the other secondary modern (Egdon Heath) suffered a similar fate to the 'old' staff at Phoenix: they were stigmatized and labelled as 'bad' teachers. They captured hardly any of the posts of responsibility in the new school and quickly recognized the poor image that they carried with them from their previous school. Describing the amalgamation, Mr Dillon, who served for twenty-three years at Egdon Heath, remarked:

We were unknown quantities. Because of what the Egdon School was, which was sitting in the oldest part of the council estate, our kids got a name for being tough and uncontrollable and of course the teachers were also classed under that heading.

The Egdon teachers were both significantly underrepresented in formal positions of authority at Casterbridge and, as a result of their low informal status, they could do little to influence decision-making in other ways. The mainlines of conflict within Casterbridge were delineated, on the one hand, by the grammar-school tradition and, on the other, by the assertive comprehensive philosophy of the ex-Shottsford teachers. In fact on many of the controversial issues which arose at Casterbridge the ex-Egdon teachers tended to side with the ex-grammar staff. Both groups were opposed to changes like the introduction of mixed-ability and in favour of measures like the retention of caning. The Egdon teachers tended to view their Shottsford colleagues as soft and unrealistic, full of 'airy-fairy' ideas and unworkable theories. As in the other cases we have considered, they stressed the primacy of the craft skills of teaching over and against subject expertise and qualifications, and hard and practical discipline over and against the 'weak', relational forms of control used at Shottsford Road. Where the Shottsford teachers talked about equality and opportunity, the grammar-school staff emphasized ability and standards. For the latter, knowledge of 'the subject' was taken to be of prime importance, together with an understanding of the pedagogical and administrative skills which were required to translate subject expertise into examination passes and university places. They wanted the comprehensive school to continue to be geared to and judged by the numbers of pupils obtaining places in university, and Oxbridge places in particular. Both the grammar and the Egdon teachers held strong views about the fixed nature of pupil abilities, and from their contrasting perspectives and in terms of their vested and self-interests both groups were opposed to innovations, like mixed-ability, which were advocated by the Shottsford teachers and supported by the new head-teacher. For their opponents, mixed-ability and the idea of subject integration threatened to undermine the basis for their assertion of special skills in being able to deal with the most able or the least able pupils as separate groups with specific and special demands and problems.

As a combined opposition, the grammar and Egdon teachers were able to inhibit or block many of the innovations put forward in the early years of the new school; the Shottsford teachers spoke of the 'pervasive influence', the 'strategies' and the 'opposition to change' of the grammar-school teachers. Indeed, the grammar-school teachers, especially those in positions of authority, may be seen to have been engaged in *strategic maintenance*; that is, the calculated defence of the values and practices of the grammar school against the threats of innovation. The following comments were made by three Shottsford teachers:

> There was a major row about the sixth form because the person who had been appointed Head of Sixth Form was a disaffected ex-grammar school bloke who started off very negative, saying, 'We're not having the riff-raff in the sixth form.' And in the first year there was a sort of major campaign by one or two people to get established the idea that the open sixth form – the one year sixth form – was valid and those were customers that should be treated with equal status to the other customers. And that worked.

> See, the whole strategy of the ex-grammar school teachers is quite simply a ratchet and it's very blatant – I mean, the History bloke, coming back once a term about selection in the fourth year. Now he's going to give me a paper in September about how he could select them at the beginning of the third year. And, of course, he'd really want to select them after the first term of the second year. And they've done the same thing.

> But it's just – it's part of this process whereby the grammar – I think, on the whole, the grammar school has had a very pervasive influence, you know, it's used all sorts of subtle strategies to keep things going, keep things comfortable.

Again we may see this as an attempt by the grammar-school teachers to defend their preferred version of the school against the assertion by the Shottsford teachers of an alternative version. The grammar-school teachers were 'to a man' opposed to comprehensivization and sought in the new school to save what they could from the past, their primary concern being the maintenance of high academic standards.

The headteacher of Casterbridge was very aware of the opposition of the grammar-school staff to change and to comprehensivize education generally, but he described this opposition as 'mainly passive'. The tension and antagonism which underlay the discussions in meetings often had to be read as a *sub-text* (Marland, 1982b), which was only accessible through asides and allusions. One commonly used tactic was that the grammar-school staff would often appear not to understand or see the relevance or point of innovations being proposed by the headteacher or the Shottsford teachers. They would often refuse to be drawn into substantive debate. Apathy or lack of interest were very effective delaying tactics, and as a result discussions would get nowhere, action would not be taken, decisions would be referred to other meetings. This appeared to be the case even in meetings of the senior management team (the headteacher, three deputies – two ex-grammar, one ex-Egdon Heath – and two senior teachers, both ex-Shottsford). One of the senior teachers described the senior management team:

> as a reacting body rather than an initiating body. It merely responds to what has gone wrong . . . and I am very disappointed about that. That's symptomatic of what happens at all the meetings. Nothing new is happening, nothing is being initiated, what has been has come from Alan and I. It's a difference in experience and background. He has been in different schools. He was a deputy in a comprehensive school, he is aware of recent developments in education. Clive Bishop has been at the same school for 28 years. Dan Gordon almost as long. They are happier with a school with tradition, not in transition. It's understandable in terms of their background.

The two ex-grammar deputies, Clive Bishop and Dan Gordon, were indeed powerful 'carriers of tradition' for the grammar school. Clive Bishop had been at the school for twenty-eight years – it was his first teaching appointment – and Dan Gordon had previously been a pupil in the grammar before returning to teach there.

There were critical moments, however, when the divisions among the staff were openly displayed. As the headteacher explained:

> Occasionally, like a bubble, certainly in the first two years, it sort of burst through. Sometimes at unexpected times . . . I can remember in the second year, when an academic board meeting was devoted to discussing provision for our more gifted children. And we had already then set up the system we have, of attaching our more gifted children to our senior staff, and I have eight attached to me, to monitor their progress and try to bring some enrichment programmes, where appropriate, to their work. And

when we disussed this there suddenly arose a nucleus of the academic board, mainly those who have been in the grammar school, that this was a totally unnecessary expenditure of energy and time on the part of senior staff; if we'd had rigid streaming, as in the grammar school, and these pupils were all in one stream, and were taught just normally, then all this other thing would come as part of the teaching programme and there would be no need for these other groups. And it was a very emotive meeting. Suddenly out of a situation I wouldn't have expected to give rise to these sorts of things, suddenly the whole anti-comprehensive feeling of these teachers came out very strongly indeed. It was a most peculiar thing at the time and really made me realise that though we appeared then to be all working towards the same end on the surface, deep down there were strong feelings against it.

The most senior of the ex-grammar-school teachers described the same meeting to me, and his comments illustrate the problems that can arise when groups with different experiences and interpretative frameworks are brought together in a single institution:

I think the Head's against any form of streaming. I don't think the Head is pro it. You see we had a meeting of the Pastoral Board, or one of these wretched boards we have that lasts for hours on a Wednesday afternoon, and he was saying 'what is the best way to encourage the bright child'. We have them in little monitor groups, you know, I see them every time they have an exam, every time they have an assessment, every time they've got to choose an option. A dozen kids in the third and fourth years who I watch all the way through the school. But what annoyed me was, as far as I could see, the best thing you could do for them, would be to treat them as you treat the remedial children at the other end. If you've got your remedial groups in small groups with a specialist, why can't you spare a specialist graduate to teach the other extreme, who's willing to take them 35 at a time. I can't see this. I can't see why. I can't see what the objection to it is. And I got up a thing, a sort of round robin not just from grammar school people, people who were Heads of Department who felt the same way. The discussion was nonsensical because the only way to teach them was to teach them according to their ability. And he got very upset about this. And said was this the grammar school clique again and was it coming to the fore and all this, that and the other . . . but I didn't do this out of any kind of spite. I didn't know what they were talking about.

Here again the teacher suggests that he simply cannot understand what the advocates of mixed-ability are trying to say; it does not make sense to him. The grammar-school staff saw mixed-ability as being one of the unacceptable features of the 'positive progressive' views of the Shottsford teachers. It may have been possible, they would argue, with a limited range of ability, but it is not possible with the full range of ability in the comprehensive school:

> I think that they did mixed-ability teaching over there [Shottsford Road] but they only had the 80 per cent who didn't go to the grammar and we had the 20 per cent of grammar school children. The grammar school people didn't want mixed-ability and the Egdon people didn't want it, it was only the Shottsford people who wanted it.

The feeling was that the grammar-school teachers were wasting their talents in being expected to teach mixed-ability classes. Their skills and experience, it was said, had prepared them best to teach top-stream groups:

> There are people who think and still think, and I agree with them, that their talents are diluted because they're trained to teach the most able children and that's what they're best at doing and they find it very difficult teaching less able children and yet they spend a proportion of their time doing that and they report to me – a common grumble – that it just tires them out so they can't give their best to the more able children. And I'm sure it's true. You get very tired of stroppy kids.

In their opposition to mixed-ability the grammar-school teachers were defending their own interests and commitments to teaching and speaking as they saw it in the best interests of the more able children. There were even some suggestions that the secondary-modern staff were not competent to teach more able groups, especially the sixth-form. The grammar-school and Shottsford Road teachers were ranged against one another as opposing cabals, each attempting to 'promote the occupational success' of its members and 'to restructure situations and values in the interests of its members' (Burns, 1955, p. 480). The alliances and coalitions thus established cut across the other potential or occasional interest-group divisions like departments. Indeed, the guerilla skirmishes between the school-based coalitions extended *into* the departments. English was strongly divided into pro- and anti-mixed-ability factions. Humanities were riven with conflicts both over mixed-ability and subject integration. This would seem to confirm the argument put forward by Bacharach and Lawler that:

> Coalitions create and define the parameters of conflict by crystallizing the different interest of sub-groups. In any organization, there are likely to be numerous differences among members and sub-groups, and it is coalitions that highlight and make salient the most critical differences. (1980, p. 105)

Thus inherent in the differences in ideologies, interests and identities at Casterbridge lies the continuing potential for institutional conflict. Clearly, none of the teaching ideologies held by these teachers would be or could be expected to be expunged overnight when their schools disappeared. For both groups of secondary-modern staff and the grammar staff, their work over a number of years had established a commitment to educational goals and values and a substantive teaching identity (Ball, 1972) which they wished to preserve, as far as possible, in the comprehensive school. Despite common assumptions to the contrary, comprehensivization represented a real threat to the careers of many of the grammar-school teachers. They maintained a vested interest in and commitment to forms of education at odds with those being asserted by the teachers from Shottsford Road. The grammar-school staff were anxious to maintain the status quo, to oppose change at all costs. The comprehensive reorganization had certainly changed the conditions within which teachers worked and pupils learned, but it did not ensure the establishment of one particular form of educational experience. Comprehensive education as a process of schooling was to be determined by the outcomes of the conflicts and disputes between opposing coalitions at Casterbridge. What this illustrates in more general terms is the politics of going comprehensive and the difficulties involved in implementing new practices by administrative fiat. Hargreaves makes this point:

> The comprehensive school, then, faces severe problems in creating a coherent and shared belief system or pedagogy. The two

occupational cultures that have developed over time [do] not merely inhibit it, but are themselves likely to outlast mere organizational change. Indeed, they themselves may exercise a profound influence on the different directions comprehensive schools take to solve their problems. (1980, p. 145)

One of the oft-quoted consequences of amalgamation as a basis for comprehensive reorganization (which incidentally is not borne out entirely by the Casterbridge case) is that in the newly formed schools it is the grammar-school teachers who capture the academic posts of responsibility, and the secondary-modern teachers who capture the pastoral posts of responsibility. The assumptions which underlie this separation, either as a real consequence of amalgamation or apocryphal reconstruction of events, are, first, that the experience and skills of the secondary-modern teachers make them best suited to dealing with breakdowns in discipline and pupils' social and personal problems – 'it was the elementary tradition which yielded the most fertile soil for the progressive movement and a concern with the "whole child" supported by new developments in child psychology' (Hargreaves, 1980, p. 140) – and, second, that the experience and skills of the grammar-school teachers make them best suited to academic leadership and examination teaching: 'of course teachers in this tradition never saw their work entirely in such simple academic terms: but a high rate of examination failure warned a teacher that he was for the most part a failure too' (p. 138). It is also implied in these stereotypes that the grammar-school teachers find it difficult to control 'unmotivated' pupils and that the secondary-modern teachers lack the academic expertise for examination teaching. The emphasis of the pastoralists is thus on the moral order of the school, both in individual and communal terms; the academic view is more instrumental, looking to academic achievements as the main measure of school success, again both in individual and communal terms. However, these differences in orientation and interpretation are not simply based upon the contrasting traditions of grammar and elementary schooling. They are to be found in pronounced form in many purpose-built comprehensives. Importantly, they represent alternative career paths through the teaching profession: one more child-orientated and administrative, the other more subject-orientated. The balance of power between the academic and pastoral systems in any one school has implications both for school policy and organizational goals, and for the career opportunities of the teachers who commit themselves to one route or the other.

Bishop McGregor Comprehensive

Burgess's (1983) case study of a Roman Catholic comprehensive provides a clear example of ongoing conflicts between the pastoral (in this case a house system) and the academic. When Bishop McGregor was opened in 1969 the local authority imposed a staffing plan on the new school and 'insisted that all heads of houses should be appointed on a scale 5 salary, which gave them seniority compared with departmental staff' (Burgess, 1983, p. 54). This was reinforced by the headteacher's (Mr Goddard) view of their scope for responsibility:

> As far as Goddard was concerned, House Heads were responsible for welfare, attendance, discipline, uniform and progress. In short, they were responsible for a range of activities similar to those of a Headteacher in a small school. Many of them saw their Houses as 'mini-schools' and organized them accordingly. (p. 58)

This created a strong power-base for the senior pastoral staff. None the less:

> When the Heads of Houses were criticized by the Heads of Departments, the criticisms related to the fact that their job did not involve 'real' teaching. David Peel (Head of the Geography department) summed it up by saying, 'If you're a Head of House you just check to see that all your kids are in uniform and that you have enough chairs for dinner sittings and your job's done'. George Jackson (Head of the English department) considered the job involved 'looking after the children of Mary'. These views were shared by other Heads of departments and many subject teachers who thought the House Heads were paid large allowances for doing very little. For them, 'real teaching' involved introducing pupils to subjects, getting them to work and obtaining examination successes. (p. 60)

The work of the school and the work of the staff were given different emphases by the pastoralists and the academics. Their priorities were different; it is not that they considered the work of the other unimportant, rather they tended to see the smooth running of the school and the achievement of school goals in different ways. Again, these groups hold and advocate competing definitions of the school and, as Burgess remarks, 'the ideas about the school, its norms and the work of teachers were therefore presented to the pupils in different ways' (p. 101) and 'there was an undercurrent of continual conflict between house and departmental duties' (p. 72). One dramatic illustration of the tensions and differences between the house staff and departmental staff at Bishop McGregor is provided by the events which surrounded a walk-out of pupils. The pupils were upset by the fact that they were not to be given a day off school to watch the wedding of Princess Anne on television. Resentment led to a spontaneous walk-out by about 600 pupils. What is of particular interest is the different attitudes and reactions of the house staff and the departmental staff. While the former were active in trying to prevent the pupils from leaving the site 'to uphold school rules on obedience and order' (p. 99), departmental staff either refused to get involved in the situation or actually gave tacit encouragement to the pupils. This, Burgess suggests, highlighted the different norms and loyalties operating among the staff. The headteacher clearly saw the actions of some staff as disloyal and disruptive, and he made some attempts to identify those teachers who had encouraged pupils to leave the school site. 'Although all the staff were supposedly responsible for the behavioural norms, it was only the Heads of Houses and a few assistant teachers (rumoured to have career motives) who attempted to disourage pupils from leavng the school' (p. 101). The result was disorder in the school, disunity among the staff and conflict between the headteacher and some teachers.

The relative strength of the pastoral and departmental systems vary dramatically between schools. In some cases the balance of power is exactly the reverse of that at Bishop McGregor; that is, the departmental goals are in the ascendant. To a great extent the link between influence and goals is a very practical one. The headteacher is normally able to determine how the points available for posts of responsibility in the school are to be distributed. If the headteacher considers it to be in the interests of the school, points can be used to build up a sophisticated structure of pastoral-care posts. Once established in post, the pastoral teachers will constitute a major power block in school policy-making and decision-making.

Their concerns are primarily, as we have seen at Bishop Macgregor, with the problems of moral order. For the academic, departmental teachers' cognitive and instrumental goals are to the fore. These differences can often lead to conflict over policy. The system of grouping pupils for teaching purposes is a common example. Pastoralists often see the advantages in mixed-ability groupings, which can avoid the creation of alienated bottom-stream groups the consequences of which they have to deal with. However, as at Beachside, many academics are opposed to the abolition of streaming, which they see as the only effective means for teaching their subject. In one of the schools I visited in order to conduct interviews the pastoral staff appeared to have achieved almost total domination of the micro-political arena. As at Bishop Macgregor, the heads-of-year meetings were the major focus of discussion and decision-making and the pastoral staff exercised primary control over policy-making and the day-to-day running of the school. One of the deputy heads in the school described what she called 'the great divide' – 'the divide between the academic and the pastoral', and she said of the pastoral staff:

> the people that kept the school going were the Heads of Year, they were the most powerful people and the most effective, and they still are. They are what I call the school Mafia ... when I came here, the academic side was absolutely moribund. ... And the Heads of Department didn't really meet whereas the Heads of Year meet regularly once a fortnight. ... And in fact I have actually mentioned from time to time why things have appeared on a Heads of Year agenda which possibly could be seen to be matters for Heads of Departments; but since the Heads of Department don't really come together, they don't get discussed in that way. And that sort of downgrades the academic side all the time and elevates the status of the other.

Here then is a situation where the pastoral staff have been able to appropriate matters of school business which would in other circumstances have come under the auspices of an academic committee. To a great extent the definition of the school rests exclusively in the hands of the heads of year. The school in question was regarded by its teachers and by local authority officials as having considerable disciplinary and social problems among its intake. This provided a strong basis for the legitimation of a pastoral bias.

Resources were devoted to coping with pupil problems and establishing an elaborate system of disciplinary referral. The difficult, perhaps impossible, question to answer is whether the hegemony of pastoral care is a sensible and straightforward response to major problems in the school or is actually serving to maintain a definition of the school's problems and concerns as one of discipline and social control. Certainly any reorientation of school goals and policies would undermine the established position and organizational interests of the pastoral staff.

There is some evidence to suggest that current economic and political changes affecting schools are having some impact on the relative influence of and resource support for the pastoral and academic systems. The increasing emphasis on academic results, which must be published, combined with a real decline in the financing of schools, has, in some cases, led to a dismantling of or reduction in resources devoted to pastoral care. Such changes will obviously have consequences for the balance of political control in the school, adversely affecting the interests of some teachers and enhancing those of others. However, the specific nature of the impact of such a change will necessarily be mediated by and through the micro-politics of the institution.

3
Age and gender: rancorous change

Crabbed age and youth cannot live together: Youth is full of pleasance,
age is full of care.   (William Shakespeare)

Through the case studies presented in the previous chapter, I
addressed conflict and change in relation to major aspects of school
organization and structure. I have also accounted for the continuing impact on school politics of the grammar/secondary-modern
traditions and their attendant affiliations, which cross-cut the
organization of the school. However, there are other cross-cutting
ties which need to be attended to. Changes in school policy or
curriculum innovations are frequently originated 'at the top'. Headteachers are, arguably, the most active change-agents in schools.
However, pressure for change – pressure which is often resisted –
also frequently arises from among the ranks of 'lower participants'
in the organization. In particular, young, newly qualified teachers
and women teachers can be a source of agitation or unrest even if
they do not have immediate access to channels of political influence.

The normal emphasis in studies of entrants into teaching is on the
effects and processes of socialization into the occupational culture.
The tyro is viewed as a naive subject responding unthinkingly to
pressures to adapt to the school and its working practices:

> By observation and experience the young teacher learns the
> appropriate codes of conduct which relate to such things as: how
> to address other members of staff in front of pupils; how to talk

to, relate to, and associate with pupils; what constitutes acceptable dress for a teacher; and in school expectations about
marking, involvement in extra-curricular activities, and so on. If
one is to have a smooth-running career it is as well to fit in (see
Hanson and Harrington, 1976, pp. 5–6) to internalize or at least
strategically comply (see Lacey, 1977, pp. 72–3) with these
informal although very important rules (see Lacey 1970). (Sikes,
1985, p. 36)

Indeed, measures of teacher attitudes do show that while during
training there are marked increases in radicalism, scores go into
rapid decline during the first year of teaching (see Lacey, 1977,
p.130). However, Lacey counsels against the attractive simplicities
of the straightforward socialization model, which can all too easily
lead to an over-socialized conception of teachers. He argues that:

> It is apparent that the streams of socialization that we identified
> as characteristic of the student teacher culture continue and flow
> into schools. . . . The student culture has now become a latent
> culture providing a reservoir of skills and values on which the
> probationary teacher can draw. . . . The school has now become
> the arena for competing pressures. On the one hand there is the
> need to become effective and accepted within the school, on the
> other hand the desire to make the school more like the place in
> which the teacher would like to teach. (Lacey, 1977, p. 136)

Junior staff have, obviously, the most recent training, they are
likely to have been exposed to up-to-date research on processes of
schooling, they may be familiar with the latest curriculum innovations, they will have had opportunities to experiment with unortho-
dox teaching approaches. In contrast, their first-appointment
schools can appear old-fashioned, out of touch and unwilling to
adapt to changing circumstances. Lacey quotes an English teacher
from his probationary year:

> My opinion from the Head down (barring two teachers) of the
> staff is that they are indifferent and incompetent and quite unable
> to deal with the problems of the school. I think that I am probably
> too close to the situation at present to write anything really useful
> – whatever I write would be simply bitter, unpleasant and would
> only reflect my complete disaffection with the situation. (p. 135)

(There are parallels here with the feelings of powerlessness and political impotence expressed by the 'old' Phoenix teachers; see Ch. 2 above). There are a number of possible outcomes to situations such as these. Such teachers may eventually adjust to the situation as found and become absorbed into the established institutional culture. They may leave the school or leave teaching altogether, in search of a setting that they find more conducive to their personal values. They may continue in the school as bitter and isolated voices of opposition to 'the hierarchy' and the staus quo. Or they may find allies who share their dissatisfactions and with whom they are able to act to achieve change, 'to make the school more like the place in which [they] would like to teach'. It is this last case which is of immediate interest here.

According to Hirschmann (1970), these alternatives represent the three basic lines of action available to any organizational member. He sums them up as 'Exit, Voice and Loyalty'. The 'exit' choice is fairly obvious, but Hirschmann makes the point that 'the presence of the exit alternative can therefore tend to *atrophy the development of the art of voice*' (1970, p. 43). If exit is easily available, then organizations will be less likely to change, those content with the status quo will remain and potential agitators will leave. However, in the current economic context exit is certainly not an easy alternative for teachers. Falling rolls and financial cuts have drastically reduced job opportunities and promotion opportunities in schools. Dissatisfied teachers are finding it increasingly difficult to move between schools in search of settings which they find conducive. Furthermore, new entrants are facing the prospect of long periods without promotion. This may tend to further increase the dissatisfaction of youth and generally reduce compliance among lower participants. Also, if there is little possibility of promotion, then there is less reason to cultivate a good impression in the eyes of superiors. As regards the more drastic exit alternative, leaving teaching altogether, this, in a period of high unemployment, is an opportunity available to only a few. Many staffrooms contain small numbers of teachers who have lost, or maybe never had, a cognitive commitment to teaching. They are trapped by family commitments, mortgages and a pension to a job they resent. They exist on a narrow platform of 'continuance commitment' (Woods, 1979, pp. 143–4) to the organization. The profit involved in staying and the losses to be incurred by leaving are reduced to a crude financial calculation. In relation to issues associated with change, such groups normally take a position of non-involvement and uninterest or respond on the basis of narrowly defined, personal, vested interests. They will oppose anything that disrupts their minimalist participation in the work of the school but may be willing to support proposals that 'make life easier'. They may at times give public 'voice' to their private grumbles. Hirschmann defines 'voice' as:

> any attempt at all to change, rather than to escape from, an objectionable state of affairs, whether through individual or collective petition to the management directly in charge, through appeal to a higher authority with the intention of forcing a change in management, or through various types of actions and protests, including those which are meant to mobilise public opinion. (1970, p. 30)

As Hirschmann points out, 'voice' may be either the articulation of individual views and grievances or a collective statement. As already suggested, collective responses in an organizational setting depend to a large degree on the awareness among a group of actors 'of the commonality of their goals and the commonality of their fate' (Bacharach and Lawler, 1980, p. 8); that is, the establishment of an 'interest group'. However, as indicated previously, the strength of subject divisions within the organization of the school and in the socialization of teachers militate against the likelihood of junior staff seeing themselves as having goals and futures in common: 'their vertical and work-based relationships are strong, whilst their horizontal relationships will tend to be limited to non-task areas' (Bernstein, 1971, p. 61). None the less, cross-cutting ties based upon shared junior status and shared problems of becoming established as a teacher should not be underestimated. Peterson (1964) certainly found a strong awareness of differences between generations of teachers. These differences provided fuel for conflicts over teaching methods and types of relationships with pupils: 'This conflict, typically, concerns the promotion and defence of seniority privileges' by mature teachers and young teachers' 'efforts to secure increased status for themselves' (Peterson, 1964, p. 283). The following interview exchange encapsulates many of the youthful criticisms of senior colleagues:

> I.: How would you say that your generation of teachers compares with the older generation? Are they different?

2s: Um-hum. Yes, I think so. I think there's quite a difference. We are more interested in children as children, they are more interested in getting the subject matter across. The older teachers want the children to sit there, and *behave* themselves, and *learn* their lesson, or *else*! The younger teachers are more interested in children as children. Oh, don't get the idea that we aren't interested in the subject matter. We want them to get so interested they will have a thirst for it. And don't get the idea that the older teachers are all like that. I've had some myself, this journalism teacher I was telling you about, who got us interested in poetry. She was a very good teacher.

Hannan also found an awareness of generational factors within the micro-politics of Redmond College:

I suppose that I would have to say that I am becoming increasingly aware of an attitude of less than total happiness on the part of some who do not feel themselves belonging to it, towards what they would regard as the establishment. . . . Junior members of staff seem to resent senior members of staff and the committees on which they sit and the decisions which they take. (Senior staff member)

the hierarchy are no longer in touch with the new developments among younger staff who are actually faced with the problem of teaching and contact with students on the 'shop floor'. (Senior staff member)
(Quoted in Hannan, 1980, p. 133)

In Hannan's quotation a classical separation between policy and execution, management and workers, is indicated. Peterson notes of his study that 'most inter-teacher conflicts reported in interviews were between "young" and "old" teachers' (1964, p. 300). Intra-generational ties emerged as far stronger than intergenerational ones in his research and he suggests that 'young teachers form into generational cliques' partly in order to protect themselves from 'uncomfortable situations with mature teachers' (p. 296). Open interpersonal conflicts arose most often in instances when young teachers were 'standing up for their rights'. Older teachers were keen to defend minor privileges and 'prestige symbols', such as room assignments, against the newcomers. The older teachers also held '(somewhat defensively) to traditionalism' (p. 312) in teaching methods, against the younger teachers' assertion of more 'progressive views'; they often responded to the criticisms of their younger colleagues with feelings of bitterness and abandonment and were 'concerned about young teachers' lack of commitment and dedication' (p. 290):

16s: They're not dedicated to their work at all. They're not going to do anything extra – activities or professional organizations or anything else. When the bell rings, they check out – school's out. Now, we were brought up to feel that we were getting a lot out of it because we were putting a lot into it. I don't think they feel that way at all. It's just a job to them. I feel that they don't have the same devotion to the teaching profession that we have.

I.: How do you think your generation of teachers compares with the younger generation of teachers?

48s: There is a great deal of difference. ... I hate to sit in judgement on others, but I don't think they have been held to the standards themselves. These teachers who have been coming out of the schools now, not the standards that we were held to. I have teachers coming from the teachers' college to do practice teaching. I can see that they haven't been held to do things just so, or maybe they are products of the war too. They aren't good spellers, they can't go to the board and write out a sentence for the youngsters and spell correctly. And some of the colleges are saying 'What if they can't spell, some of the smartest people can't spell'. Well, I say that if they can't, they had better learn, and things like that, you know – being held to correctness. I just thank teachers who did so much to wake me up. I don't know whether we will ever get back to that standard or not. I don't know.

The assertive claims of the youngsters can be invalidated by such talk, and pressures for change and innovation fended off as unrealistic or poorly thought out. The 'older' teachers have made a massive investment over the years in their occupational role, they identify strongly with their profession and are understandably keen to deflect or disparage potentially damaging criticisms. Peterson writes, 'In the course of time, sacred qualities are attached to the conditions and procedures of the school, the forms of organization and interaction in the work setting, and the model of teacher and teacher career' (1964, p. 291). Viewed in this way, pedagogical or other sorts of changes being advocated by young teachers may be profoundly disturbing to the older generation of teachers who 'take great satisfaction in competence at certain techniques and develop self-conceptions around them' (Becker and Strauss, 1956, p. 253). During periods of widespread change in the education system, the later 1960s for example, when young advocates of innovation find public support for their views, it may be that older teachers experience a sense of professional anomie. 'Young teachers, along with students and society at large, have moved away from the cherished, and now somewhat sanctified, values of their youth' (Peterson 1964, p. 291). However, as the political climate shifts traditional approaches can become relegitimated, as has been the case in British schools during the past decade.

I quoted in Chapter 1 an example from Burgess's work of junior staff asserting their views over those of their senior colleagues. By presenting a united front in a staff-forum meeting, a group of young teachers were able to achieve a redefinition of the school prize-giving – replacing the headteacher's preference for prizes for 'academic' achievement with a more informal event followed by a 'disco'. The headteacher, despite reservations, was unwilling to oppose the strength of feeling and weight of numbers of the junior teachers on this particular issue. (This raises other issues pertaining to headship strategies which are pursued in the following chapter.) Concerted action of this kind also has to be set against the norm of vertical insulation, discussed earlier, which, as Bernstein (1971) argues, separates teachers in different subject departments. If the typical pattern of collegial relationships is subject based, then there are definite constraints upon the possibility of concerted action by younger teachers. If, however, as at Bishop Macgregor, subject departments are not all-powerful, then generational factions may become more signficant in the political area. None the less, it is certainly a mistake to assume that all younger teachers automatically subscribe to educational views opposed to those of their elders. As Lacey's (1977) research indicates, not all young teachers enter school with radical views, and the degree of radicalism among student teachers is conditioned by the ethos of their training institution. Many of those who do carry radicalism into their first teaching posts are quickly overwhelmed by collegial pressures to conform or career pressure to 'play safe'. It would appear that only a few are actively and openly engaged in attempts at 'strategic redefinition' in this early stage of their career. Intergenerational conflicts normally remain as a potential and occasional source of change and reaction in schools. The public use of 'voice' is a daunting prospect for the tyro teachers. That is made clear by a woman teacher who described in interview her reactions to the regime in her first school:

> I began to get the sense that there was something fundamentally wrong with the whole way the school was organized and, if that was a comprehensive school, then, to me, that wasn't what a comprehensive school ought to be like. And actually nobody else seemed to have those kind of worries in the school. I tried talking to other people about it, I can remember, and it was quite obvious they didn't understand what I meant . . . but the interesting thing was that I got up in this staff meeting and I said it all. I feel it was quite a courageous thing to do now really, looking back. It was just foolhardiness at the time because I didn't have the sense to know how inapposite it was. Bear in mind that there were 103 teachers in the school and 102 of them were more senior than me! And I said, 'It's us; we do it to these children. If we treated them differently, if we gave them a different curriculum, this would not happen'. And there was such an embarrassed silence and the Headmaster said 'Thank you very much, Miss Welch, for your contribution', and that was the end of that. Two days later, the Deputy Head called me into his office and he said 'I've been thinking about what you said at the staff meeting. What do you suggest exactly?' (Information technology teacher, a London comprehensive)

Very few young teachers 'take on' the 'powers-that-be' in their new school quite like 'Dick', a teacher who 'tried to revolutionize the power stucture' (Woods, 1981, p. 289) in his school with 'radical departures from the school's usual customs and structure' (p. 287). Dick engaged in a series of radical innovations, became involved in direct confrontations with the headteacher and eventually resigned 'when the Head had exerted himself and reinforced the status quo' (p. 288). Indeed, it could be said that Dick's approach of all-out assault on the established norms and values of his school was bound to fail and that he displayed a lack of micro-political competence. Others who take a more restrained and less visible approach (like

Woods's Tom) may in the long term achieve greater and more permanent institutional change:

> Tom's approach to teaching carries a veneer of compliance, but he provided therapy for the pupils, an association centre in the school, attempted and accomplished the occasional innovation, had an impact on some influential opinions, and linked these efforts with his wider concerns. (Woods, 1981, p. 289)

It is difficult to estimate the representativeness of Tom's activities. Obviously, cases of individual opposition and attempts at re-definition and change are hard to trace. Realistially, perhaps, we should regard Hirschmann's third alternative, 'loyalty', as the primary response among new entrants to teaching. However, Hirschmann does not treat 'exit', 'voice', and 'loyalty' as mutually exclusive; quite the opposite. He argues: 'Loyalty, then, helps to redress the balance by raising the cost of exit. It thereby pushes men into the alternative, creativity-requiring courses of action from which they would normally recoil . . .' (Hirschmann, 1970, p. 80). He goes on:

> Loyalty is a key concept in the battle between exit and voice not only because, as a result of it, members may be locked into their organizations a little longer and thus use the voice option with greater determination and resourcefulness than would otherwise be the case. (p. 83)

In simple terms, Hirschmann's point here is that the more personally committed to the organization actors are then the more likely they are to want to influence its policies and ethos, to change the organization, making it the sort of place they would want to continue to work in and take a personal pride in. This would seem to be supported by Baldridge's (1971) finding, noted previously, that the most politically active members of the institution also reported the highest levels of loyalty. None the less, the argument here needs to be treated carefully. First, it might be suggested that new entrants are unlikely to display high levels of loyalty, loyalty is hardly an immediate response in a new situation. If young teachers do not engage in 'voice' this may be because of apathy, as Peterson's (1964) older critics suggest, or political naivety or strategic compliance 'in which the individual complies with the authority figure's definition of the situation and the constraints of the situation but retains private reservations about them' (Lacey 1977, p. 72). Second, we need to bear in mind the effects of political failure on individual loyalty. If the use of 'voice' to achieve change proves ineffective, then over time loyalty may weaken. It may be that headteachers sometimes mistake constructive criticism and arguments for change for embittered sniping and vice versa. Third, as Hirschman recognizes, the effectiveness of 'voice' may be linked to the availability of the 'exit' option. Those who are trapped in a particular institution may find themselves stifled, in more than one sense, and loyalties may be severely tested. (The headteacher's perceptions of loyalty are explored in the following chapters.)

If we accept that (some) young teachers do articulate ideological alternatives and do attempt to influence or change the established definition of their school, then we must also take seriously the political significance of that group which was often referred to in interviews as the 'old guard'. The 'old guard' typically consists of older, long-serving teachers who, it might be said, have been left behind in the flow of political activity and educational change. An 'old guard' often emerges with the arrival of a new headteacher. They find themselves at odds with the thinking of the new head-teacher and cast to the sidelines when decisions are being made. Because of long service, they are often unwilling or unable to look for posts in other schools and are destined to remain until retire-ment, discontented and frequently in conflict with those they see as *arrivistes*. In describing their own situation and their feelings, members of the 'old guard' commonly refer back with affection and approval to 'the good old days', as did Peterson's respondents, and see themselves as defending 'standards' in the face of pointless change. The idea of an 'old guard' can be aligned to some extent with Gouldner's (1957) elaboration of organizational 'locals', but here Gouldner's 'dedicated', 'homeguard' and 'older' types are fused together. Wagstaff provides one example of the emergence of an 'old guard' in a case study of Green Hill Comprehensive School. Three different views are offered:

> We had a very good school in those days; there were no grey areas; it was black and white; the discipline standards in the school were very high. Mr Flyn is very liberal and we developed one or two grey areas, espcially from the view of discipline. (Ted Bolder, Deputy Head)

> The old ruling caucus, Ethel Stone and her ilk were very put out when their status in the school was undermined with people being appointed above them – there were 2 departments which had sitting tenants who had H.O.D.s appointed above them by the Head. They tried to maintain their position and to a certain extent Ethel did although the others lost out. They've not been replaced by any other ruling caucus. (Malcolm Ogden, Head of 6th Year)

> When the Head came he swept everything away. He was too radical. His actions polarised the staff into two camps. This was only resolved with the retirement of the older staff. No negotiation was possible because of the entrenched postions that people were forced to take. (Head of 5th Year)
> (Quoted in Wagstaff, 1983, p. 14)

Another example came from a joint interview with a deputy head and year tutor in an eastern comprehensive school. Twice in the course of the interview they referred to the 'old guard' and their opposition to change.

> DH: One of the things that the old guard tend to do is to dampen or object to anything that county hall suggest. I mean advisers at our school at the moment have a pretty black name among the old guard.

> YT: One of the things we have said is that a lot of the staff don't want to change and they seem to be thinking all the time about early retirement.

> DH: This is the old guard, isn't it.

> YT: The young ones are frustrated I think, and if there is a possibility of the school moving in the right direction I think perhaps they are wary of the Head and the way that he will move.

Here, then, the politics of change are cast in terms of generational conflicts.

Women teachers

Even the most cursory review of theories of organization reveals that the existing body of work is in fact overwhelmingly concerned with theories of men in organizations. Studies of educational organizations have only a slightly better record with regard to recognizing the significance of sexual divisions in institutional life. Some writers assume tacitly that all organizational actors are men or 'treat employees as "unisex"' (Brown, 1976, p. 21). Either way the particular experience and contribution of the woman in the organization is ignored. Others treat women as a special case, whose careers and perspectives are deviant in relation to male norms. In the case of teachers in particular, women are regarded by many commentators as peripheral to mainstream organizational concerns because of:

> The larger number of women who work part-time, the concentration of women in primary schools, the lower proportion of women teachers who are graduates, and the fact that many women teachers have a break in service while bringing up their families. (NUT, 1980, p. 5)

This stereotype also wields a powerful influence within schools when decisions about appointments and promotions are made (gender and careers are examined in Ch. 8). Furthermore, the tendency to marginalize women or ignore gender obscures the ways in which coeducational institutions reproduce 'life in a bisexual, heterosexual world, in which men dominate and women learn to complement and subordinate themselves to men' (Arnot, 1983, p. 83; see also David, 1980, p. 244). One early escape from these self-confirming positions which in contrast takes women seriously as organizational actors, is provided by an act of deconstruction by Gouldner:

> Many sociologists who study factories or offices or schools . . . take little note of the fact that organizational role players invariably have a gender around which is built a *latent social identity*. One does not have to be Freudian to insist that sex makes a difference even for organizational behaviour. (Gouldner, 1959, p. 412; my emphasis)

As I have outlined so far, there are a number of bases for group affiliation among teachers. During periods of change or in attempts to bring about change, particular affiliations can provide the basis for factional conflict. The *social identity* of gender is one such basis, particularly in the case of women. In many circumstances women teachers may find that their interests and concerns bring them into conflict with some at least of their male colleagues. Given the typical pattern of promotion in school (see Ch. 8), groups of women may find common interests in their exclusion from influence over policy either through the informal or official channels. Clearly, gender affiliations are not recognized as a source of factional identity for all women teachers, but the development of women's groups in school, the articulation of the woman's 'voice' and the existence of an emotional and sexual sub-text in interpersonal relations in the organization cannot be denied. Interestingly, Simmel, writing in 1908, clearly recognizes the endemic conflict underlying male/female relations. While his language may now sound heavy-handed, this basic message remains relevant:

> Certain sociological attitudes characteristic of women appear to go back to the same motive. Among the extremely complex elements that make up the over-all relation between men and women, there is a typical hostility which derives from two sources. As the physically weaker sex, women are always in danger of economic and personal exploitation and legal power-lessness; and as the objects of the sensuous desire of men, they must always hold themselves on the defensive against the other sex. (Simmel, 1968, p. 94)

These two sources may be identified in the school. The first in the discrimination that many women experience in the construction of their careers and articulation of their views, and the second in the occurence of sexual harassment at work and in what I have called the sexual and emotional sub-text of organizational relationships. As Gouldner says, 'there is usually something occurring between people of opposite sexes, even though this is prescribed neither by the organization's official rules nor by the societal values deemed appropriate for that setting' (1959, p. 412). Simmel goes on to say that this fight, which pervades the inner and personal history of mankind, has rarely led to the direct co-operation of women against men (1964, p. 94). In the contemporary school such co-operation is not uncommon; it is increasingly employed in the advocacy of change in schools. Connell et al., writing about Australian schools, point out that:

> Forty-six per cent of secondary school teachers in Australia are women, probably half of them under thirty, and the younger

teachers are better trained. Teachers are themselves involved in a changed sexual division of labour; and a significant number of the younger women teachers have been influenced by feminism. They, with sympathetic male teachers, support the project of careers for girls, and provide a base for counter-sexist campaigns in schools: in careers advising, in the reading matter supplied to young children, in removing promotional barriers for women in their profession, and in teacher organizations. (1982, p.176)

Women's concerns about their lack of promotion opportunities and their experiences of discrimination in the organization are frequently tied to an ideological critique of the male domination of the institution as a whole. In schools it is commonly argued that the relatively small numbers of women in senior positions means the female pupils lack role models of female achievement and that decision-making is dominated by the male perspective; the 'women's culture', 'a way of looking at the world rooted in the experiences women share by virtue of being women' (Acker, 1980, p. 86) is excluded. Here, then, the knot which links vested, self- and ideological interests is tied tight. Women who experience discrimination and lack of opportunity also, as a result, experience damage to their self-esteem and sense of personal worth. Lack of opportunity for and discrimination against women ensures the continued domination of the male perspective: 'It is as if the world is thought from the position of consciousness which has its centre in a ruling class of men' (Smith, 1975, p. 365). From this position of consciousness women appear as *objects*; their views and concerns go unrecognized or are trivialized: 'Women do not appear to men as men do to one another, as persons who might share in the common construction of a social reality' (Smith, 1975, p. 365). Their marginal and subordinate position is thus confirmed and reproduced through the institution.

Events at Casterbridge High provide a concrete example. A whole set of vested, self-, ideological and practical concerns come together. One teacher explains:

I've got two girls who are genuinely upset who always knock at the door at the end of the lesson to talk to me and I cannot turn them away – it wouldn't be fair – and they say that they have no-one to talk to. But that doesn't mean that if I was a lady year tutor that they wouldn't prefer to go to someone they didn't know. I'm not saying to have a woman in that position would make it better. I just think that it's very strange to have a head, three deputy headmasters and six tutors all men, all involved with a mixed school. I think its a bad balance. . . . Well we [a group of women teachers] wrote a letter to the Head last year, and in fact we had thirty signatures on it, not because we felt the men who had been chosen for the posts were wrong, but for a variety of reasons, one of which was we didn't think it set a very good example to girls in the school to see that the men were always in positions of authority . . . and perhaps women were considered to have no promotion prospects . . . we also found several ladies* who have the same situation as I have where they have been dealing with girls who are obviously very upset for a variety of reasons and they say they haven't got anyone to talk to . . . . We did ask in the letter to the powers-that-be whether they felt that they didn't have any good women in the school.

S.B.: What was the response?

. . . the response from the Head was that the right people were given the jobs

(* This teacher had previously taught in the boys secondary-modern school where the small number of women teachers on the staff had been referred to as 'the ladies'.)

The NUT representative, a man, was also concerned with the situation in the school and offered further commentary:

The problem you've got is that the women are becoming as a group increasingly embittered at their lack of progress, and the attitude from the top is 'We'd promote them if they were good enough, but the buggers won't do anything for nothing, like the men will'. You know the men will creep around and do jobs for a year for nothing and that's the usual sort of way you get on if you're an ambitious young teacher, by sucking up to someone and proving that you can do a job and then getting paid for it later. But the women don't tend to fall for that one and they're embittered anyway so they've got a rather negative attitude towards the hierarchy. And, I mean, the simple comeback to that that is that if they appointed more people on scale one –

females – they'd be a bigger pool of females to select from. But anyway it's not true, because there are some very good female teachers here.

At Casterbridge, then, some of the women teachers were aware of a common situation and presented a collective response, even if on this occasion the outcomes were not very successful. There was no official recognition that 'a problem' existed, 'the right people got the jobs', end of story. The women were unable to register the issue on the institutional agenda of valid concerns. In some circumstances speaking up for women's issues can actually lead to an increase in tension between men and women in the school. Many men, in and out of authority, see women's claims as irrational and illegitimate. For women to speak up may actually confirm prejudices held by some men (Acker, 1983, p. 84). A women's perspective is rarely accepted by men in school as valuable or informative in its own right; a more assertive feminist perspective can produce paranoia and outright hostility. One teacher I interviewed described a situation in her school where the whole English department consisted of women. In this extract she touches on some of the problems involved in raising women's issues and points out the essentially political nature of feminism.

> I think the thinking of several of the women in the department is such because they are women. I think we're very aware of the position of women and what we are as women. And I think that's come very much into our teaching and into our life in school. . . . We have something of a reputation, I think, which to a certain extent was carried from my predecessor who was a very strong woman for the school, who was here before we had an influential woman in the hierarchy . . . and she was very much a pioneer for a particular style of teaching: mixed-ability, continuous assessment, this kind of thing. And she was seen as a representative of English teaching and that label stuck. And we are all very much her protégées because we all worked under her and have developed in our own way. And I think the English department still has this image of being the radical feminist element in the school, the ones who can on occasion be a little cranky. I think there's not so much of that now. . . . I think they look at us as individuals and they see the way we are as people; and they assume that that influences the way we think and the way we think about teaching

which, to a certain extent, it does. But, I mean, we have – I wouldn't say there are people in the school who don't – other teachers in the school who don't think or don't have opinions. I think the whole nature of English means that we are a group of people who will bring it out into the open. We disuss all sorts of things with the children. So our politics, if you like, are known, not only to the children but to the staff. Whereas some departments – their personal politics doesn't enter into their job; whereas I feel ours does. Whether that's right or wrong I'm not really sure. But the whole issue – the issues that we raise in our everyday English teaching are issues that generally cause tension. You know we're quite open about women's issues, we're open about racism and our attempts to curb racism in the school; we discuss the nuclear issue with kids in the course of our teaching. And, because we have those stances, I think that's got through beyond the children to the staff. ... I think there's an interesting connection between the image of the English department and other men on the staff. I think they are very wary of us. They're wary about what they say. You know, they will make pointed comments and then say 'Oh! I see there's somebody in the English department here. I'd better shut up'. They will often do very pointed things in meetings like, if we're all talking, somebody will say 'Oh sorry ladies first', and then they will apologise profusely.

Here then the politics of feminism are presented as a stance and a perspective that extends through the classroom, the staffroom and beyond the school, linked to other issues and struggles. The concerns of politically conscious women are on the social agenda even if they are manifest, in part at least, through the taunts and jibes of male colleagues. In the micro-politics of the school, feminism is frequently perceived by men, probably accurately, as a threat to their vested interests. It is a threat to their masculinity, and it does represent a challenge to their control of decision-making and organizational consciousness, it is an attempt to redefine the political ethos of the school.

In this case the women teachers are at least able to control the definition of what counts as school English. For inasmuch as school subjects may be viewed as social arenas within which opposed positions compete to define what is to count as authentic knowledge, then traditionally 'male studies' have been dominant. Most school subjects present and reproduce a male-populated and male view of the history of ideas: 'they have "passed off" this knowledge as human knowledge. Women have been excluded as the producers of knowledge and as the subjects of knowledge, for men have often made their own knowledge and their own sex, representative of humanity' (Spender, 1981, p. 1). Subject associations, institutions of research, higher education and teacher training have men in most positions of authority, and thus it is men 'who control what enters the discourse by occupying the positions which do the work of gatekeeping and the positions from which people and their "mental products" are evaluated' (Smith, 1975, p. 357). Significantly, those subjects which are associated exclusively with or are dominated by women are traditionally those of low status. In mixed schools it is exceptional to find women as heads of science or maths or even English or language departments. Thus at school level also, the definition and transmission of high-status knowledge is typically controlled by men. The department head quoted above is in an exceptional position.

However, even where women have established a right to participate in the formal processes of institutional decision-making and to speak out in other micro-political contexts, their problems are not ended, as is intimated in the quotation. There are now numerous studies which demonstrate the ways in which in discussion and argument men are able to exert control over topics and themes and otherwise dominate, in quantitative and qualitative terms, public and private talk. Typically, women's talk is supportive and facilitatory when interacting with men; control over the topography of conversation is thus surrendered to the men (Strodbeck and Marm, 1956; Spender, 1980). Men meanwhile may actively assert their own conversation 'rights' by finishing women's sentences, failing to respond to topics and issues raised by women and interrupting without permission (West, 1974; Acker, 1980). Within these interactional norms, not unusually women are caught in a double-bind. If individual women, or groups, do attempt to assert themselves in discussions or meetings, they are liable to find themselves labelled by men and other women as aggresive, loud-mouthed, essentially unfeminine. Such interactional constraints are policed by the moral arbitration of superordinates *and* co-workers and as a result

'Women participate in the ways in which they are silent' (Smith, 1975, p. 365).

Clearly, not all women recognize or experience discrimination (see Ch. 8); there is certainly no generalized sense of sorority among women teachers. Some women do 'get on' in teaching and achieve positions of authority and personal fulfilment through their career and in being able to exert influence in their school. None the less, women's groups in schools are likely to become an increasingly potent source of agitation for change in the organizational arena of school micro-politics as the claims of women receive greater publicity and external legitimation.

In this chapter and the previous one, I have outlined a socio-morphology of conflict in schools and have sought to identify the variety of forms of group affiliation which can provide the basis for struggle over change. Change in schools is rarely politically neutral. Interests are enhanced or threatened by change. 'Conflict and change are inevitably interlocked as any redistribution of power and privilege will be sought by some and resisted by others' (Kelly, 1969, p. 69). Furthermore, change does not usually arise within a set of social relationships which have been previously untouched by competition or dissension. Advocates and opponents typically 'dig in' along established lines of ideological dispute. Although I am not suggesting that all such disputes can be neatly analysed in terms of the structural categories outlined here. Some issues produce other cross-cutting alliances, genders may be divided by subject, age by pastoral/academic affiliations, union action may disrupt coalitions based on institutional history or shared status. (Hannan, 1980, provides some useful examples of alliance groupings around particular issues in his Redmond College study.) Furthermore, this type of analysis deals primarily with the effects of change, or proposed change, it does not necessarily make it clear where change comes from, how it enters the system, how it is initiated. Clearly, there is no single answer to these questions: change, or pressure for change can arise in a variety of ways. However, one figure is invariably crucial either in initiating or supporting change in the school: 'The evidence suggests that it is usually the headteacher who takes the initiative in introducing innovations into the school, and even where this is not the case his support is necessary for any innovation proposed by a member of staff' (Nicholls, 1983, p. 39).

Conversely, we should recognize that it is also often the head-teacher who is critical in resistance to change. Thus Wolcott generalizes in the opposite direction: 'School principals serve their institutions and their society as monitors for continuity. ... The real change agents of schools in modern societies are the young teachers, the young parents and the pupils themselves' (1978, p. 321). Clearly, much depends on the context, on what the change is, and whose interests it advances, but the headteacher can effectively block, stifle, dissuade or ignore groups in school who advocate change. As a result it is not unusual to find that conflicts in schools, particularly those related to proposed change, involve or focus upon the headteacher as the leader of the oganization. It is to the politics of leadership which I turn in the following chapter.

4
The politics of leadership

The most successful politician is he who says what everybody is thinking most often in the loudest voice.   (Theodore Roosevelt)

The role of the headteacher is central and critical to any understanding of the micro-politics of the school. The legal responsibilities of the head place him or her in a unique position of licensed autocracy. It is taken for granted by most commentators that the headteacher is 'to a large extent, responsible for devising and maintaining his school as a formal organization and so, in a most revealing way, his school becomes the expression of his authority' (King, 1968, p. 88). To a large degree this view is supported by the material presented in this chapter. However, the formal definitions of the role and duties of the head and 'reflections' on 'the changing role of the head' proffered in the existing body of literature, provide an insufficient basis for analysing the work of the head as organizational leader. In particular, the range of contextual factors that restrict, condition or otherwise affect the head's role fulfilment in specific settings are woefully neglected. British research studies on the practice of headship in schools are decidedly thin on the ground and the work that is available tends to be both abstract and atheoretical, the work of Morgan, Hall and McKay (1983) and Bernbaum (1976) being the major exceptions. Educational administration in Britain has been heavily biased towards prescription and there is a general failure to come to grips with the 'street realities' of headship. These weaknesses are as strongly marked in American research (with the exception of Wolcott's 1973 study). Greenfield in a review of relevant studies reports that:

> Among published and unpublished studies, the vast majority are either prescriptive exhortations or atheoretical normative surveys of duties and functions associated with the role. With few exceptions, the literature on the vice principalship is not cumulative, is not empirical or informed by theory, and contributes little to increasing the field's knowledge about the role or work of the assistant principal. (1984, p. 4)

Such research patently fails to come to grips with the social and political dynamics of the work of school leadership. Prescription and analysis have been divorced from the everyday social reality of school life and have failed to 'reflect the actual logic-in-use by organizational participants' (Greenfield, 1984, p. 29). Surprisingly, ethnographic researchers have done little to re-establish the balance in this area. 'Most educational studies of comprehensive schools only provide brief glimpses of the head in relation to other areas of school work. ... Even ethnographic studies with their emphasis upon portrayal have not done much more' (Burgess, 1984, pp. 204–5). My own work has provided no exception to this tale of systemic neglect, as Burgess goes on to point out. Burgess (1983, 1984) is in fact virtually the only British ethnographer to take the practice of headship seriously. His account of Bishop McGregor Comprehensive (1983) focuses upon the head, Mr Goddard, as the 'critical reality definer' in the school.

The primary assumption on which this chapter proceeds is that in normal circumstances the head is the major focus of micro-political activity in the school but that the possibilities of headship are realized within the specific constraints of a particular setting, history and context. As before, I shall be drawing upon both case study materials and commentaries elicited from individual organizational actors. In this case the commentaries draw both upon the experiences of headteachers themselves and the perceptions and experiences of other staff. The various analytical intrusions in this chapter and the next are derived from and grounded in the case study and interview data but are presented very much as exploratory forays into uncharted territory rather than as definitive statements. The chapter is long, sometimes complex, and of necessity covers a range of issues bearing upon leadership and followership in the school. One of the recurring motifs in the chapter is again that of change.

Licensed authority

Views on the power of the headteacher differ. Some commentators – such as King (1968), quoted above, and indeed HMI (DES, 1977) – perpetuate a vision of the head as all-powerful and unchallenged in the school. HMI assert that 'The character and quality of the headteacher are by far the main influences in determining what a school sets out to do and the extent to which it achieves those aims' (DES, 1977, p. 32). In more down-to-earth terms, Banks summarizes the received wisdom on headship in these terms: 'All the teaching methods and procedures, all matters relating to curricula, the relationships with parents and the control of teachers and their duties are recognized as matters for the head to decide and education committees will rarely try to interfere' (1976, pp. 134–5). Others are more dubious: Burgess concludes that 'the evidence that has been assembled suggests that head teachers do not have "freedom to do what they bloody like" but have to operate within the constraints that are established by their LEAs' (1984, p. 219). Even here the reference is to external constraints. The assumption is that headteachers maintain absolute authority in their organization. This is a misleading simplification. Whatever the extent or limits of the power of heads their organizational task can be expressed in terms of an essentially micro-political conundrum. The head must achieve and maintain control (the problem of domination), while encouraging and ensuring social order and commitment (the problem of integration). Once again this is Duverger's Janus face of power:

> Under their dual aspect of antagonism and integration, political phenomena occur within many kinds of human communities – nations, provinces, cities, international societies, associations, trade unions, clans, bands, cliques, and other assorted groups. From our point of view political sociology is the study of power in every human grouping, not just the nation-state. Each of these groups therefore serves as a structure, a framework for the enactment of conflicts and integration. (1972, p. 21)

On the one hand, the head will be faced with the problem of

maintaining control – both in an organizational sense, ensuring continuance and survival, and in the educational sense, through the making and implementation of policy. Both aspects of control, or of domination, may embody and provoke conflict and opposition. On the other hand, therefore, the head must attend to the possibilities of solidarity, co-operation and the generation of enthusiasm and commitment. Translated into the more rational and more sterile language of organization theory, these contradictory pressures and expectations approximate to the two basic leadership functions: the task function (initiating and directing) and the human function (consideration):

> Examples of task behaviour are 'stressing the importance of the object of the exercise', focusing attention on production and 'reviewing the quality of work done'. Examples of human relations behaviour are 'keeping the group happy', 'settling disputes', 'providing encouragement' and 'giving the minority a chance to be heard'. (Kelly, 1974, p. 366)

The way in which individual heads resolve this political conundrum (always admitting that some do not resolve it at all) differs. These differences are often referred to as leadership styles. In abstract terms in the school context, leadership styles are both an act of domination (the assertion of ultimate responsibility) and an expression of integration (the focus of identity and common purpose within the institution). A style is a form of social accomplishment, a particular way of realizing and enacting the authority of headship. It is eminently an individual accomplishment, but at the same time it is essentially a form of joint action (Blumer, 1971, p. 19). To paraphrase Blumer, 'the essence of organization lies in an ongoing process of action – not in a posited structure of relations' (p. 20). All heads by virtue of their position are invested with some degree of formal authority within the ongoing process of joint action in the school. Blumer defines joint action in the following terms:

> A society is seen as people meeting the varieties of situations that are thrust on them by their conditions of life. These situations are met by working out joint actions in which participants have to align their acts to one another. Each participant does so by interpreting the acts of others and, in turn, by making indications to others as to how they should act. By virtue of this process of

interpretation and definition joint actions are built up; they have careers. (p. 20)

Typically, headteachers attempt to pre-empt the form of joint action in their school by making firm indications to others, their staff, pupils, parents, advisers, governors, and so on, as to their preferred or intended style. A style embodies a definition of the situation, a proposed or perhaps imposed version of the modes of social interaction between leader and led. To the extent that the definition proposed by the head is acceptable to the staff, and a common definition is achieved, then joint action will proceed smoothly, with regularity and stability. To the extent to which it is unacceptable, involving perhaps versions of self that are unpalatable to the staff, or some staff, then conflict will ensue, or at least relationships will be strained, uncooperative and lacking in personal commitment.

> Alignment may take place for any number of reasons, depending on the situation calling for joint action, and need not involve, or spring from, the sharing of common values. The participants may fit their acts to one another in orderly joint action on the basis of compromise, out of duress, because they may use one another in achieving their respective ends, because it is the sensible thing to do, or out of sheer necessity. (Blumer, 1971, p. 22)

Most leadership styles require a greater or lesser degree of mutual alignment between leader and lead and, as the process of joint action proceeds, mutual adjustment, compromise and negotiation all play a part in the career of the social relationship. This is important, for it indicates, despite some of the literature on leadership styles, that styles are not of a piece and neither are they fixed and unchanging. There may be situations where heads, willingly or of necessity, temporarily abandon their normal style. Some members of staff may have privileged access to interactions with the head which are 'out of style', in 'back regions' where the performance aspects of style are unnecessary or inappropriate. Or it may be that as social or economic conditions change, or schools change, for instance through reorganization, heads will deliberately rework or drastically alter aspects of their preferred style. We may also think of the maturing of style, through experience, or even the degeneration or ossification of style. A style is an active process as opposed to a theory or philosophy of leadership, it is a way of doing leadership within the everyday social reality of the school. It is not, as some of the literature on school leadership would have us believe, a set of abstract duties, functions and responsibilities. To be clear, then, this view of headship rests neither upon a set of unexamined claims about authority nor upon a conception of power which gives once and for all predominance to the head. As indicated in Chapter 1, power here is conceived of as an outcome, something achieved and maintained in and through a performance, in and through joint action. Power is contested not invested. The dice may be loaded in favour of heads but circumstances can be great equalizers, and micro-politics is a dynamic process dependent upon the skills, resources and alliances of its participants. Also, to an extent, teachers are not only the joint actors in the social accomplishment of a style; they are also an audience for it. The more junior the teacher, the less influence that he or she normally has and the more predominant the audience role. Indeed, styles of headship are performances (Goffman, 1971, p. 28) (both inside and outside of the school) and as such it is certainly crucial that the head manages to convey a sense of belief in the part they are playing:

> When the individual has no belief in his own act and no ultimate concern with the beliefs of his audience, we may call him cynical, reserving the term 'sincere' for individuals who believe in the impression fostered by their own performance. (Goffman, 1971, p. 28)

Clearly, heads vary. Some are strongly, even emotionally, committed to and sincere in their particular style; others take a more distanced, cynical stance. None the less, the relationship of audience and performer stands out strongly in some of the teachers' comments quoted later. Teachers are extremely attentive to their head's performance and are eager and accomplished 'reviewers':

> T1: The Head does these occasions very well.
> T2: Very professional.
> T1: He's a very shy, very modest man but he does very well, you remember the thing at Christmas.
> (Conversation at school speech day.)

In certain situations, pre-eminently the staff meeting, but also in committees, at speech day, in assembly, the emphasis on dramatic realization in the head's performance is heightened. So too is the pressure to achieve an idealized performance:

> If an individual is to give expression to ideal standards during his performance, then he will have to forgo or conceal action which is inconsistent with these standards. When this inappropriate conduct is itself satisfying in some way, as is often the case, then one commonly finds it indulged in secretly; in this way the performer is able to forego his cake and eat it too. (Goffman, 1971, p. 50)

There are a number of significant points about styles of leadership and the role of the head suggested here. While it is natural to highlight the formal authority of the head and personal investment in the accomplishment of a personal style, we may also view a style and its attendant performances as a set of limitations upon his or her social interaction and social relationships – an interactional cage. The head must seek to maintain style for fear of being seen as inconsistent, vacillating or weak. The stylization of social relationships with others – joint actors – precludes or makes it extremely difficult to maintain strong affective aspects in such relationships. This is rarely anticipated by aspirant heads. One interviewed head expressed the problem in sad and nostalgic tones: 'I miss my friends from Wessex. You don't make many friends being a head. Well you can't really.' Headship can be a lonely business. However, the degree of the 'social' invested in joint action varies, as we shall see, between styles. Some styles rely upon an avoidance of the interpersonal while others rest entirely upon it and celebrate it. Finally, we should recognize, at least in passing, the pleasures and pains of headship. At times in this chapter heads will be cast in the role of villain, in particular where domination is asserted over and above integration. They are caught between audiences, and the demands those audiences make may be very different and are often contradictory and irreconcilable. Local authority advisers may be pressing for innovation, the parents for improved examination results and the staff for peace and quiet. When all goes well in a school, whatever that may mean, the head is 'successful' and may establish a reputation which can be exploited, traded upon elsewhere. When things go wrong it is usually the head who is blamed:

> A status, a position, a social place is not a material thing, to be possessed and then displayed; it is a pattern of appropriate

conduct, coherent, embellished, and well articulated. Performed with ease or clumsiness, awareness or not, guile or good faith, it is none the less something that must be realized. (Goffman, 1971, p. 81)

Four styles

From a sifting of case study data and the analysis of interviews conducted with headteachers and other members of staff from a variety of schools, it was possible to identify four style types in the performances of heads. As is often the case, I present these in the spirit of Weberian ideal-types. They appear here in abstract form, with an emphasis on their points of difference and their major features. Internal consistency is stressed and variations in practice are initially played down. As has been stressed already, styles are rarely allowed to evolve in a social vacuum; they are both the vehicle for and a product of joint action in the school. The three main styles are the *interpersonal, managerial* and *political*, the latter consisting of two subdivisions, the *adversorial* and *authoritarian*. Interpersonal heads rely primarily on personal relationships and face-to-face contact to fulfil their role. In contrast, managerial heads have major recourse to committees, memoranda and formal procedures. The adversorial tends to relish argument and confrontation to maintain control. Whereas the authoritarian avoids and stifles argument in favour of dictat. The styles are discussed in some detail, and data from interviews with heads and the teacher-audience are employed. However, I certainly do not assume that in the case of particular heads that they and their audiences would agree on a particular categorization. Performances, as interactional texts, are read differently. I do assume that individual heads tend towards the presentation of one style, but by definition they are not invariably limited to that style (although a few may be). Situational variations or changes over time in the institutional environment may well produce stylistic reworkings; performances may be tailored towards different audiences. There may also be some common elements across the styles. Bernbaum notes in his study of heads' work 'that heads in all types of schools tend to see themselves doing well those activities which call for generalized personal qualities, particularly in so far as they are called upon to "get on with", or manipulate, people' (1976, p. 31). ('Manipulate' is a key word here and underlines the element of performance.) Nonetheless, Bernbaum's statistical data also contain small but interesting rates of exception to the general patterns he describes. The survey method tends to illuminate general characteristics and obscure systematic variations which may underpin important differences in style, and studies which rely entirely upon self-reporting obviously fail to account for either the effects of an 'intended' style on followers or the gap between 'intended' and 'enacted' style.

Interpersonal

The interpersonal style is typical of the mobile and visible head. As the term suggests, there is an emphasis on personal interaction, face-to-face contact between the head and his or her staff. There is a preference for individual negotiation and compromises, which in some ways fits with a 'professional' definition of the teacher–head relationship. That is to say, staff members are encouraged to think of themselves as autonomous professionals whose problems and grievances can and should be sorted out on a one-to-one basis with the head. There is a concomitant de-emphasis on formal meetings and formal decision-making, although 'discussions' in staff meetings may be acceptable. This is very much the style of Wolcott's principal, whose work consists for the most part of 'an almost endless series of encounters. Most of these encounters are face-to-face, tending to keep principalship a highly personal role' (1973, p. 88). The interpersonal head prefers to consult with individuals rather than hold meetings, to 'sound out ideas' and 'gather opinion':

> I believe in face-to-face contact. I don't like putting pieces of paper in pigeon holes, although this is sometimes necessary, and if I had to choose one word to describe what goes on in this school it would be 'informality'. (Headteacher, secondary modern, Kent)

The use of the term 'informality' is significant. The interpersonal style is orientated to informality in relationships and to the use of informal networks for communication and consultation. This in turn rests upon and maintains a sense of trust and obligation. Rather than establishing principles of practice or institutional rules, the head will respond to individual requests in the light of circumstances and previous experience:

All heads have their strengths and weaknesses. This bloke's strength is his dealing with staff. He will get, almost without exception, anything he wants done because of his relationships, not necessarily with staff collectively, but with individual staff. They know that he supports them to the hilt . . . the quality of his reference writing is superb, anyone wanting to go on in-service is encouraged, and if anyone wants time off for a trip, personal reasons or whatever, there are no problems at all. (Head of sixth form, Green Hill Comprehensive) (Quoted in Wagstaff, 1983, p. 14)

Here the style of the head does become the style of the school. It is tempting to introduce here the imagery of feudalism. The stress upon personal relationships and individual favours from the head to staff members sets up a sense of mutual obligation. By the granting of 'boons' the head ties his or her teachers in a bond of fealty. This fealty is held towards the person rather than the office. In return for indulgence, encouragement and support, the head will expect loyalty (this is discussed in more detail in the following chapter). This sort of social relationship was a fundamental aspect of feudal societies.

Whatever the inequalities between the obligations of the respective parties, those obligations were none the less mutual: the obedience of the vassal was conditional upon the scrupulous fulfilment of his obligations by the lord. (Bloch, 1965, p. 228)

An exemplification of this is provided by a secondary-modern head who explains his role as protector of his staff:

A protective role for staff is also important. So that staff do not have to face outside agencies. I act on criticism personally, but they are channelled through me and I cushion them. I may haul a member of staff over the coals in private but in public they have my support. Caring for people is important at all levels in the school.

For the staff's part the head's trust rests upon them 'doing a good job'. Once selected for the job the members of a department and teachers as individuals are expected to take responsibility for their own affairs – not to seek or require interference from the head but also not to step beyond their limited sphere of responsibility. If the outcomes are satisfactory, in the head's terms, then the individual staff or departments can expect encouragement and support (personal and material):

> If she liked the way they operated, she liked their spirit, she liked the way they handled their department, the way they were able to control the work that they were doing – she believed in appointing specialists, people who were specialist in their field and giving them a free hand to do the best they could and she appeared to be pleased with certain departments in terms of the way they were working. If she didn't, she just kind of withdrew her support. You know, if the face didn't fit, people went. (Head of department describing a London comprehensive headteacher)

> She gave a tremendous amount of autonomy and respect to her heads of department. I mean she prided herself on picking people that she felt could be responsible. And if they went to her and said 'Look, I feel that it's important that this happens and, because I feel it's important this has happened, I've thought of A, B and C', she would say 'Okay', she never refused me anything the whole time I was there. (A London comprehensive headteacher)

The head is the focus of communication and dispenser of patronage. The lines of obligation and exchange are maintained through the person of the head. Such heads will frequently reiterate to staff the importance of bringing complaints and grievances to them first of all; 'my door is always open', they will say. Communication does not flow through a formal hierarchy: 'Anyone, and when I say anyone, I mean anyone, from myself right down to the lowest member of the first year can go and see him' (Deputy head; quoted in Wagstaff, 1983, p. 14).

Masters, describing a secondary-modern head, notes that:

> The staff apparently had been socialised into his [the head's] individual approach. . . . There was only one observed example of the head using his office for an interview (which in fact concerned a job application) and even when his office was in use his door was always open. One could not see into the head's office because the door was sited at the end on one side and opened inwards but its openness appeared a symbolic and inviting gesture. (1982, pp. 50–1)

A deputy head at Casterbridge High recalled a headmaster of a southern grammar school:

> The old grammar school head used to say we could always walk in and talk to him and it was really true and was really quite difficult in that – I mean you might find three or four people in the room at the same time when you talked to him. But he was really open like – but the school was run how he wanted.

Again the school is the person. The conduct of business is reduced to sets of personal relations and individual ownership. Favours are given or withheld by the person and on the basis of personal evaluation. The head of a London comprehensive was described as follows by a head of department:

> She would never say 'no'. It does sound terribly amazing but she would never do that; she'd never actually just say 'no'. She might be saying 'no', but she didn't just say 'no'. If she was unhappy about something, she would have arranged to meet that person and then said 'no' in a nice way. She wouldn't have sat in a meeting with twenty people and just said 'no' to the person.

Clearly, here there is an emphasis on 'consideration', on the human function in the organization. Consideration:

> reflects the extent to which an individual is likely to have job relationships characterized by mutual trust, respect for subordinates' ideas and consideration of their feelings. A high score is indicative of a climate of good rapport and two way communication. (Fleishman and Peters, 1962, p. 1)

However, it is important to keep it in view that it is also through interpersonal relationships that the task functions of headship are achieved. The work of the school rests upon the maintenance of these relationships. The myriad individual encounters and personal consultations between head and staff provide for organizational control through the satisfaction of individual needs and at least on an *ad hoc* basis lead to policy-making and goal-setting. Furthermore, grievances and turnover tend to be low in such organizations and thus stability is maintained. This style of working fits well with the 'preferred view' of professionalism held by many teachers:

> The head is a pragmatist – paperwork has always taken a low

priority. One of the main criteria of whether a department is successful is the way it deals with colleagues. Personal contact is stressed – this is the boss's own policy. (Head of maths, Green Hill Comprehensive; quoted in Wagstaff, 1983, p. 15)

At the heart of the interpersonal style lies an intriguing contradiction between the public and highly visible role of the headteacher him or herself and the private and relatively invisible operation of power in the organization. The mechanisms of decision-making and policy setting are not set within the public arenas, as for instance when a formal structure of committees, working parties and staff meetings are employed in the process of decision-making. Influence upon the head will normally take place in the form of lobbying. Interested parties will represent their own views and may be consulted directly. The head will tend to consult quietly and unobstrusively. Staff meetings will be used to 'air' opinions rather than arrive at decisions:

> It was this image of democracy, but really it wasn't. No vote was ever taken about anything. It was a benevolent despot, in a way. In terms of decisions that would affect everybody, she would make the decision. (Head of department describing a London comprehensive headteacher)

The sinews of power remain invisible. There are rumours of individuals who have particular influence with the head (this is dealt with in detail in the following chapter). On occasions this can create confusion and resentment. Decision-making comes to be seen as an elusive and mysterious process, as inaccessible, taking place out of sight, paradoxically, 'behind closed doors'. This according to Weber (1948) is an irrational form of leadership; it does not rely upon principles but rather upon the inspiration of the head and the outcomes of private arrangements:

> There is a definite feeling among members of staff, younger members of staff that they're just pawns, that they've got no control over anything, so they just do their own thing. (Head of department of a London comprehensive)

> On a major issue the Head will seek advice from lots of different places and then go away and think about it and then make a final decision. Staff are not necessarily aware that he has thought

things through – perhaps there could be a little more explaining to people how the process takes place. (Senior mistress, Green Hill Comprehensive; quoted in Wagstaff, 1983, p. 24)

A similar point was made about the latter headteacher by two heads of year. They stress the one-way direction of communication: up but not down. Accessibility is matched by exclusion. Decision-making is not focused. There is no one place or moment when decisions are made. This can produce a feeling of loss, frustration, even insecurity. Again, given the emphasis on 'consideration' to persons, this is paradoxical. There is an absence of structure, procedures and methods – just the person and power of the head:

The head is extremely receptive to the ideas and opinions of other people. A weakness is that he doesn't communicate back to people how and why decisions are made. (Head of year 2)

There are few meetings and one does not necessarily feel consulted. You can't really expect the rank and file to make decisions – they can't see all the angles. (Head of year 3)

The second comment indicates both a sense of exclusion from decision-making and an acceptance of the naturalness of such exclusion – the divine right of heads, perhaps.

If the teachers sometimes feel that they do not know what is going on, the heads certainly do feel that they do know what is going on. The interpersonal style is often associated with the visibility of the head around the school, in the staffroom at break, and sometimes also in the corridors – like Burgess's (1983) Mr Goddard and Wolcott's (1973) Ed Bell. The open-door policy also encourages heads to feel that they have their finger on the pulse beat of staff concerns and opinions. Staff autonomy is set against benevolent surveillance:

'I know what is going on in the school, you've got to know what is going on, the important things' (headteacher, secondary modern, Kent). The head of science in the same school explained: 'The head leaves me to get on with the job but he knows what is going on, don't you worry, and he would soon let me know if he wasn't satisfied.' And the head of the remedial department said: 'Oh he doesn't often come down, but he knows what is going on and would soon let me know if he didn't approve.'

In a number of respects the interpersonal head is much more a part of the staff of the school than is the case in the other styles. A deliberate attempt is made to reduce the formal trappings of the headship position. This type articulates well with Mitchell's (1983) notion of the head as 'senior professional' (as opposed to 'executive head'). Such heads tend to regard themselves as still being teachers and many demonstrate this and their closeness to their staff by retaining some teaching duties. Masters's head, referred to above:

> consulted with staff as individuals and not as the holders of roles within a hierarchy. He visited the staffroom on numerous occasions each day apart from serving as a member of the mathematics team, sitting at the 'mathematics table' and commenting on team matters. (1982, p. 49)

Wagstaff reports one teacher as saying that 'I don't suppose there are many heads who teach as much as he does' (1983, p. 24), and the Kent secondary-modern head referred to above explained in interview that:

> The head must be a teacher. He must lead. He should be a charismatic figure within the school for staff in particular and pupils and in the wider context. The head should know the staff, their strengths and weaknesses. (Quoted in Wagstaff, 1983, p. 25)

It should be apparent that the interpersonal style makes certain demands on the encumbent in terms of social skills. The emphasis on 'the personal' requires an authenticity and facility in social interaction. A great deal is done through 'talk', and as noted previously paperwork and written communication are accorded much less importance. Indeed, they are seen to get in the way of establishing the right kind of social relationships. A part then of 'bringing off' this style of headship rests upon the loquacity and affability (or at least approachability) of the head. (It may be that this approach is more feasible and typical in a smaller school, but not all my examples here come from small schools). Contrasts are often drawn in these terms when heads of different styles are compared:

> She would have a way of being able to make small talk to everybody. I mean she did all the talking mind! He just seems to be the other end of the spectrum. He doesn't seem able to find

it easy to get into a conversation. (London comprehensive headteacher)

I don't think he's got this ability to communicate ... someone who can do that sort of job has got to have charisma, has got to have the ability to communicate with people, has got to have this gift of the gab. (London comprehensive headteacher)

He gives people total freedom and up out of that comes initiative, you see. But I felt that he didn't actively support initiatives enough. I think you've actually got to really show that you're backing them ... and I think that that's to do with his personality: he's not a great bloke for going up and saying, 'Oh, that was terrific' you know. (Southern comprehensive headteacher)

The term 'charisma' is used twice in the preceding quotations and there is certainly an element of this aspect of leadership in the interpersonal style. It is the qualities of the head as person that is crucial, as Weber notes:

The legitimacy of charismatic rule thus rests upon the belief in magical powers, revelations and hero-worship. The source of these beliefs is the 'proving' of the charismatic quality through miracles, through victories and other successes, that is through the welfare of the governed. (1948, p. 297)

However, Weber also makes the point that charismatic authority is inherently unstable. If the miracles are not forthcoming, then the leader's authority is in jeopardy.

Managerial

Consideration of the managerial style takes us into conceptual territory well known both to sociologists and organizational theorists. Indeed, the concept of management as articulated by 'Speedy' Taylor and Henry Fayol provided the basis for the first formalized statements of organization theory. An exploration of the precepts and the enactment of the concept will also require acknowledgement of Max Weber's classic work on bureaucracy. However, at this point I intend to remain close to the data of headship I have drawn from interviews and case material. A more general discussion of the implications of management is presented in Chapter 10. At the present time, for a whole variety of reasons, management is a term of major currency in schools. There is an increasing emphasis both from central government and local authorities on the training of headteachers and prospective headteachers in management techniques. There are, however, few studies of the practice and effects of management techniques in schools.

The practical model for the managerial head is the industrial manager. The use of management techniques involves the importation into the school of structures, types of relationships and processes of organizational control from the factory. The managerial head is chief executive of the school, normally surrounded and supported by a senior management team (variously composed of deputy heads and senior teachers). The head relates to the staff through this team (and their delegated areas of formal responsibility) and through a formal structure of meetings and committees. Both these responsibilities and structures will be supported and outlined by written documentation which specifies terms of reference and job descriptions. For example:

Deputy Head Pastoral Work:
In charge East Wing.
Responsible for day-to-day running of East Wing (assisted by Mr Smith).
Responsible for co-ordinating all aspects of the pastoral work of the school, ensuring that all are working to a common aim within the philosophy of the school.
Responsible for co-ordinating work of Year Tutors by convening regular meetings to discuss social policy and case histories.
Responsible for liaising with all necessary outside bodies, e.g. Social Services, Educational Psychologist, Police Schools Liaison Officer, Education Welfare Officer, etc.
Responsible for examining new concepts of pastoral care in schools and to advise accordingly.
Responsible for general oversight of the school's system of reports and pupil records.

Deputy Head Communications and Administration:
In charge West Wing.
Responsible for day-to-day running of West Wing (with Mr Brown).
Responsible for welfare of staff, including probationers, giving

guidance on problems and having links with the Advisory
Service.
Responsible for covering staff absences.
Responsible for relations between school and the public.
Responsible for general oversight of contact between school and
parents. (School handbook, a Midlands comprehensive)

These specifications go on to outline in detail, in classical Weberian
manner, the responsibilities of the other members of the senior
management team, the heads of department, year tutors, form
teachers and some of the ancillary staff of the school. Thus, in
theory at least, the roles and responsibilities of staff are relatively
fixed and publicly recorded. The running of the school is formalized through such documentation. Matters arising and matters of
issue will be discussed within formal meetings (e.g. pastoral board,
academic board, staff association, senior management team) and
information and opinion will flow through the established channels
of communication. Meetings and committees will normally be
supported by an agenda and recorded in formal minutes, which are
kept on file. Typically, the communication between staff and headteacher will take place either from bottom to top through the
hierarchy of meetings and personnel or from top to bottom by
formal announcements or written memoranda. For example:

Memorandum
From: HM
To: All teaching staff   Date: 12.3.82

Following yesterday's meeting I should like to confirm that any
member of staff who wishes to be considered for either early
retirement or voluntary redeployment should let me know before
the end of the week. (Initialled by headteacher)

The educational concerns of the school will also be formally defined
in terms of aims and objectives; again, these will be recorded and
represent a measure against which the 'performance' of the school
can be evaluated. In some cases the setting of aims and objectives
will be extended beyond the overall concerns of the school to the
level of middle management, heads of department and heads of
year (or house). The following is an extract from a local authority
document, *Handbook for Heads of Department*:

As a Manager, you have specific responsibilities for leading a departmental team.
You must:
FIRST
Analyse your present situation. ASK 'Where am I now?'
NEXT
Define your aims and objectives. ASK 'Where do I want to go?'
THEN
Plan (and eventually put into operation) means of achieving your aims and objectives. ASK 'How am I going to get there?'
AND AT THE SAME TIME
Plan (and eventually put into operation) means of assessing whether they are being achieved. ASK 'How will I know whether I am making progress?'

The head's role-making will be set within the precepts and procedures which constitute management. This role-making will involve the introduction of ways of working and forms of relationship which are informed by the theory of management:

He's young, he became a headteacher I think when he was 34. . . . He believes in the new management approach to running educational institutions. So on the one hand he appears to be quite progressive. He talks about all the departments having to articulate their aims and objectives. We've got to have more consultations, we've got to have more counselling of students. The word discipline is out. Students don't have to wear uniform, we're going to get rid of all the grammar-school ways of doing things. But at the same time most members of staff would say, I think, that he's authoritarian. He has puritanical values, which basically he wants to impose on us. . . .

   The college is *run*. And the head has a fairly clear idea about what he wants to achieve. And a lot of it is very acceptable. The man is intelligent and he's something of a reformist. He's a liberal in some ways. So the management team are implementing that policy. (Social-studies teacher, sixth-form college)

These comments are interesting in two ways. First they indicate the use of the concepts and processes of management, but second they suggest that the system of organization as such is separate from the headteacher as person; it becomes disembodied as a policy and a structure. However, it is all too easy to portray management as a totally impersonal mechanism and neglect the ideologies and personalities of the managers (not that management is itself ideologically neutral). Management can be employed to achieve different ends. Weber, writing about the development and spread of bureaucracy (of which management is a particular type), pointed out that while bureaucracy was normally accompanied by and often supported the development of democracy, the relationship between the two is not unambiguous:

> one has to remember that bureaucracy as such is a precision instrument which can put itself at the disposal of quite varied – purely political as well as purely economic, or any other sort of – interests in domination. Therefore, the measure of parallelism with democratization must not be exaggerated, however typical it may be. (1948, p. 231)

As Weber states here, bureaucracy is a form of domination. The head as person, as above, may be viewed as liberal, open, democratic, but management as a system is not. As a solution to the political problem of organization it errs on the side of the task function and makes its claims for integration on the basis of adherence to legal-rational procedures. In ideal-typical form these legal-rational procedures ensure that the formalities of consultation are public and visible. In this case it is the head who recedes from view. It is possible and not uncommon to find the managerial head in the role of desk-bound bureaucrat, administering from behind the closed door of the office. Approaches to the head go through the proper channels, 'by the book'.

One head interviewed, recently returned from a school management in-service course, spoke with some sense of despair of the development of a deliberately styled 'distance' among colleague heads:

> I know so many of my colleagues who isolate themselves from their staff. They feel that they can't do the role of head and get close to their staff. They are no good at personal relationships, they won't open themselves up to their colleagues in school. And they become cardboard cutouts to their staff and then they wonder why nothing happens in the way they want it to. (London headteacher)

This quotation also raises the intriguing point as to whether styles of headship are independently selected or acquired by incumbents or are, in part, extensions of individual personality types or personal psychologies. This is a question which requires separate investigation.

The head may or may not value wide social contacts with the staff, but the accomplishment of managerial headship does not require close working relationships across the whole staff. The day-to-day running of the school and the ongoing decision-making and policy-making processes are focused upon the work of the senior management team:

> If I'm honest I think the influential policy initiating body is myself, the two deputies and the head of lower school. I do see them and consciously try to run them as a team. (Quoted in Radnor, 1983, p. 15)

The following is a formal exposition of the role of the senior management team (SMT) in one Midlands comprehensive:

1. Composition: Principal and three deputy principals.
2. Rationale: The SMT is the senior decision-making body of the staff. Its members share collective responsibility for all aspects of the organization, philosophy, operation and development of the campus. In consequence, specific roles will comprise a blend of curricular, pastoral, community and administrative responsibilities.

Primary principles of action are delineated as:

(a) to expound the philosophy of community and life-long education, by means of inducting staff, students, parents, community members, governors, etc., into the ethos;

(b) to augment the integrative role of the principal by promoting the harmonious development of distinct activities on campus;

(c) to promote the parity of worth and status of aspects of work on campus . . . academic community, pastoral, etc.;

(d) to promote consistency of ethos and procedure by monitoring the work of sections of the campus; this requires regular reporting, debate and planning among team members.

In the rationale the language emphasizes community and harmony, but the control and monitoring of the organization, responsibility for it, belies any sense of community. The debate about and planning for the school is the responsibility of the team. The members of the 'community' (teachers and others) seem to have little responsibility for the 'community' themselves. The concept is not a set of practices among the members but a principle to be managed. Community is used here as a focus for order and integration. It embodies claims about consensus and collective endeavour. It is deployed as a rhetoric of control. In the managerial mode the emphasis of organizational control is position-orientated rather than person-orientated. Information and influence flow through the formal channels and structures. At each level in the bureaucratic structure the duties and responsibilities are fixed and limited. The headteacher quoted above goes on to explain this:

> Slightly wider than that we have the admin. group, which has a significant effect on how policy is implemented and has also an initiating effect particularly through the four [the senior management team]. I widen the group to include the deputy of Lower School, the Senior Teacher for exams, administration and buildings and the head of Sixth Form. I use the term 'admin.' deliberately to try and not overplay the policy formation function. I do treat it as relating policy to good administrative practice and try to iron out difficulties before they arise. (Quoted in Radnor, 1983, p. 15)

Again the emphasis is upon the setting up of procedures which pre-empt the necessity of involvement from below. The aim is, in effect, to set up a system of organization (of control) which is totally unproblematic; every eventuality is catered for. A measure of its success is that it demands nothing of those it controls, they are indeed unaware of it, it runs, as Weber puts it 'as austerely as a machine' (1978, p. 402), just a faint hum in the background. Indeed, the deliberations of the senior management team are not normally made public. Weber (1948, p. 233) asserts that 'Bureaucratic administration always tends to be an administration of "secret sessions": insofar as it can, it hides its knowledge and action from criticism'. It is a frequent complaint among teachers that they are excluded from significant discussions, or discussions are pre-empted by the senior management team. The tendency is for the senior management team to become separated off from the staff as a whole. What is happening here, in the terms of Taylor's principles of scientific management, is the separation of conception from execution. The management team assume the responsibility for conception (policy), the staff perform the actual execution. Organization by principles of management brings with it an increasingly hierarchical and complex division of labour and the development of a management cadre. That is to say, the expertise of the head and the senior management team no longer rest upon their skills as teacher-practitioners; rather, it is their specific management skills that provide the formal basis of their authority. In Weber's terms this is the replacement of the 'cultivated man' by the 'specialist type of man' (1948, p. 243). There is indeed a phenomenal growth in management training for heads and deputies and middle managers. The Department of Education and Science have allocated £6 million for this purpose and established a National Management Training Centre. Increasingly, management training is becoming a requirement for headship. Again, Weber (1948, p. 198) notes that such training is presupposed in bureaucratic forms of organization. Salaman offers the following view of management training courses:

> The importance of such courses for influencing members' attitudes and motivation must be stressed. . . . The function of these courses is to adjust organizational members to organizational demands and realities; to encourage members to gain 'insight' into themselves, their colleagues and the organization ('insight' of a rather limited sort, usually); to inform members about the organization, and to develop new skills. They achieve insidious control. (1979, p. 203)

Whereas there was normally a continuity, in career terms, between the teacher and the head, management requires and produces a separation between them. The head becomes an executive rather than a senior teacher. This separation can be further reinforced by the norm of cabinet responsibility that operates in the senior management team:

> the management team are implementing that policy. I've never heard him criticized in public by members of the management team, although they may say in public 'that decision may be seen to be unwise'. (Social-studies teacher, sixth-form college)

What is being fostered here is a sense of responsibility for the organization that is separate from the persons who actually constitute it. The result is a reified and dehumanized conception of the school as a system, a set of committees, a structure of duties and responsibilities. Again, this is a danger of bureaucratic management that Weber was only too aware of:

> Its specific nature, which is welcomed by capitalism, develops the more perfectly the more the bureaucracy is 'dehumanized', the more completely it succeeds in eliminating from official business love, hatred, and all purely personal, irrational and emotional elements which escape calculation. (Weber, 1948, pp. 215–16)

Furthermore, the other members of the senior management team are primarily orientated upwards to the head; their special areas of responsibility are delegated by the head. They come to be identified as 'the hierarchy'; they are not seen as primarily a part of the teaching staff, as a head-teacher explains:

> They have to accept what the Head has to accept because a deputy is only a Head in the making if there is any meaning in the term at all. They are a head when the Head is missing and that is an overall responsibility for every single facet of any member of staff's performance. (Quoted in Radnor, 1983, p. 18)

As suggested above, those staff who are not part of the senior management team tend to think of themselves as exluded from the important aspects of decision-making. This is now a specialist function. They come to experience their work as subject to decisions being made elsewhere; the seeds of alienation are thus sown. The management structure and management processes, which in a formal sense incorporate a large number of staff, are seen as a sham:

> The school is a bureaucracy, that's how it's run. Take these fourth- and fifth-year curriculum proposals. The working party (all heads of faculty) reported to 'the hierarchy' and their recommendations were not wholly acceptable so a sub-committee was set up, all the hierarchy people, and there it was. I don't know why they bothered, they could have done that in the first place. And there was certainly a feeling among the staff that the procedure was not open enough. Generally, people feel that they do not have appropriate access to these things; the staff is on the whole lively and intelligent but the system is not open. The head is a technocrat. (Year tutor, outer London comprehensive)

Political

It is perhaps a little awkward within an overall political analysis to employ the term 'political' to refer to separate sub-categories of leadership. However, the important point here is that we are dealing with styles of leadership, forms of presentation and inter-action. In the case of the political style(s), a sense of 'the political' is to the fore. There is a recognition of political process as a major element of school life, although I want to suggest that the response to this recognition can be either an acceptance of and open partici-pation in the process, or a rejection of, and attempt to avoid or divert, the process. The first response I refer to as the *adversarial* style, wherein the political process is both overt and legitimate. The second response I refer to as the *authoritarian* style, wherein the political process is treated as illegitimate and thus remains covert.

ADVERSARIAL

The adversarial style, like the interpersonal, rests primarily upon the vehicle of talk; as Hall argues, 'the basic element of politics is, quite simply, talk' (1972, p. 51). In this case the crucial arenas of talk are public rather than private. The adversarial head encourages and is a major participant in public debate. There is an emphasis on dialogue and not infrequently on confrontation. There is a recog-nition of competing interests and ideologies in the school, and these are allowed to enter the formal procedures of discussion and decision-making. Decision-making is described by participants in the language of confrontation. They speak of 'rows', 'battles', 'challenges'. Here, then, headship is very much a public perfor-mance; the emphasis is upon persuasion and commitment. The ideological dimension is often strong, with debate being devoted to questions about 'what we are doing with the kids' and 'Have we got it right?', rather than to administrative or procedural matters; that is, 'why' and 'what' rather than 'how'. Once 'the political' is out in the open, then political skills are all-important and often, as we shall see, the head is at an advantage. Some staff will be unable or unwilling to participate in this form of organizational discourse. Some find it unhelpful or unconducive, others are unwilling to devote to it the time and energy that is necessary to 'get your point of view across'. The accomplishment of the adversarial style relies very heavily upon the ability of the head to cope with the uncertainties of the relatively unorganized public debate. That is, to deal with attacks, to persuade waverers, to provide reasoned argument, to employ stratagems and devices where necessary. As one such head explained, using a mixed metaphor, 'When I'm up against the wall I don't sink, I can survive' (Midlands comprehensive). In other words, he was able to talk himself out of awkward situations, to pit his wits against opponents. This head clearly saw the use of the public arena as a means to an end, as a way of getting his message across to the staff, but he also spoke of 'a degree of negotiation'. One vehicle for discussion in this school, the open forum, was usually held in the head's large study. Twenty, thirty or more staff would squeeze in, sitting on the floor, sharing chairs. He explained to me after one such event: 'Its in my room, on my terms, in my time.' The openness on the one hand, the use of the head's room, is set against the strategic implications on the other: he was operating on his own territory.

A deputy head in another Midlands comprehensive described her head in the following terms:

She is very much an ideas person – she thinks very, very quickly and she talks very, very quickly – and in a sense we are not compatible because I am a more reflective sort, who perhaps would go home and have a think and then come up with some other idea. She's very much a thinker on her feet type and loves discussion and loves arguments and so in a way tends to dominate many of the conversations. And in a strange way wants everything to have happened before it can have happened. Which for practitioners in a classroom can have dire consequences because they tend to feel, 'Cor, we've got enough to be doing without this new idea'. And, of course, one idea leads to another and we've got lots of ideas going on. We changed the pastoral system, we took on a school that's just closing down in the city, we will probably be a pilot for the authority's 'record of achievement scheme' and we are involved in the government's TVEI.

Here then we have the head's skills at and emphasis on argument, and a commitment to new ideas and to change. Talk is the primary medium; it drives the political process:

> She works through discussion, talk is very much her medium.
> Whereas in my previous school the mode of communication had
> been very much a written one, put it on the agenda, produce a
> paper, prepare a paper, talk to it at a meeting. We'll have a
> discussion, we'll make a decision, very, very, very different, very
> much a case of 'catch you in the corridor' or 'over a cup of coffee',
> talk about this, sow a few seeds.

Despite a willingness to engage in debate and discussion, there is
still a sense of inevitability about the prevalence of the head's view:

> She does it in consultation, not just with deputies but with just
> about everybody who she can find to talk to or who will talk back
> to her. She tends to only like hearing what she wants to hear and
> rarely will she have a discussion where people disagree, because
> when you disagree, because she is so eloquent and good with
> words, she can make you feel very inadequate and inferior. And
> as a result you may tend to feel perhaps a personal attack when in
> fact she often says it isn't and that she in fact is arguing the idea
> but arguing the idea comes across very strongly as it's the person
> who she's having a go at in a way.

Perhaps the previously quoted head was hinting at a similar paradox
when he described himself as a 'spider with slippers on'. While not
all heads who employ this style are unwilling to take on board
opposing views, the close identification of the argument with the
person, and a willingness to use personal confrontation as an
integral part of argument, seem to be strong common elements.
Social relationships provide a channel for discussion and dispute;
there is no polite formality of committee behaviour here. There is a
necessary degree of unpredictability, both of process and outcome.
This is emphasized by a head of department who was asked, for my
benefit, to describe his head's way of working:

> You use a social role, not an institutional role ... social leader-
> ship, social style its more challengeable, but you're not challenged
> because you're good at it. When you walk around the place
> people don't know what you will do, like in families.

In the adversarial mode the assertion of control rests upon the skills
of the head as an active politician and strategist both in the conduct
of leadership, the use of talk and in the choice of issues, allies and

opponents, and so on. The reliance on a social style and the public exchange of views means that any challenge to the head's authority must be a challenge to the person, or at least their views. The head is of necessity closely identified with the issues and ideologies being advocated. None the less, challenges are an accepted part of the form of micro-political process generated by the adversarial style. The important point is the head's ability to handle, to deal with, these challenges. Crucial to this is the awareness, cultivation and use of allies. The head's allies, and opponents, come to be recognized as a part of the normal terrain of competing interests and ideological divisions among the staff. Allies must be encouraged, at times rewarded; opponents must be neutralized or satisfied, as the occasion demands. A head of department in a southern comprehensive described his headteacher as follows:

> It's open and closed, he's got to all the change-agents here, he's worked hard at getting them on his side. He hasn't gone up against anyone who would oppose him. And there's no one who is strong enough to take him on their own.

On the occasion of challenges to the head's political power, allies and opponents will be called to account. These may be moments when the initiative is wrested away from the head, who will have to operate in response to issues defined by others and perhaps on the others' territory. One head gave this example:

> Well, there've been several political challenges. You see, a fortnight ago the head of maths convened a meeting of all the heads of department to talk about discipline because he was unhappy about discipline. Now maths do have problems and the kids are pretty awful in maths; so I was under enormous pressure to suspend some kids. ... I interceded because I heard this meeting was going to take place. I got suspicious because I was talking to one of the department heads and I said, 'Can I see you tonight', and he said, 'No I can't, I've got to change my duties round'. And he made a sort of excuse which made me think, 'What the hell's he doing?' So then I set about some people who, to use an expression, are my eyes and ears, and they spoke up at the meeting and said, 'Look, we know there is a forum set up for this to take place and it's on Monday evening. And it's always on Monday evenings. Why aren't we using it?' And so that meeting

just ended. It fizzled out because my loyal troops, if you like, just overcame the rest. And the head of maths ended up feeling pretty fraught. And he rang the other morning and said could he come and talk to me, and I said, 'Of course, lets talk now.'

On this occasion the head was able to divert a deliberate challenge by getting the arena of oppositional discourse redefined back into his territory, back into a meeting where his participation was legitimate. Also, the immediate response to the head of maths' request achieved a similar redefinition. The head of department would have few grounds for suggesting that the head was unwilling to discuss the issue as a matter of urgency. The head of department would be faced with a one-to-one meeting, having already failed to achieve formal support on the matter from colleagues. Like the gunfighter in the Western movies, the adversarial head likes to pick his or her own ground, time and place. If the head can pick the high ground and have the sun in their opponent's face, so much the better. Indeed, one head used a very similar metaphor in interview:

I mean, my line is that, if you think of a boxing analogy, I've been in the ring with them – we went ten rounds, then I hit the buggers on the floor. Well, I'm only prepared to pick things up with them if I know they are going to change what they're doing now. I'm not prepared to put my arm round them and say, 'That was a good round in the ring and let's just carry on the same as we were before', because the way we were before is wrong, it's completely out of line with what we are as a school. And they know that.

Of course, the battles here are battles of wits, the exchanges are verbal. None the less, there is a strong sense of 'sides', of friends and foes, even 'goodies' and 'baddies', and certainly right and wrong. Ideology again. As Hall puts it:

On the one hand, politics constitutes the transformation of physical confrontations into verbal ones, and on the other, the resolution or accommodation of these confrontations involves the use of political rhetoric, i.e., 'the use of public discourse to persuade'. We must be therefore interested in understanding the processes of political talk in determining how the audience is activated (or perhaps deactivated or deflected). The maintenance and activation of power comes from being able to convince others of the correctness of your position. . . . Alternatives are literally 'talked down'. (1972, p. 51)

AUTHORITARIAN

If the adversarial head aims to persuade and convince, the authoritarian is concerned straightforwardly to assert. Statement rather than confrontation is the primary mode of verbal engagement with others. Such a head takes no chances by recognizing the possibility of competing views and interests. Opposition is avoided, disabled or simply ignored. No opportunities are provided for the articulation of alternative views or the assertion of alternative interests, other than those defined by the head as legitimate. Indeed, the authoritarian may rely, as a matter of course, on conscious deception as a method of organizational control. Such a head would be likely to be a 'high Mach' scorer in measures of Machiavellianism (Christie and Geis, 1970). The high-Mach scorer is, according to Christie and Geis, 'good at forging strategic alliances (as is the adversarial), can subdue or display emotions when necessary and is able to look people straight in the eye when telling a lie'.

A history teacher at a southern comprehensive describes his head:

> when he's got an area that's contentious and he feels he's going to have some conflict. He will present it in a staff meeting at the end and he will present it as if it were a non-issue, and then will look surprised if there's any comment about it.
>
> The staff meetings themselves are very interesting because we moved from having them after school, when the head always began by saying 'there are several people who have said to me that they must be away by five, so the meeting must end by five whatever'. And we would get started about twenty past, twenty-five past four. But sometimes discussion would get going and he would find it difficult to stop at five. It was suggested then that we move to having morning meetings twice a month instead of the once, and have one for information where he is just a moving notice board really, reading out circulars he's received, and one for real discussion. He didn't like the idea of this but after pressure from the staff association he agreed. The only thing he hasn't got any control over is the staff association. And then he kept cancelling staff meetings and we were back to once a month and he would still leave these issues to the end and people got so frustrated they just didn't bother.
>
> If it's a suspect area, if the head thinks there might be some

opposition, he will make quite clear what his opinion is on it, so if anybody is going to say anything, they've got to appear to be going against the headmaster. . . . And there are only three of us who are willing to say anything and it would all be very reasonable. But I do it less now than I used to, because I felt it was just counter-productive. It wasn't getting anywhere, and you were considered as the token radical on the staff and you would have your say and they would say right the next person and you are ignored really.

We had this thing about putting items on the staff meeting agenda and eventually the head said we could do that if we wrote up the issue and then put our names, and of course people weren't willing to do that. He would say, 'Right, who's going to start us off', and no one would say anything. And in this way he put a stop to it and the agenda wasn't filled out. Actually putting something on the agenda was seen as being an attack on him. So even if you put something down and spoke to it the interesting thing was would anybody support you. I put down once the idea of having a school council, and I argued for it and then the head spoke against it and he said any other comments, and no one spoke and so on to the next issue. People kept coming up afterwards saying to me, 'I was going to but . . . ', and they made various excuses. But once he made his statement, they found it psychologically impossible to speak, even though they agreed with me.

The aim here is to stifle talk, indeed to reduce talk to a one-way flow. Discussion is defined as subversive, as a potential threat to the head's 'authority'. The head aims to limit talk to uncontroversial matters, indeed also to redefine potentially divisive issues as non-controversial and thus not requiring discussion.

The authoritarian head seems to have an almost pathological abhorrence of confrontation. There are similarities to be drawn with Weber's conceptualization of the patriarchical leader, whose authority is based on a 'system of inviolable norms and is considered sacred' (Weber, 1948, p. 296). It would seem that any display of opposition to the head's views is regarded as signifying a major breakdown in the normal political process. As the extract above indicates, stratagems of various kinds may be employed to avoid the possibility of discussion other than within the limits laid down by the head. Meetings are cancelled, the agendas of meetings are massaged, and when 'illegitimate' issues are indicated efforts are made to isolate and label those responsible as deviant, as operating outside the bounds of normal practice. A head of department in a secondary-modern school described an interesting example of this kind of manipulation and deception:

> We were discussing the implications of a reduction in staffing and the head presented it as just a fact of life, something we would have to cope with. I wanted to discuss the impact it would have on the rest of us, but he didn't. He said we would pick it up at the next staff meeting and talk it through. When the time of the next meeting came the head sent a message asking me to meet a visitor in another part of the school. And while I was away the head told the staff that we would all have to teach more. By the time I got back the staff meeting had finished. I was furious.

Again, the initial aim of the head seemed to be to present a potentially controversial issue as unproblematic and then when this interpretation is challenged to divert discussion, first by closing the meeting and second by effectively excluding a key opponent from the reconvened meeting. Clearly, without the head's own version of events it is difficult to be certain about the extent of deliberate misrepresentation involved in such a situation. None the less, the teachers who described their head's in these terms seemed unequivocal in their interpretations and were able to produce numerous examples to support their accounts. Unfortunately, but perhaps understandably, none of the heads I interviewed presented themselves to me in terms of this style.

This style of leadership does not rely on any separation of the formal/institutional and personal aspects of the headship role. The personal attributes of the head seem to be of less importance than their particular interpretation of their role, although a number of the teachers interviewed indicated that anger was frequently displayed in situations where colleagues were regarded by the head as difficult or uncooperative. Christie and Geis's work would suggest that such anger is strategic. The effect is none the less apparent frustration among the staff and an unwillingness to engage in open debate either because of fear of reprisals or a belief in the futility of opposition. Hunter describes exactly this situation in a case study of a northern comprehensive:

It was quite common for opinions which flourished in the semi-privacy of small groups in the staffroom not to be forthcoming in open meetings. Apathy, timidity and caution were some of the reasons presented, the latter reason some claimed through experience.

'It does you more harm than good to speak your mind.' 'The hierarchy take it out of you.' Such comments often accompanied staffroom anecdotes about the use of direct sanctions by the Head and the 'dominant coalition' of deputy heads – and sometimes heads of lower, middle and sixth form sections of the school. Admittedly the Head did possess overt sanctions such as control of resources, access to promotion, job references and even direct admonition. It was difficult empirically to substantiate use of such sanctions, and if used, they were used sparingly and discreetly. More to the point, many of the staff believed they would be used. (1980, p. 223)

(See the discussion of 'anticipated reactions' in Ch. 5, below.)

The collaboration of a 'dominant coalition' in tactics of discouragement was indicated by a social-studies teacher in a southern comprehensive. Here classroom techniques seem to be employed against the staff:

> The deputy plays the 'hard man'. The headmaster doesn't like that role, he is a liberal. So he uses the deputy who's known to be a hard-liner; he will come into meetings and rant and rave and act as though he were going to physically assault you, bullying tactics, which frighten some members off the issue and they withdraw their support.

Jago (1983), employing Harris's (1973) analysis, suggests that teachers' relations with the head and 'the hierarchy' often involve them being cast in the position of 'child', displaying responses including 'dependence, compliance, feelings of confusion, distress and unworthiness, childish behaviour and retreatism' (p. 137). Responses such as these are easily exploited. Operated together, a combination of threat and manipulation can effectively create a climate of non-engagement – which seems to be the desired end product as far as the leadership of the school is concerned. Again, Hunter's case study illustrates this well:

> Even though there were many meetings, many of the staff did not

feel that they could influence events. For example, after a staff meeting an elderly assistant teacher remarked on a discussion regarding the use of classrooms as teacher bases:

> It was waste of time last night. The Head stopped it (i.e. he ruled the discussion out of order) and what happened after was a waste of time. We didn't get our say. The important point didn't come up about having to carry all your material to classes. I cricked my back when I slipped on the stairs with an armful of the stuff. What happens is we don't carry the materials and the kids don't get any geometry.

At the same meeting, concerning another topic, a head of department commented: 'Its like banging your head against a brick wall. They never take any notice.'

The extent of participation which actually occurred in meetings by the staff was quite small. For example, in one typical staff meeting the ratio of contributions was 13 (head and two deputies): to 4 (from 20 heads of department): to 1 (from 42 other members of staff). If the volume of contributions were added, the disparity in the ratio would be much greater. The Director of Studies described this reticence of the staff as 'weird'. He went on to say:

> Take the CSE assessors who wanted periods 7 and 8 off for travelling time to their respective schools ... the amount of hot air and bombast about not having it. I know that there were people there who had come to me regarding this; but when they could say their piece in front of the big white chief they don't say a blooming thing. (1980, p. 223)

At the heart of the authoritarian mode, in contrast to the adversarial, there is an evident commitment to the status quo, to defend, almost at all costs, the established policies and procedures of the institution. This style of leadership seems most common among long-serving heads or in schools where 'traditions' represent cherished values strongly held by the dominant coalition. Hunter (1980, p. 225) points out, quite rightly, that in such circumstances the members of the dominant coalition have a considerable investment in maintaining the status quo. This would certainly make sense in terms of the analysis of interests developed in the previous chapters. If you want things to stay as they are, then a strategy of stifling alternative views and proposals for change is a rational course of action. If you want to bring about change, as seems to be the case with adversarial heads, then persuasion is almost inevitably required. That is not to rule out the possibility that a head may use an authoritarian style to force changes upon a reluctant staff.

A further strategy available to the authoritarian head is that of selective recruitment. That may seem unexceptional, but it is the type of recruitment that is of significance. Data indicate that acquiescence is a major quality sought in candidates – people, that is, who are unlikely to 'cause problems' for the head by 'making difficulties' or 'rocking the boat'. A head of department explains the situation in his rural comprehensive:

> When I was appointed seven years ago the school was expanding and fourteen or fifteen new staff were appointed at more or less the same time and they were all young, go-ahead men with good degrees. And for the first couple of years there was quite a lot of discussion and some decisions made and there was quite definitely pressure on the school to change. It was the comprehensive era. But then these people seemed to get frustrated, they weren't getting anywhere and the powers-that-be used different tactics to stop discussion, to stop decisions being made and these people moved one by one and have done very well. And they were replaced by very different people, very safe characters who wouldn't rock the boat. Especially the higher you go, but even among the probationers.

Hunter reports a similar situation in his case study school and quotes a deputy headmistress outlining the policy:

> We do an awful lot in considering the appointments of staff. We want people who fit in with this type of arrangement. There are one or two who don't toe the line. They are sparks in a sense and this is necessary. I could see a situation where a large number of people like this might bring havoc in my opinion. Those who would demand that the school be democratic, with votes, and so on. This would cause disruption. . . . On the whole, in general, the system is accepted. (1980, p. 224)

What seems to be suggested here is that a few non-conformists can be tolerated; as long as they lack critical mass support, then their efforts are an irritant rather than a threat. The sort of staff member that is normally sought, however, is the conformist, the acceptor, someone who will fit in with existing arrangements. The existing policies and practices, 'the system', is immutable. The more important the post, then the more critical it becomes to appoint the right sort of person. For the head the appointment of a deputy is probably one of the most significant decisions that ever has to be made. A history teacher described one such appointment in his school in the following way:

> The second deputy head was appointed three years ago, and was made up from head of maths, and was chosen from a very talented field, and the head fought really hard for him against the view of the governors. And my theory is that he got the job because he was safe. He is again liberal in ideology but he is someone who always argues that you shouldn't have change unless the whole staff are in favour of change and so change never takes place. And he has this idea of consensus, but he works out the consensus himself, he never takes a vote on anything. He is a man who doesn't want change. And he's also the timetable man, so he's very important because if there's any change you want to make, he's always the one who says it can't be done because the timetable won't allow it.

The same view is put forward by a social-studies teacher describing his sixth-form college:

> All the management team and a few other promotional points have recently all been internal appointments, and the people who have got those promotions have been in every case the ones who toe the line basically. People who are going to knuckle under and do as they are told. There hasn't been yet an example of an inspired promotion.
>
> The new house tutor is a good example; it was going to be a woman because each house has one woman and one man. And several women applied who were ready for that sort of promotion and were rejected. And to quote colleagues, 'the promotion devalued the post of house tutor'.

The attractions of internal appointments in such a situation are obvious. The heads are able to appoint (assuming that they can convince advisers and governors) the 'sort of person' they want on the basis of direct experience. There is little possibility of making a mistake and ending up with a 'subversive' in a key position, with access to decision-making.

Inasmuch as public channels of resistance, criticism, complaint, opposition or even positive suggestion are blocked and stifled by authoritarian leadership, greater emphasis is thrown onto the informal channels of influence and communication. That is to say, what become important are the deals done behind closed doors, the *ad hoc* agreements and negotiations or representations made in private. Smith sees such forms of micro-politics as critically important to the Machiavellian head:

> The size of the organization and the privacy a person enjoys within it may be crucial to a machiavellian. Size is a help because it probably takes a long time before the intentions of the machiavellian are known. Privacy, generally in the form of a personal office, is useful because negotiations can take place undisturbed. The office affords a haven when the climate is unsuitable for deals, but it is also a place from which one can venture when situations seem more propitious. In short, a private base provides the person with the opportunity to choose the time and place for interaction. Conversely, it allows one to choose not to interact, pleading when pressed the demands of another activity. (1983, p. 207)

There is a strong contrast here with the 'open door' policy of the interpersonal head.

The styles of headship outlined here focus organizational attention almost exclusively on the leader, as King (1968) suggests, although leadership styles do implicitly assume particular forms of followership. However, in stressing the styles as social accomplishments, the possibility must be allowed for some heads being unable or unwilling to bring off a version of the headship role which might be accommodated in the typology outlined above. Also, it must be acknowledged that many heads display a mixture of styles. Depending on the issue, the situation or the political climate a head may opt for a particular presentation of self and hope for or expect a concomitant response from 'followers'. However, such style-switching demands social skill and versatility. Not all heads are capable of achieving the authenticity or co-operation necessary to bring off these variations. Indeed, for reasons of choice, as a result of lack of experience or by virtue of circumstances, certain heads tend to retreat almost entirely from the focus of attention. Some certainly have problems in bringing off a single performance style. A brief case study will serve here to illustrate the point and also draw attention to the importance of understanding headship in relation to specific institutional contexts and histories.

Coping with headship: a case study

Hanna (1978) reports a situation in an inner-city comprehensive school where effective control over decision-making had been taken over by the deputy head, Norris. The only form of formal representation of interests lay in an unwieldly academic board.

> It was felt that that was too big a body to come to any useful conclusions. The discussions tended to ramble a bit. Also the deputy head at the time was a bit of a dictator. He felt that it was an advisory body, to him. (Head of modern languages)

The head in this case held little sway among the staff generally or over his deputy in particular. This seemed, in part at least, to be a matter of choice, but also reflected the strength of will of the deputy:

> The boss, his biggest fault is he doesn't like to make decisions; I don't dislike him as a person, but he doesn't like to make decisions. (Head of geography)

> he was just waiting for Norris to retire. We often said to him, 'Why don't you slap him down?' Personally, I think he was frightened of him. (Head of humanities)

In these circumstances the academic board assumed particular importance, but many heads of department found themselves excluded from it, to the cost of their departments:

> We found that decisions were being taken that affected some heads of department without any kind of check. . . . We felt that this was ridiculous. (Head of art)

> I was on the academic board before and I had Norris's ear, and I had everything I wanted, but despite all this, a lot of us thought that something had to be done about this misuse of power he had. (Head of humanities)

In this situation, in the face of the head's abdication of responsibility, it was the heads of department who eventually acted:

> Well, eventually, the head of science, you know, convinced every-body the academic board had to go, and he called a heads of department meeting, and he produced this [new] academic board structure. (Head of English)

The heads of department met as a committee; they were not a con-stitutional body within the school, but none the less, after some negotiation, they agreed upon a new structure of school committees including a new academic board and a formal heads of department meeting. The new structure was readily accepted by the head despite the opposition of his deputy, who was described by the head of art as 'obstructive and divisive'. The old academic board met to vote itself out of office in July, and in September of the same year the new board was convened for the first time. Five heads of department were represented on the new board, and Hanna reports that 'from all accounts, they vote *en bloc*, discussing the agenda prior to the meetings in the local pub' (1978, p. 21).

> Oh! we always have our little meeting over in the annex. Graham Lane, he's the chap who keeps us on our toes. If anything needs sorting out he'll nudge your elbow and tell you 'twelve o'clock, in the annex'. (Head of humanities)

Interestingly, neither the head nor the pastoral deputy were regular attenders at the new board. The basic ten-person membership there-fore left the heads of department representatives with a built-in majority. Hanna comments that 'It is reasonable, then, to say that the effective decision-making power has moved to the Heads of Depart-ment committee, apart from the fact that the Headmaster retains the right to "veto", exercised only once' (p. 21). What Hanna describes is a form of *coup d'état*, a palace revolution. The power vacuum created by the head's abdication of decision-making responsibility was initially usurped by the strident deputy, Norris. Norris's use of personal influence, however, left a major constituency, the heads of department, dissatisfied. They were excluded from formal authority but were able to use their effective power to overthrow the despotic rule of the deputy. The head's view does not emerge clearly from the account, but he seemed to find the heads of depart-ment more acceptable than his deputy as surrogate decision-makers.

What this account demonstrates is both the extent to which normal practice assumes and relies upon the head's role as a powerful decision-maker but also the possibility of alternative systems of decision-making where the all-powerful head is absent for some reason. Not all heads fill their role in the stereotypical fashion as benevolent despot. This also underlines the view of organizational power as an outcome of the deployment of definite means of action in particular situations and, as suggested earlier, the social accomplishment of leadership requires collaboration. Without a degree of compliance and acceptance headship would in most circumstances be impossible to bring off. Heads may be licensed autocrats but, as I have tried to illustrate in the adumbration of the styles, they must strive to achieve both domination and integration if they are to work and survive in the school. As a negative case, the example above also challenges the myth of inevitability that underpins much writing on headship. There is allusion to incompetent or inefficient heads but little indication of what this means in practice; followership practices tend to get ignored altogether when such hints are dropped. Heads do not rule by divine right; they must strive and struggle to bring off their preferred style in practical circumstances. On occasion they will retreat, compromise or even abdicate responsibility. The analysis of headship as a performance must be complemented by an analysis of followership in similar terms. Leadership styles are not unproblematic; they do not go unopposed.

5
Headship: opposition and control

In all matters of opinion our adversaries are insane.   (Mark Twain)

Integration and pseudo-participation

The four leadership styles identified above represent forms of resolution of the basic political dilemma facing the headteacher in a school. That dilemma concerns the organizational achievement of control (domination) and commitment (integration). In this respect the styles are different means to achieve the same end: the maintenance of political stability within the organization. This stability may be dynamic or radical, as in the case in the adversorial mode, or static and conservative, as in the authoritarian mode. Stability may be emphasized in terms of community and relationships, as is the case in the interpersonal mode, or in terms of structures, roles and procedures, as in the managerial mode. In each case stability is ultimately related to the head's control of the organization. Whatever else varies between the styles the role of the head as leader remains central. The head strives to establish the right, and the responsibility, of 'the final say':

> If all schools are taken into account, it is arguable that a majority of Heads and senior staff believe in strong leadership and find it necessary to use it. It may often be personalized and idiosyncratic. Many have paid tribute to or toyed with newer ideas of exercising control and direction. Nevertheless, they remain conscious of their ultimate legal responsibilities and therefore assert their own leadership. (Paisey, 1984, p. 33)

However, even if this analysis of the styles is accepted, the question of achieving and maintaining intergration, the other component in the dilemma equation, still remains. Two issues are crucial here: autonomy and participation. In each of the stylistic modes the issue of teacher autonomy remains as a sacred touchstone. It stands as a symbol of professional status for the teacher and is taken for granted as a powerful limitation on the power of the head. Many of the teachers interviewed referred to the degree of freedom allowed them by their head. A history teacher, describing an authoritarian-type head, explained:

> On the department basis he doesn't interfere at all, so it is possible that a department, as long as it doesn't upset other departments or the parents or kids, can make changes without reference to the headmaster on the whole. Anything that effects more than one department is made official at the head-of-department meeting, but the heads of department say that that's not the case, no decisions are ever made, they say what they think and nothing ever happens.

A drama teacher described the autonomy provided by an interpersonal-type head:

> If she liked the way they operated, she liked their spirit, she liked the way they handled their department, the way that they were able to control the work that they were doing – she believed in appointing specialists, people who were specialists in their field and giving them a free hand to do the best they could, and she appeared to be pleased with certain departments and the way they were working. If she didn't she withdrew her support, in a sense. You know, if the face didn't fit, people went.

These comments were typical of the accounts of autonomy in practice offered by teachers. In these terms the concept of autonomy appears weak and limited. First and perhaps most significantly, autonomy is presented not so much as a basic right of teachers as professional practitioners; rather, it is a privilege granted by the head on certain terms and conditions. If these conditions are breached then the autonomy may, it is suggested, be taken away. Support is withdrawn, decisions are blocked or not implemented, resources are denied and appointments held back. Second, accept-ance of the conditions of autonomy involves in fact acceptance of a set of practical limitations on possible freedom of manoeuvre. Other departments must not be affected, pupils and parents must be mollified, and as indicated previously, if timetable changes are involved, then a whole range of other interested parties will have to be satisfied. We might add to this list the limitations imposed by resources (normally allocated by the head), the grouping arrangements of the shool as a whole and the distribution of rooms and other facilities. Third, as the second extract illustrates strongly, the head's approval remains as an ultimate constraint upon the department and the classroom teacher. Negative sanctions of some kind, may be brought into play. In effect, there are institutional norms and expectations to be met. Murgatroyd and Gray provide a good example of these sorts of constraints at work:

> Teachers seeking to run their classes in ways radically different from the way the organization operates thus have a great deal to do. One teacher working in a school run very much as a 'top-down' institution with a 'tells' style of management ran a class along the lines of a teacher-initiated negotiation group only to be constantly interrupted by colleagues saying things like 'I came in to quell a riot, I didn't realise that this is what you call teaching!' When the teacher tried to run a participative assembly he was advised by the deputy to 'stick to the well-established formula of two hymns, a prayer and a bollocking!' In subtle but significant ways these and related incidents brought strong pressure to bear upon the teacher to conform to the normative classroom behaviour expected of teachers within the school. (1984, pp. 42–3)

In other words, autonomy is a set of freedoms to act which are a set within firm limits and which may be withdrawn or curtailed if these limits are infringed. (See also Beynon's 1981 account of the hounding of 'Poor Miss Floral' and Denscombe's 1980 analysis of the significance of classroom noise.) Autonomy is in effect a cosy illusion which encourages a sense of professional independence for teachers but none the less ties them into the institutional regime of their school. It is a major compromise between freedom and control. In terms of rhetoric the concept of autonomy may serve to enhance the integration of individuals into the organization by fostering a sense of personal efficacy, but it also involves the subordination of the individual to organizational control. Autonomy thus has a powerful ideological function, but it also has

implications for the structure of control. For in stressing the independence of teachers from outside control of their practice it also
stresses the independence of teachers from one another, it encourages isolation and separation, what Lortie (1975) calls the 'egg-
crate' conception of teaching. As one teacher put it, the maintenance
of strong boundaries between teachers and between departments
provides a basis for 'divide and rule':

> The staffroom doesn't function like a normal staffroom where
> information can be cross-pollinated at break, lunchtime and after
> school. It has meant that the school has broken down into 'safe
> units' with the power in departments. There is a kind of divide
> and rule with no togetherness over major issues. (Head of
> sociology, a southern comprehensive)

What we have here is the double-edge of autonomy:

> If I think logically about where the power is in this school, we all
> feel that it is in what is known as the 'executive', the senior
> teachers, who are the decision-makers. I have complete auto-
> nomy over the English department. I decide what syllabus we do,
> how we conduct the teaching, everything. But in terms of the
> whole school, I feel I don't have an awful lot of power or say in
> decision-making ... there ought to be more scope within the
> school for heads of departments to put forward ideas. (Head of
> English, a London comprehensive)

By granting autonomy, whatever its instrinsic limitations, over a
specific range of classroom and curricular issues, the head may also
effectively exclude teachers from 'a say' in a whole range of other
issues which affect the organization as a whole and the field of
determinations and limitations within which their autonomy is set.
The head giveth and the head taketh away. By definition autonomy
limits the range of concerns over which the teacher can exercise
influence. In speaking from a basis of special interest, each teacher
is prevented from taking up an overview perspective. That remains
the exclusive concern of the head. Furthermore, while individual
contributions are readily identified with special interests, the head
always has good grounds for dismissing them. In this way the
classroom teacher is doubly handicapped when trying to engage in
general debate. In celebrating their autonomy, teachers accept a
whole set of constraints upon their participation in school decision-
making.

This leads on quite neatly to the second key concept of participation, or more correctly in this context, what I shall call pseudo-participation. I want to argue that where autonomy provides an illusion of freedom, pseudo-participation provides an illusion of control. Again, pseudo-participation plays its part in the complex processes of domination and integration, the 'warming-up' and 'cooling-out' dilemma of political control. Forms of participation (or non-participation in at least one case) differ within different styles of leadership as we have seen. These different forms are represented schematically in Table 5.1.

Table 5.1 Forms of participation and types of talk in school decision-making

	Forms of participation	Response to opposition	Strategies of control
Authoritarian	Prevents public access to voice	Stifle	Insulation, concealment and secrecy
Managerial	Formal committees, meetings and working parties	Channel and delay	Structuring, planning, control of agendas, time and context
Interpersonal	Informal chats and personal consultation and lobbying	Fragment and compromise	Private performances of persuasion
Adversarial	Public meetings and open debate	Confront	Public performances of persuasion

Table 5.1 presents an analysis of forms of participation as articulated, literally, via talk. In each case the style of leadership gives rise to and is perpetuated by a particular form for the organization of 'political' talk – talk, that is, which is concerned with policy-making and resource allocation in the organization. In each case such talk is viewed as critical and problematic in terms of the leader's control of the organization. Talk of this kind when engaged in by the subordinate members of the organization, and when it is not controlled, is viewed as potentially subversive. In the case of the authoritarian and management styles, the emphasis is upon controlling the flow of information within the organization. For the authoritarian leader

the most straightforward means of control is to stifle; there is an attempt to prevent subordinates from public access to voice. Significant talk is restricted to one-way communication from the top down and behind-the-scenes deals made with those who wield some political influence (more of which later). Insulation, concealment and secrecy are the norm. For the manager, control is achieved by the channelling and formalizing of talk into a structure of committees and working parties. The only valid access to voice is through this structure. The structure itself creates hierarchy and limits subordinate participation and the manager's control of agendas and the timing of discussions provides a further source of veto over the content of the talk. In Gans's (1967) terms, the formal structure of committees provides a 'script' for decision-making 'performances'. In the case of the interpersonal and adversorial styles, control is achieved by the symbolic mobilization of support; the emphasis is upon commitment and persuasion. The interpersonal leader employs private performances of persuasion; the personal and informal chat is the primary vehicle to talk. Grievances and personal troubles are addressed in this way and the informal channels are treated as valid and open to all – the aim being to tie subordinates into a personal relationship with the leader. The adversorial leader, on the other hand, employs public performances of persuasion. The public debate is the major forum for airing grievances and opinions; the aim here is to persuade waverers, to expose and confront opponents and to neutralize alternative perspectives. Here informal channels for talk are defined as invalid and unacceptable. The subordinates are offered opportunities for 'voice' if they are willing to take them. Verbal skills are at a premium here and the use of public debate leads to a heavy emphasis on overt alliances (and thus team performances). Strategies and performances must be planned in advance and carefully organized in order to be effective.

In each case, to a greater or lesser extent, participation can be reduced to an appearance of participation, without access to 'actual' decision-making. This appearance of participation, pseudo-participation, is highlighted in particular by the concept of 'consultation'. Each of the heads I interviewed seemed to regard consultation as the key factor in the involvement of their teachers in the process of decision-making, be it in the form of personal chats with individuals or the setting up of a working party to make recommendations or the holding of a staff meeting to 'air' views. However, in each case the heads also underlined that they regarded the process of consultation as not binding – not part of decision-making but an adjunct to it. (The Countesthorpe Moot was a rare exception to this kind of process and relationship; see Watts, 1977.) None the less, consultation can go a long way in ensuring quiescence, especially when potential opponents and opinion-leaders are consulted personally. In Lukes's (1977) terms, such 'rights of participation' as these are merely a political 'ritual' which lends support to what is in reality a system of autocracy, by bestowing spurious legitimacy upon it. Interestingly, some teachers recognize this:

> I think there was a lot of feeling last year in terms of the new head's appointment and the fact there was no involvement. A lot of staff felt they ought to have a lot more say in the kind of head they had: and there sort of wasn't any formal way for them to have any – formally they had no say whatsoever. But the head did maintain that she listened to what the staff wanted. (Head of drama)

> On a major issue the head will seek advice from lots of different places and then go away and think about it and then make a final decision. Staff are not necessarily aware that he has thought things through – perhaps there could be more explaining to people how the process works. (Deputy head)

> There are few meetings and one does not necessarily feel consulted. You can't really expect the rank and file to make decisions – they can't see all the angles. Our main job is to get on with the teaching. (Year tutor)

> The head gives his blessing to a topic suggested for discussion by a group of staff and puts limitations on the discussions, e.g. we know that he will not agree to a 'sink group' in the fourth and fifth year. The eventual suggested policies are within the parameters set by the head. (Head of history)

> There was a feeling – there is a definite feeling among members of staff, younger members of staff – that they're just pawns, that they've got no control over things. (Head of drama)

These comments express a strong sense of non-participation. Despite, or set against, heads' references to 'consultation', there is a feeling of exclusion and of being manipulated – being unable to exercise control over decisions which directly affect conditions of work. However, on the other hand, some staff did find the existing arrangements quite acceptable, or at least natural. Two teachers in the same school (quoted in Taafe, 1980, p. 31) commented:

> The consultative machinery here is marvellous. At my last school we had regular grand staff meetings, very few people said anything, you felt intimidated. In fact the same few put the same non-representative view. (RE teacher)

> I feel that if I feel strongly about something I can put my point of view at either faculty or school section meetings. My points are noted and communicated to the top without names being mentioned. If, however, you really feel strongly enough, there is nothing wrong with going to see the head personally. (Languages teacher)

However, in the same school other members of staff offered a different view of consultation in practice:

> Coming in as senior mistress I feel I can be objective. On the surface there is a complex consultative machinery which the staff can use. The majority of the staff do feel involved. You must remember, that we have a very strong, dominant, assertive and decisive head. I get the impression that some issues are taboo. The staff only seem to use the machinery for some things. (Senior mistress)

> The staff realize that the head has very strong ideas. He won't change. He isn't flexible. It isn't worthwhile, in fact it is a waste of time to send some ideas up to the senior heads. (Head of languages)

> Last year a lot of staff felt strongly about how occasional days were used. This was an issue many people brought up at faculty and school section meetings and it went through *en masse* to senior heads. They couldn't ignore the issue. The head agreed to see to it; this means nothing happened. When the issue was raised again this year, we find the days are settled. He puts things off to the next academic year hoping we will forget about them. (Biology teacher)

Here then the head's control of valid topics, and the ultimate veto on any issues raised, underpins a system of 'complex consultative machinery'.

What we have here are forms of what Bachrach and Baratz (1970) call 'non-decision-making' – the use of power by heads to prevent the emergence of any potentially subversive opposition by their exclusion from decision-making. Saunders identifies three major categories of non-decision-making. Each works in a different way to stifle opposition. Each is well represented in the discussion so far and the examples quoted. First, there is 'negative decision-making': 'those in powerful positions may simply fail to respond in any way to the articulation of political demands by less powerful groups so that no decision is ever taken' (Saunders, 1981, p. 29). The question of 'occasional days', above, is a good example. Demands are quietly ignored, or put off, or diverted to working parties, and so on. Second, there is 'anticipated reactions'; here demands are simply not pressed because either it is assumed that there will be no reaction, as the head of languages and senior mistress quoted above illustrate, or there is a fear of retaliation from those in power, some kind of sanction. This latter seems to be the case in authoritarian school regimes where speaking up is actively discouraged. Power relations are routinized and naturalized and the reserve powers of the head are simply not called into question. Third, there is 'mobilization of bias', which:

> refers to those situations where dominant interests may exert such a degree of control of the way in which the political situation operates, and over the values, beliefs and opinions of less powerful groups within it, that they can effectively determine not only whether . . . demands come to be expressed and heeded, but also whether such demands will ever cross people's minds. (Saunders, 1981, p. 30)

Debate takes place, discussions are held, tensions are relieved, but crucial issues do not emerge. By definition such control is extremely difficult to itemize, but the existence of counterfactual models (both in terms of forms of organization and participation (say, Countesthorpe) and in terms of educational ideologies (say, Sweden)) indicate the degree to which the very possibility of debate over certain issues is constrained by existing beliefs and values. In effect, heads make claims for power, through the particular form of their leadership style, to define the political reality of the organization. The subordinates in the organization are limited in the impact they can have upon decision-making by the existence of certain 'legitimate' concepts and channels regarding appropriate forms of participation. Would-be participants must confront these. They may either limit their participation to the existing channels and accept the inherent constraints, or work outside of these channels and risk being dismissed as 'irresponsible' or 'naive' or 'Utopian' (Saunders, 1981). Levels or patterns of participation will vary accordingly.

Satisfaction, frustration and opposition

In Chapter 1 I raised the issue of types of participation via Baldridge's (1971) four types of political actor: officials, activists, attentives and apathetics. In the light of the previous discussion I intend to recast those divisions. Baldridge's analysis stresses the quantity rather than the quality (or nature) of participation, although he does make the point that 'attentives' may become directly involved on the occasion of 'hot issues'. His attention to rates of attendance focuses upon participants rather than non-participants and neglects the possibility of pseudo-participation, although again he does identify the importance of both formal and informal channels of political influence. However, we have no way of judging whether sitting on committees simply generates an unwarranted sense of political efficacy among the 'activists' or whether they have an observable impact upon 'actual' decision-making. Furthermore, Baldridge's vision of participation rests upon an assumption of freedom of action not borne out in the data available to this study. He is apparently suggesting that participation, of some kind, is available to all those who wish it. The body of data marshalled here indicates a considerable degree of unsatisfied demand or wish for participation and a strong sense of pseudo-participation, exclusion from 'actual' decision-making. Among the teachers interviewed, three categories of responses in terms of political efficacy were evident: satisfaction, fatalism and frustration. These responses represent different combinations of desire and experience. Satisfaction was expressed by two different sorts of teachers: the first type were those who were satisfied with their existing political resources, those that is with influence in the existing power structure. Many of these would in fact be equivalent to Baldridge's 'officials', members of the senior management team or members of key committees. However, others in this category do not hold formal positions of power but wield political influence either among the staff or as a result of 'having the head's ear'; these are discussed further in the following section. The second type of 'satisfieds' are those who find the existing state of things to be acceptable even though they appear to have no influence upon decision-making and irrespective of whether the state of things could be said to be in their interests. Some of Baldridge's apathetics might be found here. This kind of satisfaction can be the product of what Saunders (1981) calls 'symbolic bedazzlement'. One element of this satisfaction is undoubtedly a matter of deferred gratification resting on the possibility of having 'a future'; this would apply to those who are picked out for sponsorship or who hold key skills. In contrast, fatalism was common among those who were 'out of office', cut off from influential relationships, dissatisfied with the state of things, but apparently unwilling to do anything to alter their situation. They hold a sense of institutional politics in terms of Saunders's notion of 'anticipated reactions'. They feel that nothing would be achieved by active attempts at change and that indeed their position might become worse. Those in the third category, frustration, share many characteristics with the fatalists but not their resignation. The frustrated often hold 'intense preferences' and continue to press their demands for change irrespective of past failures or the poor likelihood of future success. Illustration of groupings roughly equivalent to those described are evident in the following extract from one teacher's account of his staffroom:

> There's the group that are very sour about the whole thing, they've been teaching for a long time, not going any further, they haven't got degrees on the whole – Scales 2 and 3 and not going anywhere. Spend a lot of time complaining about things. Very hostile to the headmaster. No influence at all in the school, don't speak up and if they did wouldn't be listened to [fatalists]. Then there are a group of women who are not interested in promotion and not interested in the way in which the school is run. See teaching as a part-time job, a secondary thing. Talk about their children and knitting patterns and that sort of thing. Again, no influence at all. Very rarely speak at staff meetings unless they

have a moan about an individual pupil [apathetics]. . . . And then there's the main group, made up of the younger, ambitious teachers, not very radical, willing to go along with the school and the way the school is run. Tend to talk about social things rather than educational things. It's a large group, if they decide someone is going to become chairman of the staff association they would probably make it [satisfieds]. . . . Then you've got a small group of people of which I am a member of, just about, who feel strongly about education, read books about education. About four or five people. And we tend not to spend a lot of time in the staffroom because it is about gossip, it's not about education somehow, it's somewhere where people put you down if you talk about education or talk about anything serious [frustrateds]. (History teacher)

This, then, is one view of the political terrain of participation and influence in one shool. It offers a partial, and sexist, account of different forms of commitment and types of investment in education as a career. Vested interests, self-interests and ideological interests all appear to play their part in creating general orientations to the political life of the school. It is against this background that the formal political structures of the school are set. From such a basis particular patterns of influence upon and opposition to the head are founded.

Influence and opposition

Outside or alongside the formal school structure of posts, responsibilities, meetings, committees, and so on, it is possible to identify the existence of other types and bases of political activity. Two of the most important I shall term as 'influence' and 'opposition'. Each, in very different ways, is a mechanism for intervening in the decision-making process. Influence is based on the exploitation of some kind of special relationship. A social and personal relationship or a relationship of power or exchange. Influence is normally exercised in private regions, backstage, behind the scenes. It is known about, hinted at, used, but not observed. Opposition is based, in a sense, on the absence of a relationship, it is a public clash of will between particular individuals or groups in the organization. Influence involves the ability to affect another's judgement or decision-making, by word or action, on the basis of informal ties of some kind – admiration, fear, obligation, expertise. From interviews it was possible to identify two arenas of influence. First, there were those individuals who had some influence with the head, people who might be informally consulted or who might take it upon themselves to speak. Second, there were those who had influence with the staff: opinion leaders, respected elder statespeople, long-serving members of the staff room, the well connected (e.g. union committees or subject associations). The former were often widely known about, frequently resented but not uncommonly used as a channel of communication:

> There are some fairly influential individuals on the staff. There are those who influence the head positively and those that influence her negatively. And one of the house heads – he's also an artist and a very flexible, nice man, in fact somebody very reasonable and easy to talk to and a bit independent really, an unusual chap. But I've noticed that the head will often ring this guy at home after a meeting when she's feeling that things haven't gone well. And as a result of what he says she changes her mind .... I think the art people do influence her – her husband's an artist and she seems very keen on the Arts in education. (Deputy head)

Interestingly, describing another woman head, another respondent also identified a special concern with the Arts:

> She had that thing about the Arts. Music, art, drama and all the rest of it. She had terrific respect for the head of English, who's a very strong personality and she always managed to get everything she wanted to get in terms of what she wanted. And the head would speak to her about things before they would come up generally in head of department meetings. (Head of drama)

What these two quotations highlight is the use of influence for specific advantage on the part of some people as against the role of influence as means for gauging staff feelings or reaction – in a sense, use for personal advantage or the 'common good'. As indicated above, the exercise of influence is not necessarily based on positive ties.

The head of maths was acting deputy during the head's secondment. He is leaving to become one of Her Majesty's Inspectors.
The head of science is now a deputy head. Both of them were
people who had been at considerable variance with the head. The
head of science is well known in the area; he's a big union cheese.
He's an eloquent speaker, he's efficient on paper, a good organ-
izer, can produce a paper at the drop of a hat, somebody who 'has
the ear' of the boss. Or rather, should I say, she has a lot of
respect for him partly as a result of his work outside the school for
the union, and he does sit on a lot of very important committees
and he more than any other person knows what's going on in the
LEA and he's got the national picture. And a lot of initiatives
come from him because he knows the way the wind is blowing.
(Head of year)

Here we see some of the technical bases of effective influence. On
the one hand, there is a whole set of 'political' skills, mechanisms
that enable influence to be brought to bear, eloquent argument,
organization, written materials. On the other, there is the access to
information provided by outside contacts. This influence is an
example of Gouldner's (1957) 'cosmopolitan', his power base and
career orientation lay outside of the institution.

Of course, with the development of more complex management
structures in shools, patterns of influence among senior staff are
more formalized. The senior management team is the most obvious
example of this. This can be a mini-arena of conflict and debate in
which different interests are put forward, influence is bought to
bear. A deputy head explained this:

As a management team, I think we're, well, good, because I do
think that we represent all sorts of interests. And I think he
knows that if he sits down and talks to me, Howard and Bill, he's
gonna get a range of views. And it's interesting to watch on
certain issues, I sit and wait sometimes to see which way he's
plumbed; you know, to see whether he's gone for my way or
whether he's gone Howard's.

To be effective, influence must normally be subtle. It must not
be overdone or pushed too far. Outrageous demands now may
jeopardize future possibilities. It must also be quiet, the private
telephone call, the word in the ear. If it is too obvious, too heavy

handed, then it begins to lose its potency for both parties. If a head is seen to be under the influence of a member of staff that is rather different from being influenced by them. Having power and having access to power are different in kind. If a staff member feels that somebody is exploiting a relationship with the head, then the individual may be compromised, other relationships may be damaged. Equally, if a member of staff is very obviously a head's person, then their value as a barometer of staff opinion may be neutralized. The essence of influence is its unobtrusiveness.

In contrast, opposition is marked by its visibility. It is an out-in-the-open attempt to change things, to challenge formal power, to overturn the status quo, to subvert the accepted channels of decision-making.

Arguably, as the size of schools has increased, as new forms of management have been introduced and as cuts have begun to have a direct impact, the whole nature of working relationships in the school has undergone a fundamental change. Schools at the present time tend to be characterized by a clear sense of 'them and us', of management and line, of employer and employee. This is perhaps indicative of what some commentators call the 'proletarianization' of teachers, the reduction of teaching from a form of professional practice to a form of mental work focused starkly on the exchange of labour power for wages (see Ch. 10). A head's view of movement in this direction is represented below in the comments of a head of a Midland comprehensive school:

> The head is there to maintain standards within the school community and to produce an educational programme. And if the resources aren't backing that up, then his relationship with his colleagues on the staff is bound to be affected and that's what's happened here. It's particularly noticeable in some of the teachers who are more vulnerable, their energy is sapped, they're under more pressure and their confidence is sapped away. They turn to the head for support and if you cannot give them that support, then there is an obvious change in the relationship and this has been noticeable. The saddest example is that over the last two years is the only time that I have had to work in a programme seeing teachers to tell them that their standard of work is not professionally good enough. This has set up a new set of relationships that borders on the employer–employee relationship, which of course was foreign to the school society.

As organizational slack (Cyert and March, 1963) is lost then flexibility is reduced and the raw essence of the work situation of the teacher is left bare. The head is not infrequently caught in a conflict of 'loyalties' between responsibility to the teacher and to the local authority or parents. Each side may expect support and want to regard the head as acting in their interests. Increasingly, however, schemes of 'teacher appraisal' require of heads that they make formal judgements about the 'professional' competence and efficiency of their staff. To quote the same head (his use of 'we' here refers to the management team):

> There's no doubt at all that they [the staff] feel we should be on the side of the teacher and when we don't carry out our actions on their side, that is letting them down, that is absolutely certain. Whereas our terms of contract as it were are to keep the school running as long as possible as smoothly as possible and we are caught between them. That is one of the new problems for the head: he's caught between the county and the staff. Seven or eight years ago the image of the head would have been the senior partner in a professional firm, as in a law firm; today the feeling is that he is the mouthpiece of the government or the county council who are making cuts and it's very difficult to talk our way out of it.

It is on this basis that some, but not all, of the opposition in school can be understood. In some senses, opposition represents a recognition by teachers of their objective interests. The changed economic situation in which they now work has revealed the true antagonisms of management and labour in the school. These antagonisms have been obscured in the past by the powerful ideological effects of the concept of professionalism. The concept of profession is both slippery and ill-used. For teachers it embodies a set of claims: claims for status and for autonomy. It also signals a particular sort of identity; the image it conjures up is of the trained, dedicated and expert practitioner applying specialist skills and esoteric knowledge with considered judgement and care. To a great extent this image is an ideology, a deliberate mystification to enhance the status and protect the practice of the 'professional' teacher. However, this image has become battered and careworn over the past decade as teachers have borne the brunt of criticisms of the education system. In the media teachers are now portrayed as uncaring, improperly trained, resistant to change, politically suspect and mercenary; in short, 'unprofessional'. The identity, so useful at times to its claimants, is now used to chastize them. Johnson (1972) indicates that professions vary in the type of control they exercise and the type of control exercised over them. Thus 'the behaviour of the profession is interpreted by referring to the way its work life is organized and to the pressures toward conformity and deviance implicit in that organization' (Freidson, 1970, p. 82). Clearly, teaching fits Johnson's category of a 'state mediated' profession. It is the state which decides the 'needs' of the client (pupils or parents or society) and how these needs should be met. Currently the state is aggressively asserting its mediative role in education to a greater extent than at any time since the 1920s. Increasingly, professionalism has assumed the role of a subtle form of control over the teaching force inasmuch as it provides a code of conduct that operates in favour of the employer. Professional status has carried benefits in the past, benefits which brought a degree of autonomy, but as the benefits are eroded, the external controls have become more obvious. Thus, while the term 'profession' is still widely used in teaching, its function in the analysis of school organization has changed. It is now difficult to conceive of schools as 'professional organizations' where work is 'directed and controlled by the workers' (Freidson, 1975, p. 9). Direct forms of control are being brought into play, and formal administration is exercised by management teams, whose members are often formally trained for the task. (Freidson, 1975, describes a similar process at work in medical practice.) Increasingly, teachers see it to be in their interests to oppose the measures introduced by management in specific instances and to be 'in opposition' to management in general terms. Morgan, Hall and Mackay certainly portray contemporary headship in this light: 'Heads in the 1980s cannot promote their policies without contest, or impose their own values or ethos without debate, bargaining and compromise' (1983, p. 11). Pratt, writing from the subordinates' point of view, is also unequivocal:

> The key issues no longer surround the question as to whether teachers can be helped to respond, in their own self-interest, to the initiatives of enlightened, benevolent heads. Today we need to understand the interaction between superordinates defending the interests of the providers of the education service, and the subordinates defending their opposing interests. (1984, p. 303)

However, as noted previously, there are problems involved in mounting opposition in school. As soon as a group or an individual decides to work outside the accepted channels of decision-making, they open themselves up to criticism; typically they are accused of being subversive and/or disloyal. To return to the views of the headteacher:

> I certainly would accept that when the authority of the head-master is challenged, and that's the area of disloyalty that would be most obvious, I object vehemently and strongly. I see it as undermining the fabric, but I also see it probably as a challenge to me as a person. Now that has happened. Eight or nine years ago it didn't happen at all. ... There has crept in a whole new social atmosphere now, not only do teachers say under the pressure they are 'Why should it be asked of me?' and demand the answer before they will do it, there are certain subversive elements in the staffroom who will actually work to undermine the authority so that they can have a little more authority themselves. Now that sounds quite bitter but it would be quite false if I did not say it was there. ... You learn new tricks when this sort of thing happens; it means you change your whole tack; now when decisions are to be taken and policy is to be changed, we think as a management team about all the things that could be raised in opposition before we introduce it.

These comments are very important in a number of ways. They highlight the extent to which consultation and decision-making is, in the heads own words, a 'trick'. The autocracy of the head is to be asserted in one way or another. There is no room for opposition. Open discussion and the airing of views is only really acceptable when the views aired are not damaging to the policy intentions of the senior management team. As soon as those intentions are threatened, the opportunities for free discussion are closed down. As soon as discussion becomes oppositional, it is redefined as subversive and disloyal – very powerful concepts. Such redefinition serves to factionalize the staff and stigmatize and isolate opponents. Saunders makes the point that 'the definition of acceptable be-haviour will often reflect not so much the inherent qualities of the behaviour in question, but more the assessment by those in power of the desirability of the demands being made' (1981, p. 63).

Many heads appear to regard any form of opposition as a threat to the stability and authority of their leadership and will go to great lengths to avoid or diffuse open conflict. Some of the strategies employed were explored in the disussion of leadership styles. The political culture in schools, as in the society generally, rests upon a limited conception of democracy and participation, again as discussed previously. Two strongly held conceptions of political possibility are embedded in this culture. First, there is the presentation and conceptualization of political problems as technical problems. Such problems need to be left in the capable hands of professional experts; the ordinary teacher, like the ordinary citizen, it is argued, lacks the skills, information and resources to deal with problems or participate effectively in the problem-solving process (Barker, 1978). Such a view underlies and is reinforced by the growth in application of 'management science' to school organization. As schools increase in size and complexity, it is argued, there is greater necessity for a specialized cadre of trained educational managers and the less possible it becomes for ordinary teachers to contribute effectively to the processes of school government. In other words, management is a powerful mechanism of exclusion. Through the application of management techniques, problems or issues which may have value or ideological aspects can be translated into technical matters and thus depoliticized. Howell (1976) identifies a similar process at work within national politics; he traces the contraction of political debate within the Labour Party from concern with ideology and national interest to preoccupation with simply making the system work. This leads to the second major assumption embedded in the political culture of schools; that is, the emphasis on empiricism – a prime and overwhelming concern with maintaining the stability of the system, a concern in which there is 'neither starting-place nor appointed destination. The enterprise is to keep afloat on an even keel' (Oakeshott, 1962, p. 127). The emphasis is almost exclusively on the survival of the system itself and the objectives of the system, so to speak, are lost sight of. Ends are displaced by means (Wolin, 1961). Once again, ideology has no legitimate role to play; efficiency becomes the key concept. Any attempt to dispute the framework within which 'legitimate' political activity takes place is viewed as disruptive and threatening. It detracts from the main effort which has become, in terms of Oakeshott's metaphor, keeping the ship of state afloat. This is most clearly evident in schools at times, as at present, when survival becomes a critical issue. With falling rolls and cuts in the rate-support grant affecting local-authority funding of education and a Conservative philosophy which stresses the cleansing effects of market forces being applied to education, some schools do indeed face the possibility of extinction. What is more, the 1980 Education Act means that schools are effectively in competition with one another for a declining number of school-age clients. In this situation, ideological issues can be defined as invalid and unhelpful diversions from the main business of convincing sufficient parents to send their children to the school.

None the less, as noted already, broader political and economic trends have also had the effect in schools of stripping away layers of ideological cushioning which had served to blunt the tensions inherent in the work position of teachers. These tensions are never more apparent than during periods of industrial action:

> The recent industrial action has created a tremendous amount of discontent in the school, a lot of breakdown in communication and antagonism and so on. Between the NUT [National Union of Teachers] and other unions and the head. Those who did not go on strike and those who did. Between management and the rest of the staff. . . . The main friction was between the head and the NUT. The action we took was a withdrawal of goodwill, a one-day strike and a three-day strike, and then we went to arbitration. Between the teachers there was a tremendous amount of acceptance that people were doing what they thought was right. (Social-studies teacher)

At times like these (industrial action is discussed further in Ch. 10) the divergence between staff and line interests are most stark. In this school the head and management team concentrated on keeping the work of the institution going, indirectly limiting the effect of the industrial action, and putting pressure on the staff to remember their 'professional' obligations:

> The most interesting thing was when the head issued a memorandum, about three weeks ago. The memo said, 'We are under a lot of strain; it is a very difficult time and I would like to say two things', and number two said, 'We should all be judged as individuals at this time of industrial action'. It was seen as a threat. The thing he was saying was, 'I'm going to write down in

my little black book the names of people who have taken action in this way'. And a lot of people felt that what this means is when he comes to write a reference or promote people we are not going to get it. There was a lot of fuss about it when we got it in our pigeon holes at four in the afternoon and immediately everyone was talking and there was tension in the staffroom. I was one of the people who said, 'we've got to have a staff association meeting immediately'. So I got the necessary signatures . . . and we had a lot of people there, well over half the staff. I said I thought the head's statement was outrageous, we were being victimized and we should say that we are not prepared to accept what he was doing. He should withdraw his memorandum or explain it. There was some discussion and then my motion was passed by thirty votes to nine. The next day the committee of the staff association went to see the head. As a result he seemed to back down. Then he called a staff meeting and at the staff meeting my reading was that he went as far as he could without contradicting what he put in the memo. He didn't say look, I've cocked this up I wish I had never written this memo, I take it all back. What he did do was talk generally about the notion of individual responsibility and went on to say he really respected people who stuck to their principles. So I thought it was a victory. (Social-studies teacher)

Here, then, we have the language of opposition and a conscious antagonism of interests between the 'rank and file' and 'the management'. None the less, however strident such moments of opposition may be and however sincere the attendant feelings of injustice, events such as these are for many teachers temporary aspects of their work relations. The same teacher explained:

I think in the normal course of events people don't bother with unions, if there was no action going on or it wasn't the immediate aftermath of action and an NUT meeting was called no one would turn up. A meeting was called six months ago to elect a new rep. (union representative) and about four people turned up. People just aren't interested. But when it's needed, then it suddenly galvanizes into action. It depends on the situation. (Social-studies teacher)

This is another example of Lane's (1959) 'closure principle', but for some teachers opposition in school is a more or less permanent stance. They take up a role almost akin to that of the official opposition in the House of Commons, constantly questioning and challenging the programme of government. 'More subordinates respond to managerial initiatives not so much as offers of collaboration as with compliance, resistance or even by ignoring the superordinate move' (Pratt, 1984, p. 302). The social-studies teacher again:

> There are different types of groups among the staff who react in different ways. The most obvious group that represents opposition are the people like me. There are four people in the humanities department who are identifiable as part of a group because we all sit together in the staffroom. There are one or two in the history department, members of the English department; late twenties, early thirties. . . . Those are the sort of people you expect to lead the resistance. They are NUT members as well. There are also those people on the staff, I'm not sure whether they form a cohesive group, who have been around for a long time and just don't like the head's new style; they hark back to the old days. To form a coherent group in the school would be to them inappropriate I would think. Because forming groups is something that does not go with being a grammar-school teacher. . . . Today one of the women teachers called a meeting to form a Women's Group, and thirty people turned up, of whom three were teachers . . . they were women who are part of the radical group in the school, the Radical Caucus, as we call ourselves, jokingly.

In this account many of the lines of conflict identified in Chapters 2 and 3 arise. The subject complexion of the opposition, in particular the predominance of humanities and English teachers, is significant, and cutting across this are the factors of age and gender, and union membership, specifically the NUT. In the background are the 'old guard' formed of ex-grammar-school staff.

For a few of the opposition members in schools their stance against the dominant coalition, the management, is an extension, an intrusion some would say, of their political affiliations outside of school. It is taken for granted by heads and many other teachers that members of radical political parties are acting illegitimately if they allow their 'politics' to play a part in their reaction to school matters. The assumption is that everyone else is politically neutral and immune to 'political' influence. Big politics are seen to have no place within the small politics of the school. One headteacher in Grace's sample defined 'poor' teachers in part in terms of their politics:

> the absence of self-criticism; fear of anything that could be labelled accountability; the resistance to it in some extreme cases; the immediate joining of way out and rather militant groups (i.e. Rank and File or International Socialist). (1978, p. 154)

Another of Grace's respondents draws a significant distinction betwen left-wing affiliations which are directed at educational issues, and doctrinaire politics. The first is valid in the head's view; the second is not:

> I: So would you say your staff has little time for a political stance? Head: I would say they are professionals. I've got left-wing people. I'm left-wing myself (not far-left: I vote Labour). I've been a socialist all my life and intend to remain so . . . but I like to think I'm an educationalist rather than a doctrinaire politician. If the system is wrong and we teach people to think honestly, then nothing we can do is going to stop them seeing what is wrong and trying to put it right. It's not our job to push people one way or the other. (p. 144)

Once again, professionalism is used as an alternative to politics. Overt politics is again unacceptable and out of place. Even here, though, matters are not clear-cut. It is difficult to disentangle actual 'political' commitment and motivation, illegitimate or not, from the attribution and labelling of opposition as 'politically' motivated. For such labelling is another very powerful mechanism for diverting opposition, casting it as outside the accepted framework of political action:

> Some of this opposition might also be from outside circumstances which affect staff I think. Primarily, I suppose, from political motivation. That's the more difficult one to deal with because that's where staff have divided loyalties. Loyalty to the school and political loyalty or to their union. And opposition can be raised not because it is good/bad for the school but because it's for union action. . . . The only time that this has really come to a

head and been a real problem in the past three or four years was with one member of staff who is a strong personality and very politically motivated and who therefore was looking at all decisions concerning the school policy, not from the first base of will this work or will it give me more work as a teacher, but whether this is something I can use to further my political views. That was quite different for us. When this member of staff arrived we had not realized that she was working on a number of members of staff at break-time and in the staff commonroom, so that when the time came for that influence to be brought into action, she had a great number of people who were discontented about this and we hadn't realised that they were a means to an end. (Headteacher, a Midlands rural comprehensive)

The language is interesting here; the powerful use once again of the notion of loyalty for example. Loyalty is a major vehicle for maintaining political integration, stressing as it does the pre-eminence of the institution or the person (usually the person of the head) over individual concerns or principles. It can act as a form of sanction. The label 'disloyal' suggest betrayal, double-dealing, dishonesty and breach of faith. Loyalty is also a form of reciprocation; it ties the member into a relationship, like it or not. The only escape from the relationship, from the reciprocation, is betrayal. Further, the teacher here is described as 'working on' colleagues, with its overtones of undue pressure; she is 'politically motivated' and concerned to 'further' her political views. There is a tone which suggest intrigue and underhandedness.

In many schools the political stance of 'the opposition' enters into the language and folklore of the staffroom. Taafe (1980) describes a school where a small side-room off the main staffroom was regularly inhabited by 'the concerned elements of the staff' as they described themselves, who had 'meaningful discussions', but who were described by other teachers as 'the reds', 'the militant lot' and 'the unionists', and by a deputy head, member of the NAS (National Association of Schoolmasters), as 'the militant-left faction of the NUT'. The language is again debunking, stigmatizing; it is an effective neutralization of perceived threat.

It would be a mistake, of course, to treat opposition as though it were inevitably a matter of radical assertion against conservative dominance. Given the overall range of political influences acting upon education, that is the most common scenario, but it is not the only one. Opposition must be defined as being based upon 'contending definitions of the situation which compete for the attention and the acceptance of the populace' (Hall, 1972, p. 53). It is important to recognize that those contending definitions have institutional specificity. I have already noted on several occasions the significance of 'old guard' formations as sources of criticism and disgruntlement in changing schools; in some circumstances such groups can constitute an active and co-ordinated opposition. One example is described and analysed in Ball (1985). This is an account of the amalgamation of three schools to form a new comprehensive (Casterbridge) – a traditional boys grammar, a traditional boys secondary-modern and an innovative mixed secondary modern. Attempts made by the head and the teachers from the innovative secondary modern to innovate in the new school (mixed-ability grouping, subject integration, an open sixth form, active tutorial work) were staunchly, and to a great extent successfully, opposed by the grammar-school and other secondary-modern teachers. As suggested earlier, the ex-grammar-school staff may be seen to be engaged in strategic maintenance – a sustained and calculated defence of cherished values and practices against the threat of contending definitions of education posed by the new head and innovative staff.

Building on the Casterbridge example, it is possible to postulate three basic scenarios for the occurrence of opposition, each of which rests on an assumption of a particular kind of leadership behaviour and organizational emphasis:

1. Where the head's major commitment is to the maintenance of the status quo; the administrative head, whose emphasis is upon running the system effectively, rather than changing it (Lipham, 1964). Here we are likely to find a 'progressive opposition' advocating change and innovation. Opposition will become entrenched and coherent across a whole set of issues – organizational, pedagogic and curricular. Procedures and structures for participation or discussion may be absent. Young teachers moving into the school, having recently completed their training, will tend to align themselves with the established opposition. Matters are likely to be exacerbated during times of rapid environmental change. Opponents will point to the dangers of

organizational entropy and an absence of responsive decision-making. For example:

> I think up to now in fact a lot of people have asked what decisions have been made; they wouldn't be able to think easily of decisions that have been made and implemented ... things have been stagnant ... he [the head] didn't really know where the school was going; he wanted to keep things as they were, by and large, because we were reasonably successful, and you know if it's successful you don't want to change it. ... The impetus has come from County Hall and some progressive members of the staff. ... Things that were accepted in years past are now being questioned ... and he has realized that he has got to bend in the wind a little. (Deputy head, an eastern comprehensive)

> I think a lot of the staff, myself included, are frustrated that we haven't been involved in anything in the way things were moving. They weren't moving, you know anyway, but if we wanted to see things moving, we would want some kind of mechanism whereby we can get things moving; there's no full staff meeting, he [the head] is a bit worried that the staff are getting power ... the young ones are frustrated I think ... he still considers the traditional values of the grammar school to be most important. (Year tutor, same eastern comprehensive)

The teachers here have a dual complaint: the extent to which the school is falling behind the times and the absence of channels of influence through which change might be effected. In two senses the status quo is under attack. The philosophy of the school and its procedures of government are regarded as unsuited to the contemporary context.

2. Where the head is a gradualist. Formal and informal channels for staff discussion are established. Structures are created, formal or informal, for staff discussion and a sense of participation in goal setting for the organization is created. Consultation is used as a matter of normal practice, but dramatic change is avoided in favour of careful adaptation. The head is seen as open to suggestions but stresses the importance of change being dependent on staff support. 'Change is impossible if you can't carry your staff with you.' Recruitment is careful and long-stay careers are encouraged; the head will use promotion strategically to reward

successful staff and incorporate them into a sense of community. This is obviously made more feasible where there is reasonable but not rapid turnover in staffing:

> The Head vets staff very thoroughly. He has candidates here for a full day on their own. They have a long session with the Head and spend a while with the department. Often there is no formal interview involving Governors or Inspectorate ... if sure, an appointment is made ... if not sure, he holds on ... uses the 'pool' or a temporary appointment which could become permanent. (Quoted in Masters, 1982, p. 42)

As a result, the institution runs on the basis of 'indulgency' (Gouldner, 1954). Individuals are allowed considerable freedom of action. 'If you've delegated something to somebody, then let that person get on with it!' (secondary-modern head). Contentious issues, when they arise, are treated as one-off events; opposition tends to be issue-based, specific and temporary. Once the issue is resolved, individuals slip back into the established pattern of indulgency. Thus Masters (1982) sums up the head in his case study by saying, 'his ideology is accepted by all but one and he commands respect and admiration from most of the staff'.

3. Where the head is attempting to innovate and promote change and is challenged by a defensive opposition. In this case the opposition is attempting to retain aspects of the status quo which are under threat. Such a situation often arises with a change of headship (discussed below). New heads often bring with them new ideas and a mandate (from governors or local authority) to initiate change:

> Now what she did when she came in was she wanted to change from the system we had, which was – it seemed a quite good system in one way – but she wanted more of an overview of how the school worked and she wanted communication. ... She is very much into the Arts and she very much wants Arts throughout the school – so she thought of the head of art, who's on a Scale 4 and the head of maths and she decided that she wanted them to be senior teachers. (Midlands deputy head)

As we have seen already, change frequently involves disruption to the established pattern of advantage and preferment, and challenge to routinized practice in both teaching and organization. On some or all counts some members of the organization will see their interests threatened.

> When the Head came he swept away everything. He was too radical. His actions polarised the staff into two camps. This was only resolved with the retirement of the older staff. No negotiation was possible because of the entrenched positions that people were forced to take. (Head of year, Green Hill Comprehensive; quoted in Wagstaff, 1983, p. 12)

There are resonances in the quotation of Riseborough's (1981) analysis of change at Phoenix Comprehensive. There, as we have seen, the arrival of a new head resulted in the effective demotion and marginalization of the existing secondary-modern-school staff. These teachers quickly developed an entrenched antagonism to the new head, the new teachers appointed by him and the innovations he introduced (see Ch. 2 above). They became an anti-school group almost paralleling the attitudes and orientations of the low-stream pupils they were assigned to teach. The 'old' secondary-modern teachers saw themselves in total opposition to the head and the new regime. All proposed changes were opposed. There appeared to be no grounds for co-operation. Any tactics to undermine the position of the new head were regarded as legitimate. The whole system of values and the attendant practices that the head was pursuing were dismissed. However, such clear-cut polarizaton may be atypical. There are certainly other modes of opposition that are more subtle and strategic. In part, perhaps, the mode of opposition will be dependent upon the formal position of the opponent. For those who are 'out of office', the alternatives to public 'voice' are limited. For those in established key positions, opposition may be limited to confrontations muted by the etiquette of committee behaviour. None the less, in both cases caucusing may be a vital preparation to ensure support from sympathetic colleagues and to devise tactics. Against this, heads have resources at their disposal which may dampen or undermine the strength of opposition. Key opponents may be offered promotion or guaranteed a good reference should they wish to leave; they may be encouraged to take early retirement; or shunted off into dead-end jobs well away from the mainstream of micro-political activity:

The old ruling caucus, Ethel Stone and her ilk were very put out when their status in the school was undermined with people being appointed above them – there were two departments who had sitting tenants who had Heads of Departments appointed above them by the Head. They tried to maintain their position, and to a certain extent Ethel did, although the others lost out. (Head of sixth form, Green Hill Comprehensive; quoted in Wagstaff, 1983)

In any organization there are probably some groups or individuals who feel themselves to be 'passed over' or 'hard done by'. Schools are competitive for teachers as much as for pupils. Promotions are limited, increasingly so, and yet the system of scale posts encourages a sense of career development and personal status based upon being promoted. Competition creates division and fosters careerism. The ideological complexity of educational issues also factionalizes teachers. The result is, as Richardson puts it, that 'the warm solidarity that exists between certain members of staff may have been purchased at the cost of other people's loneliness and sense of rejection' (1973a, p. 182). (Nias, 1985, reports several staffs where this occurs.) However, as indicated already, opposition in schools is by no means simply a matter of personal dis-affection and disgruntlement but can be a commitment to challenge and attempt to change the policies, in whole or part, of the dominant coalition. Opposition, as the term is employed here, cannot be reduced to a clash of personalities; it is a micro-political concept that at heart concerns conflicts of interest.

6
Doing headship: leadership succession and the dilemmas of headship

> There will be no end to the troubles of states, or indeed, my dear
> Glaucon, of humanity itself, till philosophers become kings in this world,
> or till those we call kings and rulers really and truly become
> philosophers.   (Plato)

As indicated above, and in Chapter 2, periods of change often
reveal the extent of latent dissensus within schools. The advantages
and threats carried by proposals for change serve to uncover
opposition which at other times remains as a sub-text to normal
business (Marland, 1982a). Thus opposition is often revealed
through and focused upon particular moments or events when the
'negotiated order' is disturbed or overturned. In some instances
these moments may arise spontaneously, but not infrequently they
are carefully planned and prepared for. They become 'social
dramas' (Turner, 1957) which 'express nuanced shifts or switches
in the balances of power or ventilate divergent interests within
common concerns' (Turner, 1971, p. 352). Burgess (1983) uses the
social drama as a vehicle for analysis in his account of Bishop
McGregor Comprehensive. They provide 'a limited area of trans-
parency on the otherwise opaque surface of regular uneventful
social life' (Turner, 1957, p. 93). Social dramas produce a 'breach'
in the predominant pattern of social relations, lead to a 'crisis', to
'redressive action' and thence in many cases to 'reintegration', or
perhaps the 'social recognition and legitimation of schism between
the parties' (Burgess, 1983, p. 116). In many instances the 'redressive action' and 'reintegration' are achieved via renegotiation
and compromise; both sides give ground and a new, temporary

equanimity is re-established. However, the willingness to negotiate, as against alternative modes of action (Strauss, 1978, p. 100), may not always be present; this will depend on what or how much is at stake as well as the social context of the negotiation (Strauss, 1978, p. 100–1). Part of the skill of political activity in an organization is to be able to read situations, to know when to give ground, when to compromise, when to run away and live to fight another day. Such calculations are evident in a Midland comprehensive head's views of staff meetings:

> Staff meetings, if they are any use at all, are bound to be occasions when people oppose things, and many times they are right and you have to think again. There are times in staff meetings when there is a sincere feeling that what we are suggesting is wrong and objections are made, they are listened to and if we think there is any truth in them we act. And if we think they are wrong, however sincere, we try to say so. There is then the other group who oppose a thing through not understanding at all what is being proposed. They either haven't listened or we haven't explained clearly. There is opposition from some staff in a staff meeting because of a feeling of crude basic fear; they can't cope with the situation as it is and you are adding a new idea; then they will draw other people together to give them support to avoid having to face the situation themselves ... in a way you have to be quite analytical about why the opposition is there in order to know how to cope with it. In some cases the opposition is real and this is a warning sign, at other times it is inadequacy and it requires giving that member of staff some support rather than to change the decision.

Perhaps the important point to reiterate here is the distinction between specific acts of opposition, which may arise when a particular interest is threatened, and opposition as a permanent stance of resistance to established authority. In Baldridge's (1971) terms, this may separate 'activists' from 'attentives'. During social dramas both types of opponent may be involved, and in a particular context their actions and interpretations may be indistinguishable.

There are a number of moments of change which could well be termed as 'grand social dramas', extraordinary events which create profound turmoil in the organization in that they represent fundamental challenges to the stability of the established order. In the case of schools there are two obvious instances. Amalgamation is one; some evidence of the ensuing problems of conflict and opposition have been indicated above. The other is leadership succession.

Leadership succession

In the United States in particular, the study of leadership succession has been a major focus of activity among organizational researchers. Gouldner's (1954) study of a gypsum mine and Guest's (1962) investigation of an automobile plant are the established classics in the field. Occasions of leadership succession, it is argued, provide a natural laboratory for the study of the organization and in particular the effects and problems of leadership. As 'grand social dramas' leadership successions have a revelatory quality which exposes the sinews of structure and power in the organization in a unique way. Some writers, however, have argued that focus on these particular 'grand social dramas' has led to an overemphasis on the leader and 'great man' conceptions of leadership (Dwyer, 1984). While I am interested in leadership here, the investigation of succession is also an opportunity to explore opposition and conflict. The focus on the headteacher serves as a vehicle to raise other issues. As Miskel and Owens point out, 'it is during the pre- and post-arrival phases that old resource allocation decisions are argued again, that suppressed ideological divisions over goals and performance are raised for reevaluation, and that job responsibilities are redefined' (1983, p. 25). Extracts from an unpublished case study will serve our purpose here.

Price (1979) presents a detailed account of the first eighteen months in the tenure of a new head in a primary school. Jim Kenedy was replacing a retiring head, Frank Jones, who had held office for eight years and had overseen the establishment of Alder as an all-through primary school, from the amalgamation of separate infant and junior schools. In Frank Jones's period in office, two senior members of staff played key roles in the running of the school. Bill Burdon, the deputy head, in his fifties, was responsible for much of the day-to-day administration of the junior department, and Dot Parsons, ex-deputy of the infant school, had responsibility for and virtually sole control of the infant and nursery departments. These two shared an office. The

new head entered a well-established pattern of allegiances, expectations and routines worked out through a close working
relationship which had developed over a number of years. These
expectations and routines were extended initially to include him.
Price notes that 'the Day before Jim's first term started Dot, Bill and
Jim met at Alder to disuss the following term. This meeting was to
bring out into the open fundamental issues which were to character-
ise the organizational life of the school in the months which followed'
(p. 29). Jim explained his view as follows:

> I was surprised to find that they [Dot and Bill] expected me to be
> timetabled in by them to teach every class once a week as Frank
> Jones had been. ... I also found that Dot was very surprised that I
> wanted to be involved in the running of the nursery, and that I
> wanted to deal with infant admissions ... when I was told that the
> infants had separate staff meetings, she again expressed surprise
> when I said I'd like to be there. (p. 27)

Jim's view of his role, his expectations about how to run the school,
were clearly in conflict with those of his new senior colleagues. What
ensued may be described without exaggeration as a conflict over the
control of the school. Both parties seeking to win over the support of
the other teachers. The head was not slow to appreciate his
problems:

> Initially I was viewed with a great deal of suspicion. They thought I
> was going to make big changes. Because of this any changes that I
> have made have been subtle ones. (p. 29)

As he saw it, a campaign began to undermine his position in the
school:

> They circulated deliberate misinformation of a mischievous nature.
> ... They also spread gossip and misinformed me about things so
> that they would appear hunky dory and I would be the villain of
> the piece. (p. 29)

The attempts that he did make to instigate changes, like the keeping
of record books, were not well received:

> I presented these ideas in all innocence, and there was a explosion
> from the staff. I discovered later that the staff had been talking
> about it beforehand. Trouble had been brewing, but I was not

informed about it. When I tackled the deputy about it afterwards, he said that he didn't think it was part of his job. (p. 30)

As numerous commentators have pointed out, the control of information in an organization is a powerful weapon of control. Here the head was effectively cut off from the normal upward flow of information through his deputy, and disadvantaged by what he saw as misinformation being communicated downwards. The deputy and Dot were able to construct a particular image of the head by virtue of their control of the information to and from the staff. He was compared unfavourably with the previous head:

The parents and children soon recognized me as the head, but my colleagues did not. There was a harking back to the days of Frank Jones, and quite honestly the idea of Frank Jones as a wonderful head is a myth. (p. 31)

Price comments that the staff began to look back:

with renewed and idealised nostalgic affection at the good old days, and what Jim has described as 'the myth of Frank Jones'. To many of the staff in these early days Jim was the ogre, and Frank Jones 'the big white chief'. All Frank's weaknesses were forgotten during this period when they saw, or imagined they saw, that their way of working, and the security they derived from that, was being threatened. (p. 31)

This kind of idealization occurred in virtually all the schools quoted in this study. There appears to be almost an 'iron law of retrospective preference' in attitudes to headteachers. The present case would also seem to parallel aspects of Gouldner's (1954) *Wildcat Strike*, with a pattern of 'indulgency' being disturbed by the arrival of the new head, a conflict of expectations and values between head and teachers creating instability and shifting the nature of the teachers involvement from 'moral' to potentially 'alienative'. In terms of furthering their own interests, Bill and Dot sought to promote 'the myth of Frank Jones' and isolate the new head from the staff. There is a further parallel with Gouldner in that Jim saw the resolution of the tensions in an increase in bureaucratization:

I need to be more positive and less democratic. They need leadership which they've never had. . . . I'm going to insist on some form of record-keeping so that teachers know where they're at, where they're going and where they've been. (p. 33)

As might be expected, Dot and Bill's version of events at Alder differ somewhat from Jim's. Dot explained:

> He said he wanted to do all the admitting of the new children, and talk to parents. I had always done this before. I knew all the parents and they knew me. I told him this, and later in fact he did back down. ... Jim had said that he wanted to learn in the first few terms, so we timetabled him in to teach like we had Frank. He didn't like that at all ... I think he was rather put out to find that we could do the job of running the school. In a way, it must have made him feel redundant. (p. 34)

In their own terms each party's view is entirely rational and reasonable. Dot went on to say:

> I find he's two-faced. He says one thing to one person, and then tells a different story to another. He's done this to me and Bill. ... Trying to split us up. ... Because of that and lots of other incidents, I can never trust him, or respect him. ... He plays people off against one another. Rings them up at home. I think that's unprofessional. (p. 35)

The other's behaviour is condemned and labelled as illegitimate. Jim was seen to wrest control of crucial information away from Bill and Dot. Dot said:

> He brought in his own filing system, completely ignoring the one we had built up. He didn't go through any paperwork with me when he arrived. In fact, I have no real access to his filing system, which is locked up in his room when he's out of the school ... my responsibilities aren't as great now. (p. 36)

Again, the power of information control is evident, with no access Dot's role is considerably eroded and weakened.

In reality, among the staff feelings about Jim were mixed: not all staff were unhappy about Frank Jones's retirement and some approved of Jim's new ideas. However, the predominant climate and Dot's role as opinion leader meant that pro-Jim sentiments were rarely aired in public. He was normally confronted with what appeared to be unanimous opposition. One teacher, promoted to a Scale-3 post by Jim (to buy support, or reward it?) took a more temperate view of events:

During the early days there was a lot of suspicion and ill-feeling against Jim, stirred up by Dot, mainly supported by Bill and Ivy. My attitude during all this was 'let's wait and see'. I tried to temper gossip with reason. ... The whole basis of the trouble is the clash between Jim and Dot. ... There will be no continuity until Dot comes round or decides to leave. (p. 49)

Indeed, as Jim began to make his leadership more apparent across the school as a whole, including the infant and nursery departments, Dot remarked, 'This is the last straw. I've just got to get out of this place next year'. There is little evidence of willingness to compromise or establish a new 'negotiated order' between the protagonists. In one respect the conflicts at Alder can be seen as an interpersonal clash between Dot and Jim, as Glen points out:

Conflict between individuals can also be of importance in organ-izational settings, particularly when those concerned occupy positions of authority within the structure of the enterprise. Such situations can arise not only as a result of disagreement in relation to work decisions but also from incompatibilities of personality. (1975, p. 94)

However, perhaps of more importance here is the competition for status and control in the institution, particularly the contest over the definition of and the extent of the new leader's authority. The organizational future of the contestants are at stake and thus the future of the organization. As has been reiterated through each of the chapters thus far, change embodies a social and personal threat at a number of levels. Change of leadership is a potentially profound threat to the established patterns of advantage and disadvantage. Furthermore, such a change can constitute a threat to the established organizational reality:

the established patterns of group life just do not carry on by themselves but are dependent for their continuity on recurrent affirmative definition. Let the interpretations that sustain them be undermined or disrupted by changed definitions from others and the patterns quickly collapse. (Blumer, 1971, p. 18)

However, it is not simply the collapse of established patterns that causes problems in the organization but also the instability created by the opposition of alternative interpretations of organizational reality. One of the ironies of the Alder case is the frequently expressed plea from staff for Jim to be more positive and assertive. They expressed a need for certainty, for some kind of stability to be re-established. In the event, this emerged as more significant than opposition to Jim's new ideas. As Price points out, 'this process of the establishment of a new group reality is necessarily a slow, and often painful, one' (1979, p. 54). He goes on to argue:

> a head needs to cultivate an understanding of how individuals react to situations and events. He needs to be able 'to get under the skin' of how another person feels, as the researcher attempts to do, and see things from their point of view. What may appear to be a trivial issue to a head may be vitally important to a member of staff, and unless it is understood and dealt with can grow out of all proportion and not only affect that member of staff's work, but begin to affect the wider life of the school. (p. 54)

It seems not uncommon that heads are surprised and taken aback by the actions and responses of their staff. Part of this sense of surprise lies in the ambiguities and lack of agreement inherent in the role of headship. Teachers, advisers, parents and heads themselves seem to disagree as to the scope and responsibilities of the role. Heads are frequently faced with irreconcilable expectations of performance within their audiences; this produces practical and political dilemmas which may be irresolvable.

The dilemmas of headship

When working with data from teachers on the issue of headship, perhaps the easiest generalization that may be drawn is that their views, experiences and feelings are highly contradictory. Heads are key figures in the vast majority of schools, and the office of headship is historically entrenched in the folk mores of teachers, and yet the role of the head may still be considered as highly controversial: 'Conflict between the different aspects of the head's role, and ambiguity in the nature of demands are potentially an ever-present element in the job of being a head' (Morgan, Hall and Mackay, 1983, p. 17). The head's power as the super-professional in a supposedly 'professional' organization is virtually unparalleled in the public sector, aside perhaps from the prime minister – 'autocrat of autocrats' (Morgan, Hall and Mackay, 1983). Like prime ministers, heads are people that their subordinates love to hate. The demands addressed to the head defy satisfaction because they frequently contain contradictory expectations. It might be said that as a head, 'You can satisfy some of the people all of the time, you can satisfy all of the people some of the time, but you can never satisfy all of the people all of the time'. It is possible to capture some of these contradictions in a language of dilemmas, vaguely akin to that developed for teaching by Berlak and Berlak (1981). The dilemmas are expressed in terms of perceptions and expectations which relate ultimately to action. To paraphrase the Berlaks, the dilemma language of headship is an effort to represent the thought and action of heads as an ongoing dynamic of behaviour and consciousness within particular institutional contexts:

> The dilemmas are not to be conceived as entities that may be physically located in persons' heads or in society. Rather they are linguistic constructions that, like lenses, may be used to focus upon the continuous process of persons acting in the social world. (Berlak and Berlak, 1981, p. 111)

Two general areas of dilemma are disussed below; each contains a number of sub-dilemmas.

PARTICIPATION VERSUS CONTROL

This dilemma covers a number of aspects of headship behaviour but is one of the more profound aspects of contradiction in the role of the head and the relationship between heads and teachers. It can be expressed in a number of ways. For example, heads are frequently attacked for being weak, indecisive or vacillating:

> Yes, he is not a very good person to approach, he's not a very easy person to talk to and he is not able to express his views very strongly, very forcefully, and therefore he comes across as very weak. (Deputy head, an eastern comprehensive)

> You didn't feel that he was taking the reins . . . even now he won't put his foot down when he needs to; we don't feel the authority. . . . A head should give a directive; an incentive. (Teacher, a London primary)

Strong and forceful leadership would seem to be the order of the day. Weak heads, so-called, are roundly criticized. Yet:

> His idea of democracy was consultation after the event. . . . We would talk for ages, and finally agree to something that he had decided anyway. On the rare occasions we didn't agree, and it was important, he would say, 'Well, it's got to be done anyway', and storm out. (Head of mathematics, a London comprehensive)

> The staff realize that the head has very strong ideas. He won't change. He isn't flexible. It isn't worthwhile; in fact it is a waste of time to send some ideas up to the senior heads. (Mathematics teacher; quoted in Taafe, 1980, p. 32)

Strong heads are equally problematic; they hold too firmly to their own ideas, they will not listen to criticism, they fail to take into account alternative views:

> Sexton came in and we were asked our views, but they were completely disregarded. We were told that if we didn't like it then we could move. Therefore, he lost the goodwill we had for him when he started. (English teacher, Millrace Comprehensive; quoted in Meadows, 1981, p. 10)

Ideal heads, it would seem, must combine strength with openness, be able to assert their own views and ideas while taking full account of the views and ideas of the staff. To err on the side of openness is seen as weakness; to err on the side of strength is to court the label of tyrant. Strength, it seems, needs to be directed to clear ends. Good heads have policies:

> The boss, his biggest fault is he doesn't like to make decisions, I don't dislike him as a person but he doesn't like to make decisions. (Head of geography, inner-city comprehensive; quoted in Hanna, 1978, p. 16)

> The trouble was, there was no school policy. The head didn't offer any policy, any direction. There was a lack of leadership in the school. (Second in charge of English, Inner City Comprehensive; quoted in Hanna, 1978, p. 16)

Again, if the head fails to assert himself or herself in the role, then the accusation of lack of leadership is always readily to hand. If the assertion is too strident then sensibilities are quickly outraged:

> Sexton told me that if I didn't agree with his policy then would I leave. I would never go to see him now. He has his thumb on everybody. (English teacher, Millrace Comprehensive; quoted in Meadows, 1981, p. 11)

Hardly any of the heads reported here seemed to achieve the sort of balance that satisfied many of their staff. Furthermore, assertive heads like Mr Sexton were frequently accused of imposing change on their staff, of moving too fast, of overriding objections, being too single-minded:

> There's a rate of change that seems to be comfortable. . . . The school has been reasonably stable. . . . My personal sympathies are for stability. . . . There's no sense in coming in with fixed ideas. (Head of lower school, Millrace Comprehensive; quoted in Meadows, 1981, p. 11)

Equally, lack of initiation from the head is criticized:

> I don't think it's unfair to say that he doesn't initiate things. . . . The boss goes through the motions – we have not arrived at a conclusion – he needs to follow things through more fully. (Primary teacher; quoted in Foley, 1985, p. 21)

> I would have thought people were concerned that the headmaster is not imposing certain things on the school. For myself, for example, I think we should have a mode 3 practically in every subject . . . it's not the sort of thing that happens unless school has a positive policy towards it. (Head of history, Casterbridge High)

It is not just a contrast between different heads that highlights the dilemmas. Individual heads often find their style and actions interpreted and responded to differently by different members of their staff. Ed Bell, the principal shadowed by Wolcott (1973), was described by members of his staff in the following ways:

1. I probably operate better in a structured atmosphere than in a non-structured one, but I like to think I'm somewhere in between.
2. Ed does not spell things out clearly enough as to his expectations, particularly along the lines of structure.

3. I have been real comfortable at this school in that I've been allowed to do as I've wanted.
4. I think Ed gives us a lot of leeway as far as how we teach. I think he realizes that each teacher teaches in a different way. He doesn't expect us to fit into any set pattern. (Quoted in Wolcott, 1973, pp. 291–2)

One interesting aspect of these comments is that it highlights the ways in which the principal's style is interpreted and responded to in terms of the individual teachers' preferred working pattern and personal preferences. As indicated previously, doing headship is a form of joint action, based on a collective but discontinuous coming together of meanings and actions.

THE PHYSICAL AND THE PERSONAL

The second general area of contradiction and confusion surrounding the head's role concerns the quality of personal relations achieved by the incumbent and their presence in and around the school. The first set of dilemmas relate to the emphasis in the head's involvement within the school. Some heads clearly choose to define and develop their role in relation to outside constituencies and audiences. The result is that they are seen as absentee heads and criticized for lack of interest and involvement and for being too interested in their own career.

Frank Jones was a disaster as a head. Always out of the school on Union business, and not really interested in the children's work. (Primary teacher, Alder School; quoted in Price, 1979, p. 41)

The head's outside activities mean that he is not in touch with the school as he ought to be; it makes life difficult, especially for the deputy head. (Senior teacher; quoted in Rillie, 1982, p. 31)

It may be, however, that such activities bring indirect benefits to the school:

The head is criticized for being out so much but it is not all justified and he brings back good ideas. (Young maths teacher; quoted in Rillie, 1982, p. 31)

The head spends a lot of time out of the school on various

committees. As a result he brings back new ideas and is well informed on educational thinking, bringing very worthwhile advantages to the school. (Head of maths; quoted in Rillie, 1982, p. 31)

It is possible to draw upon Gouldner's (1957) distinction and suggest the categories of 'cosmopolitan head' and 'local head'. The cosmopolitan head orientated to outside activities, is likely to have a high profile in the local authority, may be even nationally. This may attract attention to the school; it may even attract parents. It may also mean that the school is well prepared for changes eminating from national and local initiatives and well defended from cuts and other threats. While a 'local' head may score well with staff in terms of being abreast of school-based concerns, he or she may be less well perceived at times of external threat. The 'local' head may be regarded as less effective or less willing to be involved in politicking outside the school:

He doesn't fight for the school, not like the head at Crabtree and Mrs Smith at Melchester Coombe. They fight tooth and nail for their schools and get a better deal than us, although we are meant to be on a par. They always seem to find some points somewhere. There's a lot of bad feeling which is understandable. (History teacher, Casterbridge High)

Even within the school there are degrees of involvement. Again it is tempting to distinguish between the 'visible' and 'invisible' head, the office head and the corridor head:

The headmaster takes an introvert low-key role; philosophically, he swings towards the academic – whether he's got to or not I don't know, but I think he feels he's got to. . . . There's a little bit of criticism that he's in his office, he doesn't look around the corridors. (Head of English, Casterbridge High)

The head won't provide what the staff are crying out for – paternalism. He never comes round the lessons and says you are doing a good job. (Head of craft, Green Hill Comprehensive; quoted in Wagstaff, 1983, p. 14)

All heads have their strengths and weaknesses. This bloke's strength is his dealings with staff. He will get, almost without exception, anything he wants done because of his relationships, not necessarily with the staff collectively, but with individual staff. They know he supports them to the hilt. (Head of sixth form, Green Hill Comprehensive; quoted in Wagstaff, 1983, p. 14)

The staff generally view him as saying too much, especially about his last school, and doing too little. Their opinion is that he should be involved much more in the classrooms, particularly in allowing them more free time. ... He maintains a distance from both staff and children and does not become involved personally with either, although his knowledge of both groups is already quite considerable. (London primary teacher)

Winkley quotes an extreme case of invisible headship:

At its worst, heads have been known to retreat entirely into their rooms or occupy themselves on strange or obsessively mundane tasks. In one school the staff used to organize a sweepstake on who saw the head first during the school week. (1984, pp. 210–11)

As Woods (1979) illustrates, significantly, a great deal of staff-room humour is directed towards the person of the head; derisive comment is common.

What are being described here are different ways of dealing with the role and its ambiguities. The dilemmas present the head with essentially irresolvable sets of expectations. Thus the head who is out and about in the school may ultimately be perceived no better than the office-bound retreatist. Such a head risks either accusations of spying and interfering or is seen as wasting time when there are more important things to do:

I remember, he used to come and watch me teach and I was taking a dancing lesson and he took me aside and said 'Don't say "please" to the children'. And I just remember looking at him and thinking 'Oh!'. And any respect I held for him at that time just completely disappeared. (PE teacher, a southern comprehensive)

she takes on too much. She'll sing in the choir when maybe someone wants to see her. (PE teacher describing an independent school head; quoted in Tarn, 1984, p. 13)

Interestingly, this and other categories of dilemma cross-cut the evaluation of a head's personal relationships with staff and pupils. In this case there is a fine line to be drawn between 'distance' and 'familiarity'. Often heads are seen to be close and too close at the same time. To quote Tarn again:

> you've got to be 'with it' to a certain extent. She's on the same wave length as the girls . . . sometimes there's a lack of respect for her amongst the older girls. It depends on what dealings they've had with her . . . sometimes she goes round looking like a jumble sale. (1984, p. 14)

The problems faced by heads in their relationships with staff are to an extent parallel to those of the classroom teacher. Such relationships are sometimes easier to manage in one-to-one situations:

> Sexton is very good on a one-to-one basis. I was very cheesed off over something and I went to him. He listened very sympathetically. I know of others who have had the same treatment. (English teacher, Millrace Comprehensive; quoted in Meadows, 1981, p. 16)

Even so:

> He's very approachable but he doesn't take time to find out about people. He's not good at initiating. It's a pastoral function really. People are fed up about not knowing when decisions are being made. (English teacher, Casterbridge High)

The distinction in this last case is between a head who is willing to receive staff but who does not approach them.

> I see the Headmaster as someone, as I said before, the head's door is open to anyone. It's not a door where you've got to make an appointment. You can knock, and he will listen. As I say, it doesn't necessarily relate to school problems. He also has a sympathetic ear and will help, you know, with personal problems. (Head of middle school, Inner City Comprehensive; quoted in Hanna, 1978, p. 16)

The ever-open door is apparently not in itself adequate. Active pastoral work is needed. However, once again there is a problem: the head who is keen to become involved in staff problems risks being seen as interfering. None the less, distant heads seemed thicker on the ground than the over-familiar type. Some were seen as good with children but poor with staff. Price (1979) quotes three primary teachers as follows:

> I've got no complaints about Jim. He'll always see difficult children and he backs you up. (p. 42)

> Jim's interested in the children whoever and whatever they are, but he's not very good with adults – understanding people. (p. 43)

> I don't think he makes personal relationships as easily as he makes out. Superficially maybe, but I feel that he is a lonely man. (p. 37)

The head who does make friends on the staff, however, faces a different problem – friends can all too easily be seen as favourites:

> He is insecure and wants to be loved, but knows that he isn't . . . he loses his temper and flounces out of rooms. He likes mediocrities . . . he has favourites and allows it to show. (Primary teacher, quoted in Price, 1979, p. 39)

Damned if you do and damned if you don't – that seems to be the message.

We have here only the beginnings of a dilemma analysis of headship. There are a number of other categories of expectation which might be explored. However, what should be clear from what has been presented is that the analytical ambiguities of headship – the twin problems of domination and integration – are central to teachers' expectations of their heads. Heads and their followers are trapped in this sealed political dialectic of colleagueship and hierarchy, professional and employee. Furthermore, the work of headship carries with it the vestiges of a fixed and traditional form of school relationship which has to be set against the changing demands of a turbulent contemporary environment:

> The result is a job not only of complexity but also of unusual stress. The head is above all highly exposed, representing authority in a world in which traditional formal authority is decreasingly respected. His strengths lie increasingly in his skills as a negotiator of stamina or sheer awkwardness. (Winkley, 1984, p. 210)

What this sheer awkwardness disguises, however, are the acute political discrepancies which are now invested in the job. Headship is, on the one hand, the focus of 'innovations' like management practice and management teams, related to which is the increased divergence of 'them and us' type relationships exposed by cuts in educational funding and changes in teachers' conditions of work. The management–line relationship is at heart disciplinary and punitive. On the other hand, heads find themselves confronted by pressures for high-speed organizational and curricular change, which demands high levels of creativity and personal initiative, and it is highly questionable whether traditional, hierarchical management relationships are best suited to respond to such pressures. Indeed, recent work by Corwin indicates that such circumstances call 'for a diffuse decision-making structure with corresponding autonomy for individuals and groups' (1983, p. 226); activities need to be relatively unstructured and power decentralized. All the indications are that organizationally schools are moving in the opposite direction.

7
The politics of career

Stop, while ye may; suspend your mad career! (William Cowper)

In this chapter the basic analysis of micro-politics and the themes identified with it above will be further explored and developed in relation to the concept of career. The intention here is to set the work experiences of individuals against the backdrop of organizational conflict and the competition of interests. Within the current career and occupational structure of schools competition – between individuals, and indirectly between groups – is a fundamental aspect of individual advancement through teaching. This often leads to an orientation to work dominated by careerism. Roy suggests that:

> There is probably no topic of staffroom conversation which causes more concern, raises more hopes, and sees more hopes dashed, than that of promotion. Most teachers, at some stage in their careers, want it – whether it is a move up the ladder to the next scale, or whether the goal is headship. (1983, p. 78)

In the following chapter the position of one particular interest group, women teachers, will be examined in some detail. This provides the opportunity both to analyse the career experiences of women teachers and to explore the broader issue of the politics of gender. I shall take as a premise for this that the majority of schools are predominantly patriarchal in structure and ethos. (Virtually all of the data presented in the chapter are derived from mixed- rather than single-sex schools.)

In general terms, the concept of career as employed here rests upon the frequently quoted (if sexist) definition propounded by Hughes:

> Institutions are but the forms in which the collective behaviour and collective action of people go on. In the course of a career a person finds his place within those forms, carries on his active life with reference to other people, and interprets the one meaning of the life he has to live. Thus, a career consists 'objectively' of a series of statuses and clearly defined offices – and there will be typical sequences of position, responsibility, even of adventure, and, 'subjectively', a moving perspective in which a person sees his life as a whole, and interprets his attributes, actions and the things which happen to him. (1964, p. 18)

The analysis here rest on the interplay between personal aspirations and identities, and the micro-political processes and constraints of the organization; the use of influence and power are critical in the advancement or blockage of individual careers and the careers of particular groups of teachers. Two other general points need to be made about the conept of career. First, as will be seen, it brings into play, in complex fashion, the three areas of interest outlined in Chapter 1: vested interest, self-interest and ideological interest. The first two emerge fairly obviously from most analyses of teachers' careers. Career advancement through promotion certainly brings increased material rewards for the individual and often also increased power and/or influence, and autonomy (given the peculiar nature of teacher autonomy discussed in the previous chapter). As Hughes suggests, career development can also provide for self-development, the fulfilment of projections and conceptions about the self, becoming more the sort of person, or worker, one wants to be, one is aiming to become. This is particularly relevant in relation to the possibility of increased role specialization that is now apparent within the complex division of labour of many schools – the possibility of becoming an administrator, a pastoralist or counsellor, or head of department, and so on. Bound up with these areas of interest, for some teachers at least, is a sense in which career advancement can also provide for the achievement or fulfilment of ideological concerns. For example, the NUT survey *Promotion and the Woman Teacher* (1980, p. 31) asked its 3000 respondents to rank-order a list of factors which might provide strong encouragement for promotion. The factor most often placed first in rank (by 38.4 per cent of respondents) was 'Opportunity for putting your own ideas/organizational ability into use'. Second, it has been usual to study teachers' careers at the individual level, focusing on the unique trajectories of particular teachers or aggregates of teachers. This, for example, is the approach employed by Lyons (1981). Lyons interviewed 122 teachers from five comprehensive schools but presents an analysis which takes no account of the difference between or particularities of the individual schools. In other words, careers are presented in abstract, out of context. The collectivity is ignored by such studies, although as we shall see, many teachers seem to be highly aware of the institutionally contingent nature of their career – both in subjective and objective terms. There are, however, a number of exceptions to the acontextual approach – Lacey (1970), Riseborough (1981), Burgess (1983), Beynon (1985), Cunnison (1985) and my own accounts (Ball, 1984, 1985) – each present analyses of careers within the context of a particular school. From these studies it is possible to recognize the relational nature of careers, the competition between groups and individuals for advantage and preferment. Both individual and contextual data are discussed in this chapter.

Strategies and ploys

If we begin at the individual level, Lyons (1981) has identified significant differences among teachers in their degree of careerism; that is, in the extent to which they are actively engaged in the pursuit of objective career advancement through promotion. At one extreme there are those who enter teaching with little real sense of a career plan or map, neither accordingly do they have a timetable for measuring their pace of advancement, neither do they employ deliberate strategies to achieve such advancement. Their careers are guided and determined by luck, chance opportunity and circumstance. As one teacher explained: 'In those days one went into teaching and one taught, and one thought that the powers that be would appreciate worth and one would get some sort of promotion' (quoted in Lyons, 1981, p. 42). Perhaps also there is an element of reticence among these respondents. Within some institutions, among the teacher peer group, expressions of ambition are discouraged. However, in contrast to these non-planners, at the other extreme, Lyons found a group of active strategists who entered teaching with a firm and often long-term career map and who sought to keep to a timetable of promotions benchmarks, measuring their progress against that of their peers. Thus:

> I became aware of the career prospects at college, because I was older – young people do not become interested for some time. I saw it because after other jobs you can see where things are leading: at my age with a family, etc., one needs to assess the prospects. I'm obviously not going to be a headteacher, but I have a good hope of getting to Scale 4. (Quoted in Lyons, 1981, p. 45)

It is these strategists who are the most interesting in terms of the micro-politics of the institution, for their strategies and ploys involve an awareness of and engagement with the micro-political structure. For example, Lyons suggests that one index of career motivation is to be found within the overall pattern of communication in the school. Those teachers, outside of top positions, who scored high in terms of their patterns of communication with others were also more likely to have long-term career aspirations. It could thus be argued that those who have such aspirations attempt to further their careers by ensuring high visibility among their peers and superiors; they deliberately attempt to get themselves noticed. It might also be deduced from this that such strategists see themselves as being in competition with their peers for scarce promotion opportunities. There may be particular ways of achieving (appropriate) visibility. For example, Sikes, Measor and Woods (1985) suggest that the choice of appropriate forms of dress can be a deliberate career ploy for some. By making themselves 'fit in', they also make themselves acceptable to those who make career decisions. It is clear that many teachers also consider involvement in extra-curricular activities to be an important factor in obtaining promotion (Lyons, 1981, p. 66), being seen to 'be willing': 'If you're prepared to give up your time, it helps. The more time you put in with the children, the better it looks in the eyes of those who count' (quoted in Lyons, 1981, p. 75). In the United States such activities are referred to as GASing, getting the attention of superiors:

> Advancing up the 'ladder' requires more than simply acquiesing to the system, however. One must actively demonstrate willingness and aptitude for assuming greater responsibility. In the parlance of educational administration, such people are sometimes referred to as GASers. (Wolcott, 1973, p. 196)

Whiteside (1978) suggests that involvement with or interest in educational innovations may also play its part in getting the young teacher or would-be head noticed. Attendance at in-service courses may serve a similar function and also look good on a curriculum vitae when applying for jobs. The danger with such an analysis is that it can easily shade over into a totally cynical view of teachers' work. What is being suggested here is that for some, but by no means all, there is a degree of strategic planning and presentation of self in their career development which is deliberately aimed at achieving promotion.

However, it seems clear that individual strategies may ultimately prove fruitless without active support from senior colleagues; that is, the acquisition of a sponsor. When attempting to move between schools, sponsorship may be of lesser importance, but in the case of internal promotion such support may be critical. As with other forms of relationship discussed in this study, the relationship of sponsor to acolyte demands that advantage be gained on both sides. The acolyte requires that the sponsor advance his or her reputation; the sponsor may expect political support during discussions or disputes and certainly the successful fulfilment of posts of responsibility that may be obtained. If the acolyte fails in a promoted position, then the sponsor's reputation may suffer; if the acolyte succeeds, then both the sponsor's reputation and influence will be enhanced. As Lyons explains it: 'A characteristic of those seeking sponsorship is their *political acumen* and their instinctive understanding of what the Head, or who ever is in authority, thinks; the courtier is unlikely to follow a course of action of which the king disapproves' (1981, p. 55; my emphasis). There is a strong indication here of the feudal type of relationship discussed in Chapter 4. However, sponsorship also seems most typically to be an all-male affair. Aspiring women confront what Lorber calls the Salieri phenomenon: 'Those of devalued status get less opportunity to show what they can do, and when they do perform well, their work is undervalued. As a result, they get a smaller share of rewards and resources' (1984, p. 10). Also, as Reskin argues in the case of science, professional relationships between male and female workers are riven with inequality: 'male scientists deliberately respond to female co-workers in terms of sex roles rather than collegial ones in order to hinder women's careers' (1978, p. 11). Data presented in the following chapter suggest that this may be equally true of teaching.

Very often the head is the critical reality definer (Riseborough, 1981) of the arena in which careers have to be constructed. Bargains, understandings and deals are frequently associated with the matter of promotion in schools. What is significant is not just who does get promoted but also who does not and what the consequences are. Jago examines a series of promotions and non-promotions at Millrace, a southern comprehensive. For example:

> When mixed ability for the first year was being discussed, early in the Preparation year, the Head (according to one source) asked Mrs Browning, an experienced teacher, new to the school, to coordinate mixed-ability work in English, thus bypassing the Head of Department. This teacher reported that she had been:
>> Promised a Scale 2 from last autumn for mixed-ability responsibility but it hasn't materialised. (June, Preparation year)
> Having worked extremely hard in initiating the new and elaborate plans, she was so disillusioned at the non-appearance of the promised reward that she felt 'contempt for a system' in which this was possible, and began applying for Scale posts elsewhere (Jago, 1983, p. 126)

Meadows who researched the same school, quotes Mrs Browning directly:

> I am very bitter. Last October, I was promised promotion for organizing the year-one course. [The Head] also said he wished to extend mixed-ability to the second and third years and I would receive more promotion as it developed. ... I worked for nothing on the promise of a promotion. (1981, p. 16)

Here the problem is a promise, as the complainant sees it, renaged upon. The Millrace English department was further disrupted by competition and preferment. The appointment of a new second-in-charge produced another bitter reaction:

> He [the head] made Sally the number two, on Scale 3, when he could have had both of us on Scale 2. It would have been fairer. I asked for the promise to be kept. I wrote to the adviser. I said that at least there should have been an advert in the press. Sam Kimber was also interested in applying. I was told that all the points had been used up. But they could have been used in another way. ... I'm too outspoken and forceful for my own good. I finished the situation by my anger afterwards. Not many would talk to the head as I did. This head operates on the principle of personal likes and dislikes. To think that I was given the definite promise of a Scale 2, and better things to come! (Quoted in Meadows, 1981, p. 17)

The key decisions and the resulting bitterness and frustration focus on the headteacher. These examples underline Riseborough's point that the head is 'the critical reality definer' with regard to teachers' careers. Individual careers and attendant commitment are made and broken by these sorts of decisions. One newly appointed head I interviewed described the problems from his point of view:

> you inherit, you never start off with a virginal state, you inherit, don't you. You inherit a sort of track record, you inherit a past regime. And undoubtedly the way that things were done [here] was really closed in terms of staff promotions ... they were just pinned up on the wall. People would be seen but very rarely would it be advertised. It was much more that you were nobbled and it was said to you, 'Looking at this head of Welsh then. ... ' And it went through that way. And it wasn't just announced like that. I mean, there was a lot of sort of politicking going on. (Head of Midlands comprehensive)

The obvious point made by each of these examples is that the promotion process appears closed, secretive and biased. The criteria for promotion are regarded as unfair or politically distorted; they are open to interpretation. Promotions are regarded, rightly or wrongly, as political acts. The newly appointed head found himself faced with this fact:

Now, I had some promotions last year which I stuck on the board and said to people if they were interested come and see me about it. Though they were highly suspicious about that, very suspicious indeed. . . . I actually promoted two women to Scale 4. So the women's lobby saw this as being really good, power supporting women. I didn't know I was, I mean, it wasn't a conscious act in that sense. More consciously, I actually promoted people who were very – not quiet people, because they're not – but people who didn't sort of get on the big stage in terms of really doing the politicking or getting things organized or going to conferences, but did an excellent job in terms of their classroom work and excellent in terms of contact with parents and their care for kids. (Head of Midlands comprehensive)

What is particularly interesting here is that the head perceives that his criteria for promotion in this case are out of the ordinary. That it is normally not the good classroom teacher that gets promoted but rather those who cultivate a public performance of competence. This seems to confirm the importance of promotion strategies, discussed above. Clearly, no promotion is entirely neutral in its effects. The head will make friends and enemies, store up goodwill and cultivate opposition. In this sense promotions are future-orientated, they can undermine or reinforce the position of the head, alter or reinforce the balance of political influence within the staff group. Wolcott says of the principal he studied: 'Ed's second means for reducing the impact of variation to which he was exposed was to surround himself with coteries of like-minded confidents whose opinions and judgements he sought because they were customarily sympathetic and inevitably supportive of him personally' (1973, p. 295). The distribution of scale points can also act as a powerful indicator of the head's definition of the school; the sort of school he or she wants to create will be advanced (or not) by virtue of both who is promoted and what sort of posts are deemed worthy of additional points. A last example from Millrace:

The allocation of Scale 4s to the new Heads of House was a powerful statement by the Head that they were to be equal in status to the Heads of major Departments, and thus that the pastoral system was as important as the academic in the life of the school; but in 'putting his money where his mouth was' he risked disappointing a significant number of staff who had applied for Scale posts and being seen by others, who had not, as having been unfair. (Jago, 1983, p. 125)

Patterns of advantage

Over time particular patterns of advantage (and disadvantage) tend to become established within schools. In-groups and out-groups can be identified with the attendant possibilities for preferment being different for each. These patterns are, however, not infrequently disturbed; the arrival of a new head (discussed in Ch. 4) or the onset of falling rolls (see below) can disrupt established systems of status and can effectively truncate some careers (Riseborough, 1981) and facilitate others. However, there are some ingrained patterns of career that extend across schools to provide structural advantage for certain groups and disadvantage for others. The most significant of these structures is the organization and differential status of subject departments. While acknowledging that there are exceptions, it is possible to specify fairly simply, and trace the consequences of, a common pattern of status. This pattern tends to privilege certain of the 'academic' subjects over and against the practical and expressive. One simple index of this can be obtained by looking at the subject background of headteachers – which subject specialists are more likely to become heads and which are least likely. Hilsum and Start indicate that 'If a headship is the target, then for *teachers of equal experience* the best chances of achieving that goal lie with history, physics, French and maths' (1974, p. 82). (See Table 7.1.)

It is also possible to find support for this pattern in the perceptions and experiences of these teachers who are disadvantaged by it. The disadvantages are not simply structurally produced. Bennet, for example, found clearly cut evidence of this in the case of art teachers:

> Art teachers don't get promoted as readily as academic disciplines. You may get shortlisted, but somebody with an academic training will always get given the job. They seem to think that someone with a degree in maths is going to be more intelligent than someone with a degree in art – which is ridiculous!

Table 7.1   Percentages of subject specialists holding headship status

Subject	Promoted (%)	Promoted/eligible*	Rank
1 History	9.9	31	1
2 Physics	6.3	27	2
3 French	5.4	19	3
4 Maths	4.3	16	4
5 English	3.5	10	6
6 Geography	2.3	7	8
7 Biology	2.2	13	5
8 Art	2.0	9	7
9 Music	1.4	4	11
10 Chemistry	1.0	7	8
Woodwork/ Metalwork	1.0	3	12
12 PE	0.5	6	10

Note
* Eligibility – fifteen years or more of teaching experience

Source
S. Hilsum and K. R. Start, *Promotion and Careers in Teaching*, Windsor, NFER, 1974, p. 83

It *is* more difficult to get promoted if you're an art teacher. (Teacher 1)

We're not looked upon as people who could cope with administration. Running a department like this, obviously we can. (Teacher 2)

Art teachers are too discomforting in schools – subversive – and the subject, by its very nature, is about the development of individuals, and that's not what schools are about. . . . Top men are 'Yes' men. (Teacher 3)
(Quoted in Bennet, 1985, p. 124)

The same also applies to other expressive subjects:

[Music] is not really accepted in the school; they pay homage but that's all; exam subjects are everything in this school, you don't count if you aren't churning out regular O and A level results. I, therefore, will never get on here. (Teacher 4) (Quoted in Lyons, 1981, p. 55)

those who want to offer something a little different, drama, music, counselling – at least they feel their offerings are judged as not main line. It is because there is a lack of interest in what they are doing by the hierarchy of the school. (Teacher 5) (Quoted in Lyons, 1981, p. 92)

A number of points may be drawn from these quotations. First, they indicate a strong feeling that these subjects are not valued in the school, and as a result their teachers are not valued. Second, as teachers 1 and 2 indicate, it is assumed that these subjects do not provide the necessary background for advancement. Third, as teachers 3 and 4 point out, these subjects do not contribute to the simple measures of school effectiveness that may be derived from examination results. Fourth, as teacher 3 suggests, teachers of these subjects may seem unconventional; they often do not dress like or share the aims and attitudes to teaching of teachers in the academic subjects. They tend to be marginalized and stigmatized as a result. A similar picture can be developed for teachers in other areas of the curriculum which are regarded as non-academic; that is, craft, design and technology, PE, domestic science, dance and rural studies. In micro-political terms these subjects lack credibility and thus lack influence. Their pedagogies, philosophies and forms of evaluation frequently deviate from the simple class teaching methods of the 'academic' subjects, but they gain little credence as alternative versions of the schooling process. Clearly, in part this is a chicken-and-egg situation. If more artists or PE teachers were to become heads, then such subjects might gain greater influence. While they lack influence, their teachers are unlikely to become heads. Goodson makes the following point:

in secondary schools the self-interest of subject teachers is closely connected with the status of the subject in terms of its examinable knowledge. Academic subjects provide the teacher with a career structure characterised by better promotion prospects and pay than less academic subjects. Seen from this viewpoint the conflict over the status of examinable knowledge is therefore partly a battle over the material resources and career prospects available to each subject community (1983, pp. 35–7)

Burgess provides an example of the relationship between micro-political status within the school and career disadvantage in the case of Newsom teachers:

At first sight it might appear that gaining an appointment in the Newsom department was relatively easy, as negotiation between the headmaster and an intending Newsom teacher resulted in promotion and financial incentives for the teacher. In these circumstances, it might appear that the same rewards were there for any teacher prepared to take Newsom groups. However, in making appointments Mr Goddard had only given the teachers one scale point for their work *within* the department. Each teacher, therefore, had equal formal status in terms of their salary within the department, regardless of their general status within the school, and there was no head of department. These factors contributed to the conflict and competition among Newsom teachers, because they had to develop a strong commitment to the department if they wished to gain promotion. (1983, pp. 189–90)

Thus careers need to be examined within the context of subjects as well as within the context of institutions.

Structural uncertainties

As indicated above, established micro-political structures inside the school can be disrupted when changes are thrust upon the institution. The arrival of a new head is one such change. The effects of falling rolls is another. Amalgamation or reorganization is a third. Increasingly, the careers of teachers are being disrupted by the effects of such changes. Indeed, it may be, as suggested earlier, that the work of teaching is being profoundly reconstructed. Teachers are certainly becoming more and more accountable in cost–benefit terms, and with greater state intervention in the curriculum, the introduction of forms of graded assessment and attempts to achieve direct quality control over teachers, 'we find the capitalist mode of production increasingly impinging on, invading and restructuring the technical job of teaching' (Harris, 1982, pp. 71–2). Teaching is no longer a secure occupation. There is both a surplus of trained teachers in many subject areas (in relation to the way in which requirements are currently defined) and, as a result of falling rolls, declining demand. At the same time, more is being expected of teachers in terms of curricula innovations, the adoption of new technologies and the establishing of links with industry. Teachers are increasingly becoming, in Harris's terms, 'economically oppressed'. In most dramatic terms these 'structural uncertainties' are manifest at institutional level by school mergers, redeployments, redundancies and pressure for older teachers to accept early retirement. Some groups of teachers and individuals, especially those teaching minority subjects, seem particularly vulnerable.

Reorganization and amalgamation

Riseborough's (1981) study of Phoenix Comprehensive, previously referred to, analyses the structural uncertainties that derive from comprehensive reorganization as they affect the careers of a group of secondary-modern teachers. For these teachers the appointment of a new head committed to the creation of a 'pressured academic environment' (Lacey, 1974) resulted in the effective truncation of their careers. The view of education they had held and practised over a number of years was defined as irrelevant to the new school. The teachers experienced 'vertical' and 'horizontal' demotion (Becker, 1952). They were not allocated to posts of responsibility (although their salaries were protected) and found themselves timetabled to teach lower-stream classes. They were deliberately kept away from examination and top-set groups. A similar but by no means identical state of affairs are outlined in my own account (Ball, 1985) of the amalgamation of three existing schools (two secondary moderns and a grammar) to create a comprehensive, Casterbridge High. Here, once again, one group, the staff from the boys' secondary-modern school, found themselves losing out in the process of reappointment to the new school. Table 7.2 shows the distribution of posts of responsibility in the comprehensive school.

The teachers from Egdon Heath Boys' Secondary Modern clearly lost out in the reappointment process: they are underrepresented in all three categories. Krekel, Van der Woerd and Wouterse argue that 'Every merger has its victims; this is apparently inevitable' (1967, p. 162); here the Egdon Heath teachers were the victims. Like the teachers at Riseborough's school, they found themselves

stigmatized for their views about teaching and their previous practice. The head of history in the new school, an outside appointment,
described them thus:

> I think the Egdon teachers would have the classic secondary
> modern thing of 'it hurts the poor little sub-normals to push them'
> and 'They are happy knowing where their place in life is' you
> know, 'all you do is stir them up and give them ideas beyond
> themselves'. And there is also this sort of craftsmanlike
> approach: 'if you give me a well streamed group, I'll push them
> through' and 'I used to get fantastic results from streamed
> groups' you know, 'This mixed-ability, well!'.

Table 7.2   Senior posts of responsibility (% in brackets)

	Managerial[a]	Academic[b]	Pastoral[c]	Total staff
Shottsford Mixed SM	2 (50)	10 (59)	5 (50)	35 (51)
Melchester GS	2 (40)	5 (29)	3 (30)	18 (25)
Egdon Heath Boys' SM	1 (10)	2 (12)	2 (20)	17 (24)
				70 [d]

Notes
(a) Members of the senior management team
(b) Heads of department or teachers in charge
(c) Heads and deputy heads of year
(d) Other appointments: 13. Total: 83

In career terms this distribution of initial posts of responsibility is
both an evaluation of the worth of the schools and teachers involved
and a basis from which future promotions and appointments were to
be fought out. The social interactions between the groups were, to a
great extent, constituted in terms of on-going conflicts between
competing educational ideologies. Here, as suggested earlier, we
can see career in the broadest sense being closely bound up with the
ideological conflicts between the constituent schools of the new

comprehensive. The expectations carried by these more or less permanently mobilized interest groups and their claims for recognition and career advancement rest on 'logically distinct and competing' claims for legitimacy. Careers are intimately related to the struggle for control over the definition of the school. As Bailey argues: 'A key factor in the politics of organizations is the way in which individuals are able to justify their actions as reasonable and normal' (1982, p. 101). The claims put forward by the three schools link views of good practice with assumptions about pupils (and teaching and learning) and particular goals and policies. That is to say, values are linked with vested interests, self-interest with self-image (which Nias, 1985, explores). The case of the Egdon teachers rests upon claims about their ability to handle difficult and less able pupils, and other teachers are judged by them on the same basis. They stress the primacy of the craft skills of teaching over and against subject expertise and qualifications (of the grammar school) and contrast their down-to-earth 'realism' with impractical 'theories' (of the Shottsford teachers). Discipline and control are keywords in their vocabulary of motives. Conversely, the sense of legitimacy asserted by the grammar-school teachers rests upon their ability to 'handle' the most able pupils. Knowledge of 'the subject' is taken to be of major importance, together with an understanding of the pedagogical and administrative skills which are required to translate subject expertise into examination passes and university places (one grammar-school teacher was recommended to me as 'the best writer of UCCA references'). (The inadequacy of the secondary-modern teachers in these respects was often alluded to.) Again, discipline is a key word but perhaps for the grammar-school teachers their claims to control and respect are based on reference to *traditional authority* rather than the *charisma* (the importance of a 'forceful personality' and making relationships) cited by the Egdon teachers. Both groups saw caning as a legitimate part of the establishment and maintenance of discipline, and both groups held strong views about the fixed nature of pupil abilities. The Shottsford teachers made their claims, in part at least, on exactly the opposite basis. Both their previous experience and their commitment to comprehensive education were bound up with a belief in offering all pupils the opportunity to participate in an academic curriculum and to strive for examination success. They stressed the need for teaching across the abilities and the postponement of selection. This was also linked to advocacy of the need to change and to innovate. They also argued for the virtues of co-operation, between teachers and between subjects. While the Egdon and grammar-school teachers laid stress on coping at the chalkface, alone in the classroom, the Shottsford staff urged the need for meetings, discussions and the airing and sharing of problems. The Egdon and grammar-school teachers were suspicious of meetings, of talking rather than doing, and this was linked to their view of the Shottsford Road reputation as being a façade, with difficulties being 'swept under the carpet'. As we have seen, the system of legitimation put forward by the Egdon teachers receives little recognition in the new school, it carries connotations of 'dirty work' (Hughes, 1964), associated as it is with pupils regarded as low status by the grammar-school teachers and with teaching methods and attitudes regarded as outdated and repressive by the Shottsford teachers.

As these three systems of legitimation compete in conflicts over policy and preferment, the outcomes, in terms of teaching and organization in the school, were often messy and confusing (Bailey, 1982, p. 102). The political process was most apparent in the contest over critical decisions (like mixed-ability, caning and open sixth form) and over critical appointments and promotions. Significantly, some of the grammar-school teachers who were effectively de-moted during the reappointment process were later able to achieve a degree of 'career recovery' (the same was certainly not true of the Egdon teachers). Of particular interest are two appointments made at sixth-form level which maintained the sixth form as a bastion of grammar-school influence in the new school. First, the head of languages from the grammar school, who had failed to gain that post in the new school, was appointed as assistant sixth-form tutor. After five years he obtained a post as head of sixth form in another comprehensive. Second, he was replaced by the unsuccessful ex-head of English from the grammar school. His appointment rein-forced the grammar-school control over the ethos and running of the sixth form.

Rogers makes the following point:

> By far the most vulnerable group in a merger is the teaching staff. They see career prospects diminish; they have to compete for

what many see as their own job; they face redeployment even redundancy. Many fail to see any benefit in a merged school. A few acknowledge the value of 'a good shake-up'. But the overwhelming feeling is insecurity. (1981, p. 16)

What is more, Beynon's (1985) account of Victoria Road Comprehensive shows how the effects of decisions made during amalgamation can make themselves felt over many years. He studied Victoria Road some fourteen years after amalgamation and found that 'the former secondary modern teachers still saw themselves (and were recognized as) a distinct group' (Beynon, 1985, p. 160). Appointments made at the time of the amalgamation were now a part of the folklore, and micro-politics, of the organization. One teacher explained to Beynon:

Peter Montgomery was the first headmaster of the new comprehensive in 1966. He had the difficult job of integrating the grammar staff and the secondary modern teachers. He had a great belief in the value of the practical arts and so appointed Craft and Art teachers and such like to be heads of year, and Lower and Middle school. He saw them as blending the imaginative and the practical – something naive like that! That's how Bill (Mr Changeable) got his job – he used to teach Art. It was little to do with talent, but being in the right place at the right time. The next thing was that people who'd been wielding a paint brush or a chisel one term were sitting behind a desk issuing orders the next. The whole business caused a lot of bitterness and a number of good people were overlooked. (Quoted in Beynon, 1985, p. 171)

Here again the importance of the head as critical reality definer emerges, and also we find an exception to the marginalization of 'non-academic' teachers described earlier. Mr Changeable, one of the non-academics appointed, was under no illusions about the way he was regarded by some of his colleagues:

Some of the senior staff look down on those, myself included, who were in the secondary moderns, when we all amalgamated to form the comprehensive. They regarded us as a threat to what they held to be their province, their little academic empire! The jealousy when I took over as head here was quite blatant! (Quoted on p. 172)

Decisions which advance the interests and careers of certain groups and individuals in these circumstances also inhibit the interests and careers of others; competition is inevitable.

Falling rolls

In some senses the career problems and insecurities created by comprehensive reorganization are limited compared with the threats created by the combination of cuts in funding and falling rolls. In a situation of falling rolls the issue shifts from 'Who gets what job?' to 'How many and which jobs will be lost?'

> I write to confirm that your allocation of teaching staff in 1982/83 will be 69.8 FTE [Full Time Equivalent] staff. This figure is made up of a basic allocation of 61.8 FTE on the estimate numbers in January 1983, with an addition of 8.0 FTE for falling rolls, based on the number of pupils shown on form 7 for January 1982. There are currently 80.2 full-time equivalent members of your staff and a reduction of 10.4 FTE therefore has to be made. In view of the size of this reduction I feel that it will be necessary to consider the redeployment of some members of your existing staff.

This is a letter written by the Chief Education Office to the head of Casterbridge High School (Ball, 1984). In the first instance the headmaster was able to respond by indicating that two resignations were aniticipated from women teachers on maternity leave, and that there would be the redeployment of a science teacher on a LEA contract, a secondment, three possible early retirements and one teacher who had expressed an interest in voluntary redeployment. The CEO noted these possibilities and replied:

> Having taken account of all the above factors I have decided that formal redeployment measures will need to be taken in respect of the reductions which are sought in history/sociology, mathematics, science, art, and remedial. In accordance, therefore, with paragraph 1.3 of the Authority's Code of Practice on the Redeployment of Teaching Staff I am writing to ask you formally to seek volunteers for redeployment in the subject areas mentioned where, in my view, it appears unlikely that the reduction can be achieved by any other means.

The letter went on to say that:

> In applying section 3.3, I propose that every teacher who has a major teaching commitment in one of the five subject areas listed earlier who is employed on scale 1 or scale 2 should be interviewed by . . . , the Area Secondary Adviser.

The interviews duly took place and for the remainder of the school year the redeployment issue became a major focus of conversation, speculation, gossip and disgruntlement among the staff on Scale 1 and Scale 2 posts. The interviews themselves were not well received by some of the teachers involved. One history teacher explained this to me in the following way:

> We got through the pally bit, 'Nice to see you again, how are you', and then 'What teaching do you do in the school?' 'What responsibilities do you have?' Then came the crunch question. 'Can you justify yourself?' 'What value are you to the school?' he said. 'What have you done for the school?' Well I got a bit narked by that time and I turned around and pointed out of the window. 'See that minibus out there, the new one, I collected one sixth of that.' I wouldn't do it again mind you. They walk all over you. Like Alan Atlas with the summer fair last year. 'A young teacher', they said, 'it would be good experience for you and all that', and not a word of thanks. And this year they've got John Bunsen doing it, and he's now been nominated for redeployment. I would go, I would go to Crabtree Community. It's a lot more friendly than it is here.

Another member of the history department, who was eventually nominated for redeployment, commented on her interview that 'It was a formality, they always redeploy the Scale 1s. They only interviewed the others to make it seem fair'.

The flow of information to the interviewees and the handling of the subsequent procedures were also criticized by the teachers involved. An English teacher explained:

> It's always the same. They don't tell you anything. It was three weeks before Karen Thimble got a letter after her interview with the Adviser and then they sent her for an interview at the Church School and offered the other candidate the job while they were both in the room. Morale is at rock bottom.

Another colleague said of Ms Thimble: 'She says that she could not teach properly for a month after the interview with the Adviser.' The head came in for particular criticism. Typically, a languages teacher said:

> This redeployment thing is demoralizing for people – and the head, I don't know, I would think that he would keep people more informed about what is going on. He's playing it that the Authority are the villains, but he must have some say in the appointment of his own staff, about who is to be redeployed. He's very approachable but he doesn't take time to find out about people. He's not good at initiating. It's a pastoral function really. People are fed up about not knowing when decisions are being made and what stage has been reached about their redeployment. He's very rarely over here [the West Block]. We're beginning to feel like an imperial outpost on which the sun never sets.

There are many other examples of this kind of talk which could be quoted. Grumbling about the head seems to be an almost universal characteristic of staffroom talk in schools, and at Casterbridge disgruntlements about leadership style were freely aired during the redeployment crisis. None the less, it would be a mistake to dismiss these grumbles as either simply examples of personal discontent or as reflecting the failings of an individual head. They illustrate a more general shift in the role of the headteacher and in staff–head relationships, a shift that is being brought about by the increased level of intervention by local-authority officials in areas of policy and decision-making previously left to the responsibility of the headteacher. Briault and Smith, from their study of schools hit by falling rolls, make the point that:

> In the many difficult decisions to be made, which in total result in the size and character of the staff establishment of the school, the role of the head is bound to involve some conflicts of loyalty, particularly when the roll falls and staff reductions are required. Is the head primarily responsible upwards towards his employing authority or downwards towards his school? (1980, p. 127)

Hunter adds the point that 'the head thinks in terms of general rules and uniform events; teachers think in terms of concrete situations, unique individuals and extenuating circumstances' (1980, pp. 133–4).

The views, attitudes and response of the threatened staff at Casterbridge with respect to the actions of the LEA and their interpretation of the head's role demonstrate both an apparent weakening of normative and professional commitment to the school and an increasing exposure and recognition of the straightforward employee–employer relationships within which they worked. Much of the teachers' knowledge and understanding of the process of management was based on rumour and hearsay, and they resented the lack of consultation and communication (see Ch. 9). The separation of policy-making and executive decision-making from the day-to-day work of teaching revealed for some, perhaps for the first time, the contradictions in their view of themselves on the one hand as being 'professionals' while on the other labouring 'according to the dictates of those with authority over them'. To a great extent, the professional mythology (see Bailey, 1982, p. 97 on school mythologies), through which the teachers had interpreted their work relationships and attendant sense of personal autonomy, was being stripped away by the depersonalizing experience of the redeployment crisis. Even the role of the unions, at least for those teachers on Scales 1 or 2, seemed to be merely that of providing an agreed procedure, which gave them a minimum of personal protection and security. Interestingly, one teacher at least saw the teaching unions as too 'gentlemanly' and deferential: 'The dockers are getting £22,000 apiece for fifteen years service. Perhaps they've got a better union than ours. Ours is always too pleased with anything they can get. "Yes sir, thank you very much sir"' (history teacher).

There was little evidence of collective strategies of defence at work in Casterbridge High, although collegial relationships among the younger staff did provide psychological and emotional mutual support and commiseration. The important decisions were being taken elsewhere. Wallace *et al.* (1983) report a similar lack of coherent response to cuts among middle-school teachers they interviewed. Again, it is not difficult to identify the victims of falling rolls. In this case it is those teachers who by chance of circumstance, being in the wrong place at the wrong time, find themselves viewed as being surplus to requirements. This is not simply a matter of the financial, familial and career problems posed by redeployment or redundancy, there is also the damage done to the sense of personal identity and the self-esteem of the people who find themselves no longer needed, no longer valued. This is the direct interface between the objective and subjective elements of career (Hughes, 1964). Changes in the teachers' sense of self-worth may also be accompanied by a change in political consciousness and attitude to authority, as the following interview extract indicates:

I got a year's secondment I think because it was easy for them to lose me for a year. I teach history. I was appointed as a year tutor not a history teacher; a term later a new deputy was appointed who was also a history teacher. So in one term the school acquired two history teachers that they didn't need or want. So for four years the school benefited by having extra history teachers and very small history classes of nine up to fifteen. And consequently good academic results. So when I applied for the [secondment] year they had no trouble covering my timetable and they had a year head as acting head of lower school and another year head as deputy. Two people doing the work of three.

During the year, in January/February, I had a letter right out of the blue from the director of education: would I go and see him. So off I went. I didn't know anything about this until I got there but apparently each school had to lose approximately five staff. . . . And the director said that my headmaster had suggested that I was one who might like to go somewhere else, because the school didn't really have the teaching opportunities for me there and there might be somewhere in the borough where they could provide better career prospects. So I was invited to see a headmaster of another school, and they had a position there supposedly comparable to the one I had at the moment. I got to the school, it was nothing of the sort; it was a Scale-1 history post and they'd obviously created other things for me to do, to make use of my scale points. That head wanted me to stay for at least three years if I took the job and I wasn't prepared to do that because it wasn't the job I wanted to do. So I declined. And then I saw my present headmaster, who denied all the story I had been given by the director of education and that it had never been his intention that I be seen by the director and he'd never wanted me to go to this other school. The situation then was when I last saw the head that obviously I had to go back in September and there was no question about me not going back, but there would be no history teaching for me on the timetable, because there wasn't any and my position as a year head would be different to what it was when I stopped in September. Further to that, the only thing is that I am advised by the union that they must maintain me in a position comparable to the one I had before I had the year off, but the union can't do anything about guaranteeing what I teach there. So I will go back as a permanent supply, but I should remain as a year head.

The worst of it is, as I pointed out to my head, I am trying to do a degree and it didn't help me that from February I have had all this anxiety of not knowing where I am going. And if you are given the opportunity to further your education it should be to the benefit of the pupils and the local authority, but of course they are not using it in that way. It's really to my detriment at the moment. I felt quite devastated really because I had thought I had given a lot to the school as year head, and when I started at the school I did not have a degree and I did my BEd part time, and I did that because I thought teaching is becoming an all-graduate profession so I worked hard to get that and then I carried on believing that the profession should have the best-qualified people. So I worked towards bettering my own qualifications and obviously it means I've given up a lot of my own time to do it. And here they were saying that your reward for working for us for five or six years is to come back and not have a job. Really, I felt that they should be saying to me what have you learned on this course; how can we benefit from what you've learned on this course? What about this sort of position? And offer me something better. But it's the other way. I don't think it's affected my own personal commitment to teaching, but it may have affected my attitude towards 'the hierarchy' and 'the powers that be' in the system. I've now got less respect for them, if I ever had a great deal of respect for them in the first place. And I think it has also enabled me to see where I've met an awful lot of complacent teachers I can now understand how they've become complacent, the different things that could have caused this. They've tried, they've been 'good' in their career; they have made them give up and you can see how this has happened.

In such circumstances the 'victims'' view of things is rarely taken into account. Indeed, as this quotation illustrates, they will often be confronted by conflicting information, misinformation or just no information at all. From the point of view of 'the Authority', 'the problem' is one of numbers, not people. The person is unimportant; decision-making is driven by the need to 'manage' falling rolls.

RB: But you've received your official notification?

ST: No, no, because everything's going to be done nicely and smoothly and in a gentlemanly way and nobody's actually going to say to me, when I say it to them first, 'You are being made redundant?': They will say to me, 'Wouldn't you like to retire?' and if I say 'Yes', then they will say I asked for retirement, and if I ask for retirement I'm not made redundant, am I? (Quoted in Beck, 1983, p. 29)

JD: Again, it is a rather delicate subject. I wasn't informed clearly and openly last year. I eventually found out because there was no timetable for me. So I found out eventually from the paper that went up on the wall. There had been hints, suggestions, because first of all I had been told I wouldn't be doing any English, but as I was converting to maths anyway I thought I'd be doing all maths, but when the timetable appeared on the wall there wasn't even any maths for me. So then at the end of the year I had to find out what was happening. The Authority were not insisting that I move, so I was able to stay for another year, but I feel that definitely this year, I hope openly this time that I'm going to be asked to volunteer for redeployment. (Quoted on p. 30)

We have two staff now who at least until the beginning of July thought that they were going to be redeployed and the Authority couldn't find places for them, and they tended to find out from the deputy who did the timetable, and Mr Austen [the head] would have directed that Mr X was not to be given a timetable and the deputy would have to say, 'Well, off the record no, but officially I'm not allowed to tell you. You'll have to go and ask Mr Austen'. And they must have felt bitter, and it spread to a certain extent to the rest of the staff because we sympathised with them. They weren't kept in the picture enough about what was being done. (Quoted on p. 31)

Planning here, such as it is, is invisible. In these moments of crisis the formal principles of control in the organization are laid bare, and the powerlessness of the subordinate stands out. The results in organizational terms are aptly summed up in Argyris's analysis of the problems of mutual adjustment between the organization and the individual:

1. There is a lack of congruency between the needs of healthy individuals and the demands of formal organization . . .
2. The results of this disturbance are frustration, failure, short time-perspective, and conflict . . .
3. The nature of the formal principles cause the subordinate . . . to experience competition, rivalry, insubordinate hostility, and to develop a focus toward the parts rather than the whole (1975, pp. 246–7)

Despite the sympathy mentioned above, individuals and groups are in competition for the declining number of available jobs. There is little evidence of solidarity or resistance emerging in response to situations of redeployment or redundancy. The 'problem' of falling rolls is defined solely in technical and financial terms by central and local government. Within the limits of such a definition no other 'solution' is possible. Subordinates have little or no opportunity to canvass alternative solutions and indeed, as Argyris suggests, the sense of crisis directs attention towards the parts (the 'need' to reduce maths by one post) rather than the whole (e.g. the decision not to take the opportunity of falling rolls to reduce class size). Thus within the organization micro-politics are to the fore. The careerist or survivalist strategies of individuals are of prime importance. Interests are at stake. Departments, pastoral staff, administrators compete for resources from a reduced overall allocation. The exercise is one of minimizing damage, but less damage for some means more for others. The misery is spread unevenly and unfairly as a result of lobbying, the use of influence, deals struck and the control of critical information. The development and defence of group and individual presentations of self, and the debunking of others' presentations, assume great importance. The larger issues are rarely addressed, and conflicts become focused around control of and influence over arenas of decision-making within the organization.

8
Women's careers and the politics of gender

This chapter builds upon the analysis of women teachers begun in Chapter 3 but concentrates specifically on career issues. Women teachers may validly be regarded as a distinct interest group within the school if only because the overall pattern of their career development is so clearly different from that of men teachers:

> If we consider the modal location of men and women teachers, we observe that men and women typically teach different subjects to different groups of children, hold responsibilities for different functions within schools, and generally have different chances for rewards within the system. (Acker, 1983, p. 123)

In addition, the comparative focus upon the careers of women serves to highlight the profound micro-political tensions which exist between men and women in the school. Marland makes the point that 'In the growing literature of school organization insufficient attention has been given to the politics of power and the stereotyping of role resulting from the male–female inheritance we have in schools management (1982, p.11). Women are severely disadvantaged in career terms by the male dominance of schools, although most teachers vehemently deny this. Deem makes the point that:

> like secretarial or office-work, or nursing, teaching has promised more to the women entering it than it has actually given them, in

terms of status, financial rewards and career prospects . . .
women who enter teaching have been no less strongly socialized
into accepting the existing sexual division of labour than have
other women. (1978, p. 109)

To all intents and purposes, mixed schools, particularly secondary schools, are male institutions. The definition of the school
reflects the values and meanings of men's culture. The language and
structure of schooling are predominantly shaped by patriarchy.
'From their social position, women have not had the same opportunities [as men] to influence the language, to introduce new
meanings where they will be taken up or to define the objects or
events in the world' (Marshall, 1984, p. 51). Connell suggests that
schools are denoted by a particular 'gender regime':

The way it embodies patterns of authority is an important part of
the political order of the school. The association that our society
makes between authority and masculinity, more specifically
adult heterosexual masculinity, is a significant underpinning
of the power structure of a school system where most administrators, principals and subject heads are men. (1985, pp. 138–9)

The structural aspects of this sexual division of labour are
straightforwardly demonstrated.

As we see in Table 8.1, 77 per cent of primary-school teachers are
women and 44 per cent of secondary-school teachers, and yet
women are concentrated in the lower-scale posts in both sectors,
and are massively underrepresented in senior positions. In the
primary sector this frequently creates a situation which Tyack
(1974) has dubbed the 'pedagogical harem', where a male headteacher is working with an all-female staff. Various theories have
been put forward, usually by male commentators, to account for the
underrepresentation of women at senior levels in teaching. Two
are most often quoted and both are inherently sexist. One attributes
the relative lack of promotion among women to a 'low promotion
orientation' (Hilsum and Start, 1974). This is the view that women
are less committed than men to the idea of teaching as a career. In
other words, they are less interested in 'getting on'; they see
teaching as a convenient means of providing a subsidiary income
and a job that can be easily accommodated to the demands of family
duties (see Simpson and Simpson, 1969). The second relates to the

'break' in career experienced by married women who leave teaching for a period to have and raise children. The assumption is that all women teachers are or will be married and mothers. Deem quotes Hoyle explaining the careers and salaries of women in terms of 'the "special conditions" [see Hoyle, 1969, pp. 87–8] attaching to female employment such as the fact that their careers are often intermittent, that they are only secondary breadwinners in the family, that they tend to be residentially immobile' (Deem, 1978, p. 116). This is what Lortie calls women's 'in and out engagement'. (1975, p. 87).

Table 8.1 Scale posts in primary and secondary schools: men and women, 1979

| | Nursery and primary | | Secondary | |
	Men	Women	Men	Women
Headteacher	13,441	10,274	4,348	857
Deputy heads	7,725	12,143	5,234	1,135
Second masters/mistresses	210	373	1,152	1,896
Senior teachers	11	5	4,927	1,097
Scale 4	88	92	21,484	5,920
Scale 3	4,803	9,153	33,289	18,392
Scale 2	13,735	63,369	34,184	31,307
Scale 1	5,891	58,243	31,088	45,838
Total	45,904	153,652	135,706	106,442
	(23%)	(77%)	(56%)	(44%)
	199,556		241,698	

Source
DES, *Statistics in Education*, London, HMSO, 1979

There are a number of problems with each of these arguments and they have been soundly criticized (Deem, 1978; NUT, 1980; Acker, 1983). The NUT/EOC survey *Promotion and the Woman Teacher* (1980) found that 81.5 per cent of their 3000 respondents considered themselves 'as consciously pursuing a career', 77 per cent saw themselves teaching until retirement and 77 per cent of married women teachers saw their careers as being as important as those of their husbands. Furthermore, 51 per cent of the sample had applied for promotion within the previous five years.[1] Interestingly, there is no comparable data for men teachers. No one seems to have considered it worthwhile to ask men as a group such questions. Furthermore, extrapolating from its figures the report estimates that:

> about 65 per cent of women would have a break in service to rear their families . . . the predominant pattern appears to be that the teacher works for four or five years, spends up to eight years raising a family, then returns to teaching with the prospect of spending 25 years or more in service. (NUT, 1980, p. 49)

There is little support here for either lack of commitment or the break in career being the main reasons for the inequalities outlined above. They may play a part in some cases but we need to look elsewhere to complete the picture. We should note that the NUT/ EOC report found that 23 per cent of internal candidates for promotion and 20.5 per cent of external candidates in the sample, believed that they were discriminated against because they were women:

> Our head will not promote any women under the age of 42 – for what he calls 'obvious reasons'.

> The head said that promotion would be a reward for long service and loyalty to the school; then he promoted a man who had only been there 15 months.
>
> (NUT, 1980, p. 36)

> I was informed by the head of department that it was an unwritten rule that women under 40 were not considered.

> I was told after the appointment was made that if a woman had been needed I would have been shortlisted.

> The head of English wanted a male teacher to balance the department.

> A man with only three years' experience was awarded the post [deputy head]. I have been in a Scale 2 post for three years.
>
> (NUT, 1980, p. 37)

If such attitudes are employed when appointments are being made, then we may certainly attribute significant blame for lack of career development for women to discrimination. It certainly seems to be the case that men making appointments employ stereotypes about women applicants which severely disadvantage them. The study by Morgan, Hall and Mackay (1983) found some evidence of this from the views of local education authority officers. They say that 'The nature of officers' perceptions of women candidates for headship can be summarized as initially welcoming, expecting a higher quality from them than from male candidates, and fearing lay selectors' doubts at the final stages' (Morgan, Hall and Mackay, 1983, p. 67). The NUT/EOC survey also asked applicants seeking external promotion whether they were asked questions at interview about matters other than their professional life, because they were women; 41 per cent replied that they had. Morgan, Hall and Mackay also found such questions being raised, 'non-explicit, non-job-related factors dominate' and 'Many more models of men teachers are available to selectors as a basis for stereotypes' (1983, p. 77).

Clearly, such questioning constitutes a form of discrimination and again betrays fixed, disadvantageous stereotypes at work. They also display the working of an essentially patriarchical institution. The gatekeepers here are predominantly men, as in other professions (Lorber, 1984, pp. 4–7). The basic problem is 'that male gatekeepers do not yet believe that women are trustworthy colleagues, either because of their supposed characteristics or because of their competing family roles' (Lorber, 1984, p. 8). (See Lorber, 1984, on women physicians; Epstein, 1981, on women laywers; Marshall, 1984, on women managers.) Several respondents also argued that a male headteacher tended to foster a very different school ethos from that to be found under the leadership of a female head, although it is certainly possible to envisage patriarchy flourishing under a female head:

> I have now taught for a number of years in a school with a woman head: this has been the most important factor in promoting equality of opportunity and in marked contrast to other experiences under male heads; nor have men suffered under our present head.

> Having previously worked in a school with a female head, the whole environment was one of equality. Male heads perpetuate the myths of female staff as teamakers and floral artists.

(NUT, 1980, pp. 21–2)

There is little hard evidence on this particular issue, although Gross and Trask, in their study of male and female elementary school principals, found 'women exerted greater control over their teachers' professional activities than men and that women associated more frequently with members of the faculty outside of school than men' (1976, p. 219). (See also Marshall, 1984, on women managers' styles.) It is certainly difficult to find examples of female heads being accused of discrimination against men (see Byrne, 1978, p. 221). In contrast, Beynon (1981) paints a vivid picture of the problem of career survival faced by Miss Floral, a drama teacher in a South Wales boys comprehensive, where 'schoolmastery' was the dominant approach to teaching. She faced constant criticism and harassment from male colleagues who would not accept her teaching methods and educational aims as valid or worthwhile. They did not fit with the dominant male ethos. Even so, institutional sexism cannot simply be reduced to the wilful acts of individuals; it is structured into the daily practices of organizational life. It operates through covert acts of omission and by indifference. However, there is increasing awareness that women in organizations may be subject not only to discrimination but to various endemic forms of sexual harassment and male violence. Such violence consists not so much of an experience of 'fisticuffs and flying chairs, as one of diminishing other human beings with the use of sarcasm, raised voices, jokes, veiled insults or the patronizing put down' (Ramazanoglu, 1985, p. 4). These expressions of violence may also confront women teachers in the classroom. Jones (1985, p. 27) reports the prevalence of 'woman-hating' graffiti in one secondary school. This was often aimed at female teachers ('Miss Smith is a pro'), and Whyld comments that the female teacher, 'If she admits that she is intimidated by male pupils, she will not be seen as an able teacher, and will jeopardize chances of promotion and other jobs' (1983, p. 37). Ramazanoglu is describing the woman's lot in higher education and solely relations between colleagues, but her comments may be equally relevant in the school staffroom and department meeting. She says:

> In my first academic jobs I was truly amazed by the effort and emotion that certain male colleagues would put into trying to impress my inferiority upon me. As I had no self-confidence at the time this was not a difficult task, so why was it so important to them? (1985, p. 9)

She goes on to argue that:

> If women fail to learn their place, or do not keep to it, they are effectively a threat to the system of male dominance and will be seen as unnatural, sexually undesirable, aggressive women whose personal peculiarities must account for their deviant behaviour. (p. 2)

Delamont finds just such a situation in Woods's (1979) account of the male-dominated staffroom at Lowfield Secondary Modern:

> The data presented on how these men relax show an unthinking and deeply embedded sexism in the teachers, from which Woods makes no attempt to distance himself ... . Apart from the headmaster, who was a frequent source of humour, the senior mistress was also the butt of jokes, for example, because of her mannerisms: 'They amused themselves during staff meetings by taking bets on what she would do first, this – rubbing her arms crosswise, or this, – smoothing and straightening her clothing' (p. 219). The women staff, especially the 'attractive' ones, received overtly sexist commentary, such as the example (p. 223) where the males are discussing a female colleague's bruise saying 'some people get a private viewing, but I didn't get one'. (Delamont, 1980, p. 81)

The threat posed by women may be countered by overt sanctions or through the apparently insignificant behaviours and attitudes embedded in working relations and social interactions between men and women. Thus, even when femininity is confirmed or fulfilled in a woman's work role, those particular aspects of femininity which posit women as desirable sex objects can and do interfere in relations at work (see Bland *et al.,* 1978).

> The 'trivia' of everyday life – touching others, moving closer or further away, dropping the eyes, smiling, interrupting – are commonly interpreted as facilitatory social intercourse, but not recognized in their position as micropolitical gestures, defenders of the status quo – of the state, of the wealthy, of authority, of all those whose power may be challenged. (Henley, 1977, p. 3)

It may also be that there are factors deriving from outside the school context which disadvantage women. Many men are able to pursue their work life via what Acker (1980) calls 'two-person careers'. Non-working wives will often play a part in directly supporting their husbands' work while at the same time taking responsibility for household duties. Married women teachers on the other hand are typically a part of a two-career family. Not only do they not have the support of their husbands, many seem to take most of the responsibility for domestic duties as well. One busy advisory teacher explained in interview:

> But my husband was very supportive. He knew that I thoroughly enjoyed what I was doing and I never had any repercussions about it. I think the biggest problem has always been rushing home after school, getting meals in time to get the children out to their activities. . . . My husband, once he left the office at half-past four, then virtually that was the end of his day and he was free very much to do the ferrying of the children and this sort of thing. Though I never landed him with the housework and the ironing – I mean, he'll put the Hoover round, this sort of thing but I've never landed him with the ironing and the washing.

Clarricoates demonstrates how the twin pressures of home and work produce guilt and emotional and physical stress for women teachers:

> The overall pressure to be proficient in all aspects of their lives is generally felt by the [women] teachers, who strive to work out patterns and rigid routines in their attempts to 'fit everything in' and 'get everything done'. Some teachers told me their husbands felt that the 'quality of home life' had deteriorated since they had started or resumed teaching. Instead of questioning this presumption they felt they had to justify themselves and offer excuses as to why they couldn't excel at being *both* the perfect wife and perfect teacher. (1980, p. 72)

Langrish (1981), in a study of women workers, found that the women regarded home life as a pressure, it was for them hard work, they had little time to themselves. In contrast, men saw home as a place of refuge, somewhere to recharge their energies.

Negotiations over the issue of female labour will be resolved differently in different households according to whether tradition (patriarchy) or rationality (maximization of economic interests) prevail: 'where both models have equal or similar importance for household members in explaining their social world, negotiations will tend to conflict' (Yeandle, 1984, p. 169). The costs arising from such conflict may be high; working wives may find that they face difficult decisions in weighing up their marriage and family against their career. 'It seems possible that the conflict within the family household which is generated by the ideologies of patriarchy and capitalism may sometimes be sufficiently intense to provoke the breakdown of the marital relationship' (Yeandle, 1984, p. 171). Even when resolution within the household is achieved, the organization of family life alongside work life may prove problematic. As research demonstrates (Novarra, 1980), the contemporary conditions of employment continue to be orientated to the male employee. Married women find that they must adapt themselves to the conditions based upon the male norm. Some feminist writers have also argued that women pursuing careers do so in ways that are different from men. This may lead to differences in emphasis between work life and social life (although this can come close to recasting the lack-of-commitment argument mentioned above). For example, Sharpe argues:

> For men, the active pursuit of ambition can consume their lives and destroy intimate relations with other people, especially women and children. The changes that women wish to make in their role in this society should never be equated with the self destructive position of men. (1976, p. 68)

Bland *et al*. suggest that for women:

> When they enter wage labour there is immediately a contradiction between their position as mothers and wage workers (as well as a contradiction in relation to men). While men are affirmed as men in their double relation as fathers and wage-labourers through their role as 'breadwinner' – which is why masculinity as a construct can so often be overlooked – feminity is cast in doubt by such a relation. (1978, p. 64)

As Cunnison notes, 'The world of work is made-to-measure for men who do not get pregnant and have family responsibilities' (1985, p. 32) and Marshall (1984) described the lives of the women managers she interviewed beset with 'often-conflicting undercurrents of stereotypes, self-perceptions and values', which 'could not be easily or permanently reconciled'. They were 'continually forced with dilemmas and choices' (Marshall, 1984, p. 189).

Women's careers in context: three brief anecdotes

MALE TAKEOVER

One factor often quoted in explanation of the declining number of women headteachers is the amalgamation of schools and the reduction in numbers of single-sex schools. At the turn of the century women constituted 75 per cent of the teaching force and held 55 per cent of all headships, but by 1978 their proportion of the teaching force had declined to 59 per cent and they held only 38 per cent of headships. (The figures for 1982 indicate the same 38 per cent.) The amalgamation of single-sex schools may have profound implications for women teachers throughout the organization as a whole. Beck (1983) describes the aftermath of the amalgamation of a boys and a girls grammar school to form the basis of a sixth-form college. In the process of the amalgamation many of the women staff clearly began to feel that they were being taken over rather than amalgamated; this may be a common factor in such situations – 'when schools merge, one inevitably feels the underdog' (Rogers, 1981, p.16) – but here it was seen as a male takeover of what was to be a mixed school:

> It seemed to us, at the high school, that we were being taken over by the grammar school ... it seems incredible to say this of the 1970s and I try to look at this dispassionately, I did at the time, but there was amongst some of the men an impression of an attitude that the women were inferior, that any position put forward by the high school had to be inferior, and I suppose it was inevitable to a certain extent because you had Mr Austen appointed as principal and Mr Tennyson appointed to his deputy and they had their status quo, the organization, their way of working. It would have been extremely difficult for them not to have given that impression. And the majority of the executive staff, the senior posts, went to men, and whilst I have no evidence for saying this, I very much got the feeling that my appointment as one of the three senior tutors was the compulsory woman. (Quoted in Beck, 1983, p. 35)

Not only does the new institution emerge with a male-dominated hierarchy but one of the few women in a senior position feels that she was not appointed on merit but rather because of the existence of a stereotyped role which required a woman to fill it. However, some of the women involved felt that the problem lay with the attitudes and commitment of the high-school staff:

> I do have strong views on that. I can see two points of view. Firstly I can see that, oh dear it's awful saying this, I don't like saying this, but if I think back to the staff in the high school and the staff who could actually or would be prepared to take on responsibility within the new set up, they were very few, so that was one problem, but also I do feel very strongly that it was a male take over to a certain extent. But I think that if there had been a more dynamic and forceful female staff then there might have been more appointments in the hierarchy. It's part of a whole social problem that women don't get executive jobs and appointments since have confirmed the male dominance. (Quoted in Beck, 1983, p.36)

For some the 'take over' was not only of male personnel but also of male visions of what the organization should be like, the male definition of school organization: 'I would agree we have had to adapt often against our will and very sadly to a structure that seems to us very hierarchical and outmoded' (quoted on p.35).

From the male point of view the situation could be accounted in terms of the different attitudes and temperaments of the men and women involved. A senior male teacher commented:

> There was lots of apprehension up at the high school, some of it was justified, that there was going to be a male takeover. Lots of the ladies had never taught boys and thought they were creatures from another planet. ... In particular it was felt by them that when the two traditions came together it was the grammar school tradition that was going to take over, and this was largely because Mr Austen was to be the new head and had taken the initiative in lots of things. ... The men didn't really see it in those neurotic terms, we were looking forward to the challenge, we thought it was going to be quite fun. (Quoted on p. 35)

The women are seen as neurotic and fearful (commonly used derogatory stereotypes) for anticipating a takeover and loss of their own sense of school tradition, but as the respondent admits this is exactly what happened.

RESISTANCE?

Analytically, it is easy to fall into the trap of assuming that, stereotypically, women who are attempting to pursue careers are

helpless victims of a male conspiracy. Two points of objection can
be raised to that assumption. First, as we shall see, women teachers
have become increasingly aware of their position of disadvantage
and have begun to oppose the male dominance of the school.
Second, and conversely, there are many women teachers, especially
those who are 'successful' in their careers, who see no evidence of
discrimination against themselves or their colleagues. (I will return
to this point later.)

One example of opposition to male dominance was provided by
an interviewee who described a primary school where the head
attempted to run his 'pedagogical harem' with a rod of iron.

> in the third year I was there the headship changed – he was an
> absolute swine. If the other one had been authoritarian, this one
> was even worse and he thought he could manage the young girls
> on his staff and expect them to do exactly what he said, the way he
> said. And, having been there two years before he'd arrived, we
> were not – we found our feet; we were in our sixth year of
> teaching: no way was I going to be pushed around by him. And by
> sheer coincidence, a woman came to teach on the staff who had
> been [working abroad] and was about ten years older than us;
> however, she was in a similar position and she was much stronger
> in her arguments with the head and we formed a nucleus – you
> know certain girls on the staff, and we managed to combat
> various things that he was expecting us to do.

In response to such a situation it is tempting to turn to Willis's
(1977) analysis and suggest that this might be seen as a form of
female 'resistance' to male dominance, arising out of the 'penetration', partial at least, of the institutional patriarchy in which they
were working. Cunnison (1985, p.35) describes another example,
but neither case moves much beyond the level of interpersonal
conflict. The third anecdote provides more evidence of collective
awareness of structural inequalities.

THE LETTER

When Casterbridge High was formed as a comprehensive school
it was composed of two boys' schools and one mixed. When the
reappointment process was completed the senior posts were over-

whelmingly dominated by male staff. By the third year of the existence of the comprehensive school there were eighty-four staff in all (full and part-time) – fifty-two men and thirty-two women – but in senior posts there were just three women in all (one assistant head, one year tutor and one major department head). Thus there was only one woman out of seven members of the senior management team, two women members out of thirteen on the academic board, and six women members out of twenty-one on the pastoral board. Consciousness was raised and resentment heightened by the fact that a series of internal promotions made in the second and third years after reorganization all went to men. A group of women teachers based in the West Block got together to write a letter to the headmaster to express their concern:

> We wrote a letter to the head last year and got about thirty signatures on it . . . it seems that there are no career prospects for good women in the school and we did ask in the letter whether the powers that be felt that they did not have any good women in the school. . . . The response from the head was that the right people had been given the jobs. (English teacher)

Feelings were running particularly high in the summer term of 1983 when two internal appointments made in the same week both went to male candidates. As the outcome of the second appointment became known in the West Block staffroom, one of the women's group declared aloud to the assembled staff: 'What do you expect, it's the same everywhere; in commerce and in industry. In a time of crisis, it's women back to the kitchen.'

For the women teachers at Casterbridge (and newly appointed young men) the declining prospects of promotion inside the school, and locally and nationally outside, created a situation of 'career truncation'. 'They could not see any future possibility of movement up the career ladder and no way out of their career impasse' (Riseborough, 1981). Such realizations, Riseborough suggest, can have profound implications for 'perceptions of self and role performance'. In particular, for the married women, as is the case in other occupations, there was a double handicap to be faced. Not only were there fewer posts being advertised but most of the married women saw themselves as limited to local opportunities by their husband's employment and their children's schooling. The cutting of part-time posts as a first recourse in the efforts to meet reduced staffing numbers also affected women teachers disproportionately.

Women who make it

Another factor which does contribute in part to the continuation of discrimination against women pursuing careers in teaching is to be found in the attitudes of some women themselves. Many, especially those who *have* attained senior posts, hold strongly to the view that no discrimination exists and that the problem lies in a lack of commitment among their female colleagues. They quote their own experiences as proof of the career possibilities available to women, if only they persevere. Radnor (1983) interviewed two comprehensive school deputy heads who certainly fit this pattern:

> Women don't apply for jobs at a higher level out of choice. They decide to concentrate on their families. I'd be surprised to find that women are blocked. (Kate)

> I am sure that there are so many able women who can't take the pressure of high challenge and home responsibilities, children, husband, etc. so they decide not to move upwards. (Susan)

Behind such statements lies a form of logic which Harris (1982) calls the 'anyone can, therefore everyone can' fallacy. 'These fallacious arguments (or examples of "individualistic logic") impute to everybody, as discrete individuals themselves, things which not all of those discrete individuals could achieve when put together in the same situation' (Harris, 1982, p. 18). In other words, what is being argued is that 'if I can achieve a senior post in school then anyone can, they simply don't try'. However, as we have seen, the NUT/EOC survey would suggest this is not the case. What such an argument ignores is the limited number of senior posts available, the competition which results and the mechanisms at work in discriminating between candidates. None the less, Cunnison suggests that in the male-dominated school culture the response in terms of personal project makes sense, 'the weight of this culture is such as to cramp into conformity all but the bravest and most independent spirits' (1985, p. 45).

There is a second significant aspect to the position of the two women quoted. Both occupy the role of woman deputy in a management team, one under a male head the other under a female head. Neither was willing to accept that any relationship existed between their role and their sex:

> I never feel I am working in this role because I am a woman in a particular way. In other words, I never think of my sex in what I'm doing. There is no deliberate way I act and think about my sex at all. (Kate)

> No, I don't accept it at all. I really don't know, I genuinely don't know, where personality ends and being a woman begins. I can't sort it out myself. (Susan)

Yet clearly many women who do make it to senior positions find themselves in sex-stereotyped roles. The position of 'woman deputy' represents a particularly dramatic nexus between seniority and gender. Thus Byrne observes that:

> Twenty years of staffing schools had taught me that senior masters, apart from occasionally caning boys, typically deal with school organization, curricular reconstruction, major administration, CSE examinations, and resource allocation, while senior mistresses typically deal with social functions, pregnant school girls, difficult parents, coffee for and entertaining of visitors (in my experience) and school attendance. Equal is not held to mean the same here. (1978, p. 233)

What is happening is that a role emerges which comes to be defined in terms of the sexual stereotypes associated with women's role in society at large. Women who achieve such positions are not in any direct sense competing with men, and when other senior staff are being appointed it is always possible to point to the 'token' woman already in office. Women's demands are apparently satisfied, but neither in micro-political terms nor in the provision of role models for pupils is a great deal being achieved. Indeed, the messages implicit in such appointments can be read entirely in negative terms. What is being indicated is that women can only achieve senior positions when a specially reserved role is carved out for them. Several other problems are associated with such a role when participation in policy-making is considered. First, given the specialization associated with the role, the woman deputy may find herself marginalized in discussions of policy issues except when asked to represent the female point of view. Baldridge *et al.*, in a study of college administration in the USA, found that the majority of women in senior academic posts were still excluded from the main arenas of policy-making and influence and that 'Not only do women serve on fewer committees, but they also report that the committees they do serve on are trivial' (1978, p. 192). (This gives support to Smith's (1975) view of the ruling class of men, quoted in Ch. 3.) Richardson discusses this sort of problem in the case of Joan Bradbury, the senior mistress at Nailsea Comprehensive, who expressed her frustration at having 'a feeling that the staff wanted to keep her in the role of a kind of "school mum"'(quoted in Richardson, 1973b, p. 228). Despite having responsibility for time-tabling and areas of administration, she reported that there was a 'reluctance of staff to recognize this side of her work', and in staff discussions she felt that her contributions were generally ignored: 'It seems nobody takes any notice until it comes out from a different face', she said (quoted on p. 230). Richardson goes on to comment that:

> [Her] feeling of having been unheard or ignored or forgotten was very strong; and it appeared to me that it was carrying something more than her own sense of frustration in the committee – something about the shared experience of women in general in a staff group like this, something about a sense of leftoutness, of being considered of little account, of having to leave the major-decisions to men, of denying their own capacity to take executive leadership even in a school in which girls had consistently out-numbered boys through its eleven years of existence. (p. 230)

Women in senior positions may also be diminished by ridicule (see Ch. 9). Cunnison (1985, p. 29) found in her High School study that the women on Scale 3 or above were the butt of jokes. Second, and clearly related to the sorts of frustrations experienced by women like Joan Bradbury, is the fact that women in senior positions are virtually always in a minority. This is discussed by Kanter in a study of the working lives of women in an American industrial corporation:

> The numerical distribution of men and women at the upper reaches created a strikingly different interaction context for women and for men. At local and regional meetings, training

programmes, task forces, casual out-of-the-office lunches with colleagues, and career review and planning sessions with managers, men were overwhelmingly likely to find themselves with a predominance of people of their own type – other men ... the culture of corporate administration and the experiences of men in it were influenced by this fact of numerical domination, by the fact that the men were the *many*. (1977, p. 206)

The question of numbers has its impact in a whole variety of ways on the personal experiences and likely success of the *few*, the women. They are often highly visible as a result of their minority, which can have its disadvantages in terms of the additional pressures it brings to bear on those who have 'only women' status and who 'become tokens; symbols of how-women-can-do, stand-ins for all women'. Some find themselves cast as outsiders, unable to enter the culture of an alien social world, constantly left out or ignored. This can lead to a *fear of visibility* and attempts to play down differences (Acker, 1980). Women in these positions may hide or minimize traits or behaviours that they see as distinctly feminine: 'They are under considerable psychological pressure to identify with the dominant male members rather than their own social category in all settings' (Marshall, 1984, p. 103). Or specific characters may be carved out for the token few which embody various stereotypes of female behaviour and male–female relationships – Kanter suggests mother (like Joan Bradbury), pet, seductress and iron maiden. Richardson supports Kanter's analysis: 'Ironically, the situation of being in a minority group of women, although considered quite an enviable one in a purely social setting, and usually experienced as such, can be an extraordinarily painful one in a work setting' (1973b, p. 232). Third, and again related closely to the two previous points, is the fact of discrimination against competent women. Several studies have explored attitudes towards successful and competent women. The argument is that men who find themselves challenged and beaten by a woman will experience a particular threat to their self-esteem and their belief system. One way of dealing with such threats is to develop hostility towards that which poses the threat – the high-performing woman. In one study, Hegen and Kahn found that:

a competent woman will be given the status commensurate with her performance, but the men she is working with will not like her, and she will be more likely than an equally performing man to lose her job. The fact that she will not be liked when competent, however, implies that the atmosphere – the reinforcement of categories – will work against her performing well. Therefore, high ability women may not perform up to their potentials. (1975, p. 372)

Buchan, in her autobiographical account of teaching in Australian schools, faced exactly this situation:

Efficient and competent females are constantly diminished. Seen as threatening, they are the target for denigrating comments about their femininity. There are numerous overt and covert pressures designed to encourage women to step gracefully aside and let men move up the ladder. (1980, p. 87)

Such a situation is based on the classic double-bind that high-achieving female students at school also face. If the woman outperforms men, she risks unpopularity and sometimes charges of being unfeminine; if she underachieves, she merely fulfils stereotypes about incompetence or being unable to deal with pressure or being unable to cope with the demands of a family and a job. For women, Marshall suggests, 'Organizational life can thus be seen as a continuing sequence of acceptability tests' (1984, p. 104).

Fourth, research indicates that women may find themselves disadvantaged in discussion situations by male dominance of talk. Again, Joan Bradbury suggests some of the difficulties. Researchers observing discussions in mixed groups have found a tendency for men to finish women's sentences, to interrupt women at will without incurring rebuke and to give limited response to those topics which are introduced by or advocated by women speakers. Smith suggests that 'Characteristically women talking with men use styles of talk which throw the control to others' (1975, p. 364). In these ways women involved in policy-making discussions may still find themselves and their views excluded from consideration.

Bearing these points in mind it is perhaps not surprising that a large proportion of women in organizations exempt themselves from participation in micro-political activity. The Baldridge et al. (1978) study of American colleges found in their sample that 40 per cent of men and 60 per cent of women considered themselves to be politically 'inactive'; that is, they rarely participated in policy-making activities. Furthermore, such involvement as is available to women may be yet another form of pseudo-participation; it suggests equality but in fact passes control. Either their contributions are confined to 'women's issues' or they remain totally unheard and unattended to; their presence is all that is required. In general terms the tendency is that women occupy a marginal position in the micro-politics of the school.

Race

If we still know relatively little about the employment experiences of women teachers and the dynamics of gender in schools, we know almost nothing at all about the employment experiences of teachers from racial and ethnic minorities. What does seem clear, however, is that almost all of the processes of discrimination outlined above with respect to women apply equally strongly to black teachers. They are massively underrepresented in the teaching force as a whole, and further underrepresented in posts of responsibility. This underrepresentation holds even in schools where the majority of pupils are black.

Interview material and case studies from a report on the experiences of West Indian teachers in London schools offer some insights into the micro-politics of race in the school and the effects of institutionalized and interpersonal racism:

I think it is a great struggle to get promotion if you are black. I have applied for other jobs in other schools. The heads seem to think about the image of the school and not your ability. To them the image of the school means that if a black person is seen about the school white parents will not send their children to the school. As a result of such thinking none of us at . . . school ever had the chance of visiting the primary schools or interviewing parents. That's one thing. With regard to head of department posts, it is easier for a white teacher after a year or two to get such jobs. For example, when X left, the head of department post was vacant. They did not consider giving Y the job. Instead, the scale was split. I'm sure it would not have happened like that if Y had been a white teacher. They also ask for experience where black teachers are concerned but they do not insist on it where white teachers are involved. I say this because the last head of remedial got the job – a Scale 4 – two years after she came out of training college. After two years, and she wasn't trained in remedial work. (Quoted in Gibbes, 1980, p. 13)

I must tell you, though, that between 1970 and 1978 I applied for various jobs – I must have written about 270 to 280 applications. During this period I had an interview for a head of department in a Catholic school. I was told by the head of the school: 'Didn't you realise that one of the things that I will have to take into consideration if you are appointed here is the fact that you are black?' I replied that if he had told me that my qualifications were not good I could do something about that. But I could not do anything about my colour. I told him I had good relationships with whites. I did not get the job. It was between this other chap and myself. There was no doubt about it – I had far greater experience than this chap and better qualifications (MA, Diploma in Educational Technology, and a Diploma in Education), but I did not get the job. I'm not going to say it could have been colour; it could have been a number of other factors, but the fact remained, I did not get the job. (Quoted in Gibbes, 1980, p. 15)

These two extracts indicate the operation of different criteria for appointments and promotions when black teachers are involved. These teachers see themselves as having very different promotion opportunities from those of their white colleagues:

The first year I was there two vacancies arose and those who left thought I would get the job. I used to cover for them. But the head got two white teachers to replace them. When I asked her about this she said to me: 'Oh. .... I forgot that you were here.' The school has about 60 per cent black children and only one and a half teachers on the staff. Myself, and the other black teacher left last term. The other teacher was asked to leave. I was told to find another job in another school. The head made it quite clear I could not expect to stay on there.

If this school had more black teachers at least it would give the children moral support, identity and some sort of ambition to know that a black person can be a teacher and can be in a position of authority. Some of the children would ask me: 'You have been here so long and you haven't got a proper post yet; how long is it going to take you? Why don't you walk out of here?' (Quoted in Gibbes, 1980, p. 19)

This extract raises again the issue of teachers acting as role models for pupils but it also points to the sense of marginalization confronting a black teacher in a predominantly white society. This is confirmed in the final quotation, from my own interview material:

> at the moment we are going through an amalgamation and they have three schools they are amalgamating and I went for an interview a few days ago for a senior post and the first thing that struck me was that there were twenty people on this [interview panel] and there wasn't a single black person. I mean, 50 per cent of the kids in that school are black. It really shook me. Because I've been going to all these ILEA conferences and they state categorically that their aim is to remove prejudice and to have black representation. And then they seem not to get straight round to that level for some reason. It's always that these things are contemplated but do not really happen in actual fact. (Year tutor, a London comprehensive)

The Swann Report noted that 'Although evidence of racial discrimination is hard to come by, it is clear that ethnic minority teachers have been and still are subject to racism both in gaining employment and in advancing their careers' (1985, Ch. 9, para. 5). In its own visits to schools the committee found numbers of ethnic-minority teachers 'in posts far below both their capabilities and experience'. The Commission for Racial Equality's (CRE) response to the Swann Report comments: 'We share the Committee's concern about the fact that few black pupils aspire to a career in teaching because of the "climate of racism ..."' (CRE, 1985, p. 16). The CRE's response also notes the danger that attempts to increase the numbers of ethnic-minority teachers may simply result in the creation of 'experts on race relations': 'Ethnic-minority teachers should be employed and accorded equal treatment because of their worth as qualified teachers' (p. 16). In some schools anti-racism is a topic of concern among the staff; in a few, black teachers' groups have been able to make a micro-political impact on policy-making. However, the role of race and ethnicity in school organization is often obscured by the 'noise' created by 'equal opportunity statements'. What is needed is more research.

9
Resources and relationships

Politics is an occupation for people who have great regard for themselves, little regard for others, and no regard for the truth. (Anon.)

In Chapters 4, 5 and 6 the main emphasis of the analysis was upon the vertical relationships between teachers and their senior colleagues. In Chapters 7 and 8 the competition between individuals produced by the organization and conceptualization of careers in teaching was examined. In this chapter the focus is upon horizontal relationships between individuals and groups within the staff of the school – the network of social relations. This network will be examined from two vantage points. First, via the 'informal' relations of the staffroom: this will lead us into the area of 'interpersonal politics' and will involve a further examination of some of the sub-groups of the school staff identified in Chapter 2. Second, via the 'formal' arrangement of teachers into departments: this will be based upon an investigation of conflicts over and access to and control over scarce organizational resources – time, territory, personnel, finance and influence. This will be extended into consideration of the public conduct of school business through the work of committees and meetings. As we shall see, the separation of 'formal' from 'informal' arenas in this context, a separation so often used by writers on the 'sociology of the school', is not sustainable for very long as a useful analytical device. It will serve here merely as a heuristic tool for the presentation of material. The social dynamics of school organization can only sensibly be understood in terms of the interpenetration of the professional and the personal. The structure of social relations in the school is the outcome of ongoing tensions and rivalries, conflicts and realignments which are played out in and through both formal and informal types of context. Organizational problems which are unresolved in one type of context may reappear, in a different guise, in the other. Also in this chapter I will be attempting to provide at least a flavour of the processes of micro-politics – the constitution and experience of politics in action.

The staffroom

Some accounts of staffroom life suggest that their action and culture may be understood primarily in terms of laughter, cynicism and anti-intellectualism (Woods, 1979). In many ways all staffrooms are alike. The categories of talk are remarkably similar, the jokes are the same and the grumbles and complaints virtually identical. However, beyond these similarities each staffroom also has much to reveal about the peculiarities of the school of which it is a part. The social relations of the staffroom are often a near direct reflection of the micro-political structure of the institution. Furthermore, these social relations will almost inevitably bear the marks of the particular political history of the institution – battles lost, ambitions frustrated, alliances which crumbled and trusts betrayed. This history will continue to have its impact in the interpretation of new events and the taking of sides in fresh disputes. As Cyert and March put it, 'The "accidents" of organizational genealogy tend to be perpetuated' (1963, p. 34).

Let us look at an account of staffroom social structure provided by Burgess (1983) describing Bishop McGregor Comprehensive. (Another example of this sort of analysis is to be found in Ch. 5 above.)

> It appeared to me that there were five major groups that formed in the common room during the morning breaks: the heads of houses, heads of departments, men's sports group, Newsom group and young women's group. None of these groups had exclusive membership. (Burgess, 1983, p. 73)

In each case the conversations of the groups reflected their main preoccupations in and/or outside the school. As Burgess goes on to say, 'the informal relationships among the teachers seemed to reinforce the basic divisions and duties which I had already recognized in the formal organization of the school' (p. 73). Such a social structure of relationships also operates to check and disseminate information and gossip (more of which later). It indicates a basis of shared interests and perspectives and the potential for political alliances. It may also act as a vehicle for the pursuit of career interests. Burgess again:

> many teachers considered that Sylvia Robinson sat there (with the Heads of House) in an attempt to gain membership of the group who helped run the school, and in the hope that she might one day take up a senior appointment. (p. 75)

As Burgess's groupings suggest, the co-identification of members cross-cuts the pattern of power and authority in the institution in a number of ways. There is a basic, but by no means absolute, division between houses and departments, between men and women, and between young and old (in organizational terms). (These divisions were discussed in Chs. 2 and 3 above.) This illustration points up the existence among the school staffs of two basic types of allegiance. The first type is based on the organizational categories of the school, departments, pastoral systems and administrative structures. Social relationships develop out of the roles that individuals occupy within the organization. The second type of allegiance cross-cuts and to some extent even undermines these role relationships. This is allegiance based upon shared interests (social, ideological and material), shared experience (of domination or subordination) and mutual obligation. The statuses, lines of communication, interpretations and relationships embedded in and revealed by the total social network, and the institutional meanings and understandings invested in this network, underpin the politics of what is, as well as what may be. The social network, both its formal and cross-cutting elements, embody and carry the working arrangements, the negotiated order of organizational life. This is the framework of social knowledge and political power and influence through which the organization functions. Those in favour and out of favour, the privileged and the excluded, the interested and uninterested, the conformist and deviant, the strong and the weak are represented and reconstituted in the structure and process of the social network. Thus informal talk is often essential for hearing about formal matters. The social network imposes boundaries upon the distribution of informal talk, and certain groups may be disadvantaged. Reskin suggests that this is the case in scientific research and that women may be particularly disadvantaged:

> Information flows into a local system through its members' contacts with outsiders and is transmitted within it during shop-talk in the labs and corridors and at lunch, in the locker room, over drinks ... the exclusion of women from conventional collegial relations, the substitution of gender-based role relations for collegial roles reduce women's access to informal communication. (1978, p. 21)

Marshall (1984) and Kanter (1977) observed the same situation affecting women in business organizations. A grasp of the network is essential (both for an analyst and political activist) in order to understand the processes and possibilities of decision-making. Who is consulted and who is not, whose opinion carries weight and whose does not, who is likely to oppose and who will support, who will support whom. What will elicit widespread agreement, what will provoke dissensus and disagreement. It is through the social network that the negotiated order is arrived at, maintained, and/or changed. Through gossip (as we shall see) the social network is a system of policing and sanctioning; through rumour it fills the gaps in official communication; through opposition it acts back against the formal hierarchy. There is a twin emphasis here: on the one hand, we must take account of the exercise of claims to power; on the other, we need to recognize that 'day-to-day interactions, agreements, temporary refusals, and changing definitions of the situations at hand are of paramount importance' (Day and Day, 1977, p. 132). The emphasis on the enactment of power is an emphasis on structure, on the relatively fixed quality of relationships between actors. The emphasis on interaction is an emphasis on process, on 'the fluid, continuously emerging qualities of the organization' (Day and Day, 1977, p. 132). Structure is obvious and fairly visible in organizational categories and roles. It is on occasion deliberately displayed in public events; rituals are employed to confirm order and celebrate and reinforce institutional verities. Process and interaction are less obvious and visible, normally available only in private and backstage settings where agreements may be tested and altered, verities challenged. In these settings attempts to interpret the organization through a rational code, and as something separate from the lives, motives and personalities of its members, breaks down completely. Role relations shade into friendship or hatred. Decisions are influenced by revenge, spite and personal preferences. Here the emotional life of the organization is played out. Grievances, complaints and grumbles are articulated; antipathies are allowed to surface and are 'acted out':

> Beneath this formal pattern of roles and relationships there are informal, largely emotional groupings in existence also, and all kinds of built-in attitudes and personal prejudices that affect people's behaviour towards one another and their ability to work together as a cooperative group. (Richardson, 1973a, p. 181–2)

And

> not only a family but any moral community contains relationships of enmity, as well as those of amity, and the former are as much a part of the fabric of a community as are the latter. (Bailey, 1977, p. 104)

This emotional milieu is not separate from the world of micro-politics; at this level 'the personal is political' and 'the political is personal'. The personal and the person are very much at stake. As Bailey asserts, politics 'is about institutional façades, make believe and pretence, lies and hypocrisy, and other such performances' (1977, p. 2).

Gossip, rumour and humour

To a great extent the backstage realities of organizational life have been neglected by theorists and researchers. They have been mesmerized by the obvious and deterred by the messiness involved in the analysis of the personal and emotional aspects of organizational functioning. Gossip, for example, has received considerable attention from anthropologists but few analysts (excepting Bailey, 1977) and researchers (excepting Burgess, 1983) appear to have recognized its role in the organization:

> Of the subject departments which were responsible for pupils in the whole school, only the head of the mathematics department did not hold a scale 5 post. Current gossip among the staff

attributed this to the fact that he was not a Catholic and because the department had some very poor examination results. (Burgess, 1983, p. 64)

When the teachers met in house heads' studies, it was a time for gossip to be exchanged about children, about fellow teachers and about the headmaster and his views on school routine. (Burgess, 1983, p. 66)

In my circle of friends there is quite a lot of gossip. There are one or two interesting personal relations on the staff. It's also about people applying for jobs and there's quite a lot of bitching. People say quite a lot of unpleasant critical things about others, behind their hands. There's a tremendous amount of speculation and comment about promotions, who's going for it, their strengths and weaknesses, this sort of thing. Gossip is one of the things that make the job bearable at times. (Social studies teacher)

In these examples some of the key features and functions of gossip in the organization are illustrated. As Gluckman points out, 'gossip does not have isolated roles in community life, but is part of the very blood and tissue of that life' (1963, p. 308). The classical anthropological interpretation, associated particularly with Gluckman, views gossip as a powerful but informal vehicle of social control. By its concentration on the untoward and illicit, gossip serves as a form of moral arbitration which penetrates beyond the surface features of apparent conformity. Using informal networks of communication gossipers bring into the half-open, 'behind the hand', infringements of social convention and potential threats to stability. They make the 'private' public. Indeed, the use of informal networks in this way can allow the maintenance of outward displays of harmony and friendship, public image can be maintained. Intimate relations between staff members, doubtful promotions and changes to established routines all, in different ways, threaten the social and moral order of the organization; they are the stuff of gossip. Thus:

gossip, and even scandal, have important positive virtues. Clearly, they maintain the unity, morals and values of social groups. Beyond this, they enable these groups to control the competing cliques and aspiring individuals of which all groups are composed. (Gluckman, 1963, p. 308)

Viewed negatively, however, gossip may act to stifle change and maintain outmoded values and expectations. It promotes power without responsibility: 'the listerner is expected to take the information on trust, not asking for evidence' (Bailey, 1977, p. 117). The tendency toward cohesion or fragmentation in gossip will vary. According to Du Boulay, the general state of affairs in the community is the critical factor: 'In the case both of a society that is getting stronger and one that is getting weaker, it is not that gossip changes its nature but the balance of forces working within it alters' (1974, p. 212). Gossip is invariably addressed to the person and to the personal. It may undermine people directly and their policies or interests indirectly. (See the case study of leadership succession in Ch. 6 above.) It is also, Bailey suggests, a form of experimentation, a way of testing in private what may later be said in public. In the micro-political arena gossip can be a devastating weapon in the hands of an unscrupulous opponent. In the struggle between competing interest-groups in the organization, denigration, in the form of 'slander and ridicule passed in gossip' (Paine, 1967) can be effective where rational argument has failed:

> Gossip is not used by the Sarakatsani to separate morality from self-interest, but to cast doubts upon the abilities and achievements of other families in order to improve one's own self-interested and competitive claims to moral recognition. (Paine, 1967, p. 281)

It generates unpleasantness and motivates argument. 'Quarrels, therefore, like gossip, are built into the structure of social relations, and it is a very rare person who can consistently rise above the pressures towards open conflict with others' (Du Boulay, 1974, p. 226). Gossip related to self-interest reinforces and exacerbates basic divisions. It gnaws at the cracks and gaps in the mutuality of an organization. It fosters antagonism, accusation, insult, exaggeration and indignation. Gossip is virtually impossible to anticipate and difficult to defend against. It constantly breaches the separation of public aspirations from private dreams. It undermines credibility and reputation. It is archetypically a political vehicle; as Bailey asserts, 'Politics is the art of bringing unacceptable myths into, and preserving one's own myths from derision' (1977, p. 8). Although, as Du Boulay (1974, p. 205) points out, not every piece of gossip is purposive. Gossip can be an innocent form of entertainment, a way of passing time.

Clearly, gossip is closely related to rumour. Indeed, gossip may be thought of as the communication channel for rumour, but I would want to reserve a particular role for rumour. As Shibutani (1966) puts it, rumour is a 'response to ambiguity'. It is a way of filling in missing information or explaining the inexplicable. Rumours operate in and around formal decision-making as a form of second-order accounting. The rumour looks beyond the obvious for 'the real reason for things':

> when Pat resigned a lot of people came up to me and said that she was pushed but she wasn't, but people wanted to believe that she was. (Deputy head)

> What do you do about rumours? I am currently suffering quite badly because of my deputy, who I'm very fond of. I get a right hassle because people keep saying he's having an affair with another teacher. I think he probably is. And this other teacher's been promoted recently so there's a big tension because people say 'Well, because they go to bed together, it means that if you go to bed with him, you get promotion'. (Headteacher)

The rumours here serve to explain promotions. It tells us why it was that one person got the job while others did not. In this way it fills in and explains where there is no other information. Rumours are at their most rife in the absence of other more reliable sources of information. Rumours may 'spread like wildfire' during periods of uncertainty, when redeployments are proposed or amalgamations are in the offing; they provide a temporary respite from collective insecurity and individual ignorance. Like gossip they are usually unaccountable, their source cannot be traced. They are passed on with their provenance always once removed. Some rumours turn out to be true of course; others, probably the majority, have only fleeting credibility.

In most organizations useful information is scarce and communication networks are usually tightly circumscribed. The 'professional' gossiper plays a crucial role in the informal management of information and is both a giver and receiver of information: 'He has "long ears" and part of his art lies in arranging a constant flow of information to himself' (Paine, 1967, p. 283); 'there are certain dependable sources of information to which people may go when other informants fail' (Du Boulay, 1974, p. 207). Information is a source of power in the organization, and the person 'in the know' may be sought after and favourably perceived by colleagues. We can distinguish between 'information' that is most effective when disseminated widely and that which has best effect with limited circulation. Thus, while the gossiper has an ongoing vested interest in talk, he or she may on occasion want to make strategic decisions about who to tell and who not to tell; in other words, what audience to address. A similar problem arises when humour is deployed. Gossip and rumour are powerful but fragile channels of communication. They are arts of subversion. Humour may be used in a similar way. It is one of the most effective presentational styles for debunking in any situation.

Hostility can be expressed 'through the medium of sarcasm, ridicule, irony, satire, invective, caricature, parody, burlesque and so on' (Woods, 1979, p. 212). Humour and gossip are frequently paired in political machinations. The funny remark is often camouflage for derision and can be a potent equalizer between otherwise unevenly matched opponents. It may:

> express approval or disapproval of social form and action, express common group sentiments, develop and perpetuate stereotypes, relieve awkward or tense situations and express collective sub rosa approbaton of action not explicitly approved. (Stephenson, 1951, p. 570)

Thus humour is deployed defensively, as a form of indirect, informal social control, but it is also an aggressive medium. Political points may be scored through the witty riposte. An opponent's frailties or past failings may be alluded to via the apparently innocuous jest. As Woods points out, humour may be employed as a political weapon either to deride those in positions of authority or to ridicule rivals: much staffroom humour takes the form of mocking, embarrassment, or compromise of senior personnel, often by "subversive ironies"' (1979, p. 216) and 'Interdepartmental rivalry frequently hovers on the borders separating humour from malice' (p. 234). Again we are tapping the emotional dimension of organizational life, the personal antipathies and long-held grudges which both fuel and inevitably arise out of the political process. The 'mindless hostility' (Bailey, 1977) which underlies at least some of the surface rationalities of institutional discourse should not be left out of account when trying to explain policy and decision-making. It is easy to assume conditions of mutual trust and consideration from the theorist's armchair but difficult to sustain such assumptions from the ethnographer's armchair in the corner of the school staffroom.

A great deal of lip-service has been paid in organizational theory to the importance of the informal aspects of organizational life. However, the informal has been treated effectively as a residual category beyond analysis and beyond study. Little is really known about organizational behaviour in backstage settings. None the less, the interpenetration of formal and informal is real, and the informal needs to be incorporated *analytically* into any comprehensive attempt at theorizing. Indeed, in a micro-political analysis the informal assumes even greater significance, as I have tried to demonstrate. Social relations are frequently, by default, a vehicle for decision-making, amendments to rules and formal arrangements and information exchange. Informal channels of communication are crucial in the development (or loss) of status and reputation, in the maintenance of influence and in the subsidiary decision-making (in corridors and offices) which accompanies resource allocation and budget distribution. All three aspects are represented in interdepartmental relations in the school and in the maintenance of departmental status.

Baronial politics

In the middle ages the conflicts between English barons were essentially concerned with two matters: wealth and power. In the school the concerns and interests of academic and pastoral barons are fundamentally the same: allocations from the budget, both in terms of capitation monies and in relation to appointments, timetable time and control of territory (teaching rooms, offices, special facilities), and influence over school policies. Clearly, to a great extent, in the micro-political process these concerns are inseparable: 'If politics is regarded as conflict over whose preferences are to prevail in the determination of policy, then the budget records the outcomes of this struggle' (Wildavsky, 1968, p. 192).

In Chapter 2 the general conflict between the pastoral and the academic was considered. Examples were quoted where one of these coalitions of interest had achieved supremacy over and against the other. Here I want to deal more specifically with the disputes and struggles *between* subject departments, particularly in and around the concomitant issues of resource allocation and departmental status.

In the secondary school, leaving aside the pastoral-care structure, subject departments are usually the most significant organizational divisions between teachers as colleagues. On the one hand, the department provides and maintains a special sense of identity for the teacher; it can be a basis for communality. 'The pedagogic subject department forms an epistemic and spatial boundary maintaining community that its members share as an experience of being a common "kind" of teacher' (Smetheram, 1979, p. 1), they share a speciality. On the other hand, as I have indicated, the department is the basis for special interests and internecine competition; it is a political coalition:

> definitions of centrality and marginality arise through the superimposition of departmental boundaries on speciality boundaries. One of the significant consequences of this is a budgetary separation which creates competitive groups. Boundaries are rationalized through decisions taken about what is central and what is peripheral as they are exemplified in allocation of time, money, and staff and even students. (Esland, 1971, p. 106)

Thus budgets forge and perpetuate (and occasionally change) a pattern of status and a distribution of influence. The competition between departments is a competition between unequals. Relative status and influence become embedded in the curriculum structure of the school and more immediately in the timetable. (Once established, this fixed structure is difficult to alter, either by outside agencies or internal interest groups.) In practice the 'voice' of any particular department, both in relation to policy issues and/or resource decision-making, is effectively limited by whether it is expanding, remaining static or on the defensive.

The specific distribution of the strong baronies and weak baronies *will* differ between institutions and will change over time; it is the outcome of on-going conflicts and rivalries. None the less, there are typical patterns, and clearly the expectations of influential outside audiences do enhance the claims made by certain subjects and detract from those of others. Richardson gives a flavour of strengths and weaknesses in her account of Nailsea Comprehensive:

> Two of the most persistent images that I carried over from the 1968–9 session into the following one concerned the modern languages and science departments on the one side and the geography and history departments on the other. The former I saw as the 'giant' departments which seemed able to make their own conditions regardless of changes elsewhere in the system – almost, at times, to be holding the staff up to ransom. In contrast to my impression of power and independence in these areas, the departments of geography and history seemed to me to be suffering more than any others (except perhaps classics) from the problems of encroachment, erosion and loss of wholeness. (1973b, p. 90)

The metaphor of baronial politics seems particularly apt in this case. As Richardson expresses the situation at Nailsea, it is the curriculum that is at stake. With curriculum control comes influence and control over resources; without it there is political impotence. In addition, the strength of modern languages and science also raises the question of the state of their mutual relations as well as their disposition towards weaker departments:

> Were their departments allies, rivals, or equally powerful independent forces in the school? Both were staffed almost entirely by specialist teachers; neither did any appreciable sharing of personnel with other departments; both insisted, or appeared to insist, on finer setting by ability throughout the school than any other departments did; both were concerned with the development of new methods of teaching that involved the purchase, control and maintenance of expensive technical equipment. (Richardson, 1973b, p. 92)

However, as Richardson goes on to point out, there were occasions when the giants clashed. Although these clashes did little to weaken their entrenched positions. It was the geography and history departments that seemed to be continually losing out in the battle for resources and control over the timetable:

> I began to think of geography as a department that was trapped – or perhaps suspended – between the arts and the sciences, having

allegiances to both sides and a visible link with both sides through geology, but fearing encroachment from the arts side because of the uncertainty about where the subject was rooted. In the recurring discussions about the humanities course, geography was always linked (uneasily perhaps) with history, as mathematics seemed, in the recurring discussions about mixed-ability grouping, to be uneasily linked with science.

If I saw geography as an area that was being crushed between opposing forces or being stretched in opposite directions, I saw history as an area that felt itself to be shrinking. The encroachments on its territory from humanities in the lower school, from social studies in the middle school, from general studies in the upper school, and perhaps also to a lesser extent from ancient history through classics, had to do partly with the loss of recently acquired subject matter, even of new approaches first worked out in terms of history, and partly with a loss of contact with younger children. (pp. 95–6)

Several processes affecting the status and political 'voice' of subject departments are evident in the examples drawn from Richardson's study. It is apparent that the fortunes of certain departments are rising while others are in decline. In some areas, like humanities, new empires are being carved out. In others, like history, declarations of independence are undermining status claims which previously seemed inviolate. In the first case, smaller, weaker subjects areas are being swallowed up in expanding conglomerates. In the second, smaller subjects are emerging as separate entities to make their own claims for time, territory, money and personnel.

The impetus for the emergence of new subjects can take several different forms but is inevitably surrounded by political struggle and intrigue. In some cases the arrival of a new subject, and its struggle for departmental status, is shortlived. Goodson (1987) provides one example in his examination of the birth pangs of European studies. The 'subject', such as it was, developed from a combination of idealism, what Bucher and Strauss refer to as a sense of mission, in this case the creation of European consciousness among British school-children, and pragmatism, 'as a vehicle for motivating the less able in languages lessons' (1961, p. 9). In schools it was the latter that was the main driving force; Goodson quotes a number of examples, among them:

> Well you see ... I think as far as we are concerned this was a conscious turning away from what was beginning to develop and then people were starting to say 'what are we going to do with the youngsters who are not learning French or German?'. ... From the point of view of timetable convenience they ought to be doing something associated ... 'let them learn about Germany, you know and what you have for tea in Brussels or something' ... we were so frightened that this was what European studies was going to become, some sort of dustbin ... I think we have consciously turned away from that and although we haven't got to lose sight of it eventually, I think we've got to come back to terms with this after we've done the other things. ... I think we've got to go ahead from our middle school into our sixth form first and get that thing right and get the subject established with status ... then we may be able to add on these less able youngsters.
>
> Well, when I became Head of Humanities they also made me Head of European Studies ... which had been taught on and off for several years to the 'dumbos' in languages. ... So I organised a meeting to discuss it as a subject – only the young assistant teachers were interested. I went to the Head and asked for money. I was given £150. (Quoted on p. 215)

Here we have both the strengths and weaknesses of an assertive claimant for subject status. On the one hand, European studies teachers can claim to be heard and make demands on school resources in so far as they take responsibility for problematic groups of pupils, the less able. On the other hand, one crucial measure of subject status is taken from access to the most able pupils, particularly in the establishment of sixth-form A-level courses. Here European studies has a problem. The first teacher clearly recognizes this and is suggesting a strategy which will distance the 'subject' from its less able clients and go instead for recruits in the sixth form. But this is exactly the sort of strategy that is likely to meet with opposition from other subjects. To capture sixth-formers for European studies means luring them away from other subject choices. This threatens access to sought-after teaching allocations, capitation, status and perhaps chances of promotion within other departments. The second quotation also suggests contradictory pressures and possibilities. The interest of young teachers can provide important inputs of energy and commitment necessary for the development of new ideas and materials. However, these teachers lack institutional status; there may be considerable political disadvantage as a result of this and not having friends in high places. None the less, from the point of view of the young adherents a new 'subject' area can offer the potential of career enhancement and increased promotion possibilities, although these possibilities clearly rest upon the successful establishment of that 'subject'. Again Goodson provides a clear example of the problems:

> I'm very disillusioned about my future. Well it hasn't given me a future after five years so I can't see that it will suddenly give me a future in the next few years. I don't think I could have done much more than I have done. I got involved with the County syllabus, had a lot of contacts with the European Resources Centre, one thing and another, and I thought this can only be of benefit to my career. But it's been going on and I've been doing things and doing things and it's done me no good whatsoever. You know I'm still where I was when I came here seven years ago. I just don't know really . . . obviously I've become disillusioned, disheartened. (Quoted on p. 17)

This teacher clearly sees his career tied closely to the development of his subject. The success of work put in is measured in terms of creating a 'future'. To a great extent the teacher is the subject. Their fortunes are inextricably linked.

The conflict potential posed by the rise of a new 'subject' like European studies is increased further if claims are made which actually involve enchroachment into the subject matter of other departments. This is often a problem for the 'subjects' which, like European studies, have an interdisciplinary orientation. Much of the failure of interdisciplinarity in the 1960s and 1970s can be accounted for in terms of micro-political resistance. While in content and pedagogical terms interdisciplinary work makes perfect sense, in micro-political terms it looks like empire-building, and it is rational for those who see their interests threatened to resist, to defend their patch. Again Goodson's European studies teachers recognized the problems:

In a place like this departments are huge and they like to keep their legality. It's [i.e. the construction of a new subject] all a problem of trying to cross barriers which have been there for a long time. However well you get on with people it's still a thought in the back of their mind that their empire could be chipped away at. Interdisciplinary studies are always going to be in that situation. (Quoted on p. 220)

When attempts are made to separate off a new subject from its parent discipline – European studies from languages, drama from English, humanities from history – there are material interests at stake. The new boundaries involve a new distribution of resources – someone gets more and someone else less. Many a proposed innovation has floundered upon the opposition of potential losers in subject restructuring. As we saw in Chapter 2, change cannot usefully be examined without attention to institutional micro-politics.

When structural change does occur the new divisions are quickly reinforced by new allegiances. New identities are forged:

What ties a man more closely to one member of his profession may alienate him from another: when his group develops a unique mission, he may no longer share a mission with others in the same profession. (Bucher and Strauss, 1961, p. 227)

Where relationships between teachers are poor almost any attempt at innovation can be seen in terms of the political motivations or career aspirations of the instigators. One of the headteachers I interviewed described a group of teachers who had pressed for the school to become involved in PGCE work with the nearby university as 'suffering from frustrated ambition'.

European studies provides one example of a 'failed' innovation, a 'subject' which, with a few exceptions, was unable to establish itself as an independent department with its own resources and career structure. In contrast, classics provides a case where a once great subject has declined and virtually disappeared from the timetables of most comprehensive schools. Stray (1985) offers a case study of the declining fortunes of classics in Llangarr Comprehensive. The department and its teachers experienced a series of setbacks during the 1970s which marked a gradual loss of political credibility and status for the subject. The first blow came when Latin was made optional:

> In the head of departments' meeting ... the head confronted us with a sheet of paper which showed the options ... we were horrified to see that Latin had been put against History. Whereas at present in the third form it was a class subject for the top two classes. (Stray, 1985, p. 39)

Such a change has both practical and symbolic implications. Symbolically, it indicates the removal of Latin from the assured status position of being a compulsory subject, a crushing blow. Access to pupil numbers is threatened and valued teaching, to the top classes, is at risk. Politically, two points are significant: first, the lack of consultation – the department was faced with a *fait accompli*; second, the inability of the department to mount a serious defence or call upon support from colleagues in other departments. The classics teachers were soon to find themelves further beleaguered. To add insult to injury, the reorganization of the option system also redefined classical studies as a subject for the less able, for those pupils who were prevented from continuing with French or Welsh:

> We get the poorer children, the difficult children. Now in a sense you may say this is justice, since we've had the cream in the past ... but by virtue of the choice, the pupils we're getting, they're the rejects. (Quoted in Stray, 1985, p. 216)

As noted already, a critical indicator of the status of a subject is the status of those it teaches. Once again the fortunes of the subject must be associated with the career opportunities of the teachers. The classicists began to find themselves under pressure in this regard from unsympathetic colleagues:

> One remarked that there were 'several people who don't see why a subject they think is on the decline should have two graded posts'; points are taken away from their own departments such as ... practical subjects. They see themselves as more relevant to the comprehensive set-up than Classics. (p. 41)

Stray notes that the rivalry over promotion in Llangarr became ingrained in the micro-political processes of the school. The processes of influence were through these informal channels discussed above:

> The merger of the three different staffs and the tensions caused by 'overpointing' and the scarcity of promotions, in particular, discouraged open discussion; instead points were made via sarcastic jokes, the mutter in the corridor, separate trips into the 'administrative suite'. (p. 42)

Classics was often the subject and butt of these informal pressures and behind-the-scenes manoeuvrings. It was clearly a subject on the slide. There were few collegial scruples preventing the subject from being kicked when it was down. By 1974 Stray notes that 'The Llangarr classicists had thus suffered successive dislodgements towards an uncertain and marginal position. Underlying this process was a shift in the relations, and relative power, of the knowledge, occupation and organization systems' (p. 44).

In many schools both classics and European studies teachers find themselves locked into a rather precarious and often unrewarding existence on the periphery of the curriculum. Their 'missions' (Bucher and Strauss, 1961) have failed and in the battle for institutional status they have been, for the present at least, routed. Falling rolls, a teacher who leaves, or any other contingency might extinguish the subject entirely. But clearly, in contrast, some new 'subjects' do make it, do establish themselves as secure and (relatively) permanent, taken-for-granted parts of the school curriculum.

Here again we must recognize that the rise and fall of subjects and departments is not solely dependent upon the outcomes of micropolitical manoeuvring. The impact of changing patterns of external legitimation is also significant, Reid makes the point that:

> For while it may appear that the professionals have power to determine what is taught (at school, district or national level, depending on the country in question), their scope is limited by the fact that only those forms and activities which have significance for external publics can, in the long run, survive. (1984, p. 68)

While I would accept this statement in general terms, I would still want to argue that the legitimation of external publics is essentially a constraint upon or opportunity for the interest-groups and coalitions at work in the school. These constraints and opportunities are mediated through the micro-politics of the instituition (see Ch. 10 for further discussion).

The impressive growth of computer studies is a good example. The high level of public awareness of 'high-technology', the massive infusion of government support and monies, and programmes to get a computer into every school, have provided a powerful base for the take-off in computing courses. Certainly, in some schools, departments of computer studies have emerged, in others such initiatives remain under the auspices of the mathematics departments. In some schools battle ensues to ensure that computing is seen to be relevant across a range of subjects; in others it is a specialist subject in its own right; in still others the impact of new technology has been minimal. The differences between schools can be explored and explained in terms of micro-political factors. The control of expensive, high-status hardware is at stake. So too are the reputations and futures of departments. The ability to respond to and cope with the new technologies may be critical in the long-term survival of certain subjects. This is not simply a matter of responding effectively but being seen to be able to respond. Once again it must be said that new curriculum initiatives like computing or TVEI or CPVE provide new career avenues; they also threaten established patterns of preferment. Indeed, a whole range of scarce and valued resources are subject to renegotiation. New skills are in demand, older skills are threatened with extinction. Interestingly, newer, younger teachers may be better trained and prepared, while others, keen to exploit the new opportunities, may turn to in-service courses. Awareness of new developments and up-to-date contacts, especially those which might provide equipment or money, are themselves important resources in the ebb and flow of status and influence.

External legitimation, or delegitimation is just one factor at work in affecting the standing of departments and teachers. Innovations can be stifled by established interests or 'knowledgeable' young teachers may find themselves being sponsored by older, more influential colleagues. Outcomes, in terms of curriculum change cannot be assumed to be the result of rational, bureaucratic procedures. The departmental barons will not concede control easily. To a great extent, change or resistance to change will depend upon the relative influence of protagonists over organizational decision-making.

Influence at court

The complex political calculus which underpins the actual distribution of status, and resources, in the school is by no means easy to unpick. One way to begin is by examination of those cases which fall outside the typical pattern. For example, where mathematics, or science or English departments have failed to achieve status and resource preferment, or where departments like drama, CDT or music have done so.

Oak Farm Comprehensive (Ball and Lacey, 1980) provides a case of the former kind. Here the English department is to be found in a marginal position. The head of department explained his predicament:

> We have three full-time English teachers including myself. . . . So that at the moment we have ten people who are teaching partly in the department or wholly. I've been fighting for more full-time English specialists since I've been here. We ranged from 22 teaching English, for a while it was 17, now it's ten. (Quoted on p. 42)

Despite the improvements, the head of department faces a difficult situation; he is unable to draw upon the support of a group of teachers committed fully to the English department in any negotiations over resources. Indeed, the status of English as a department in its own right is questionable. Most of his staff have major commitments elsewhere:

> it involved one trying to bring as much pressure as possible to bear on the Head and Deputy Head and other influential people in the school to make them see that English was being too much fragmented. And the most important subject, at least I consider it so. . . . I know that every teacher is a teacher of English, the old tag, but it doesn't work out that way. (Quoted on p. 158)

The head of department seems to acknowledge his own lack of influence in the school and the failure among those who have influence, to recognize his case as valid. English has failed to acquire the infrastructural base which accompanies and underpins subject status:

> It's only for three years that I've had a second in charge. It was

thought that there were other priorities. And also physical things like an office. Which is quite a sore point, it hasn't been recognised in that way. But this was determined not so much by a positive opposition but by the circumstances which prevail in the school which make it difficult. I just asked in this financial year that some provision be made whereby I could get a base to work from, but although it appeared on the list of requests, when it was sorted into priorities, it missed the priorities and was shelved again. (Quoted on p. 159)

Without a group of specialist teachers English cannot establish its credibility and assert demands for resources and facilities. There is a vicious circle. While the head of English continues to have no influence over the definition of new appointments, there is little possibility of such specialists being appointed. English will continue to be regarded as something that anyone can teach. Once established in the culture and history of the institution, collective assumptions of this kind are difficult to break down. As the head of department sees it, the preferences and background of the head-teacher are crucial factors at work here:

it so largely depends on the backgrounds and previous careers of Headmasters. My present Headmaster has done quite a lot since he's been here for the science department; which is a good thing. But I feel that English is not recognised as firmly and as widely as it ought to be. (Quoted on p. 159)

In the same vein, St John Brooks (1983) provides an account of an English department in a Bristol comprehensive which as a result of ideological differences with the headteacher is also excluded from influence over school policy. Indeed, to a great extent the department was unwilling to engage with the accepted procedures of debate and policy-making.

The department as a whole could not defend their position in a manner comprehensible or acceptable to most of the other teachers, especially the Headmaster. By rejecting the bureaucratic world of institutions and the realm of public argument and debate, along with the kind of justification it demands, such romantic individuals or groups are destined to remain forever marginal. (St John Brooks, 1983, p. 56)

By opting out of school micro-politics, the department marginalized itself and put itself under pressure. Sponsorship by the head can clearly do much to advance the position of a department both in terms of status and resources. An antagonistic head can make life very difficult. As suggested in Chapter 4, the relationship between headteacher and head of department will to a great extent rely on mutual obligation. The head will expect efficiency or loyalty or both, in return for continued support. This relationship will thus depend both upon the *quality* of personal relationships, a matching of styles and some sharing of goals and ideologies. However, this is not the only relationship to be attended to: the head of department must face in three directions, towards the headteacher and senior management and a concern with whole-school policy, towards the interpersonal arena of departmental relationships and the specific policy interests of the department, and across towards other heads of department as colleagues with shared problems or competing interests. Taafe quotes a head of creative arts from a London comprehensive on the qualities of a head of faculty required by his headteacher:

> To be a senior head you must be very flexible and devious. Flexible to fit in with the headmaster, back off if necessary. Devious, to get your faculty to do what the headmaster wants. (1980, p. 23)

Careful tending of their patch, positive support from colleagues and positive indicators of department success can put the head of department in a powerful political position. In some cases, from the headteacher's point of view, heads of department can become too powerful. From Taafe's study again, the head of mathematics explains:

> If you look at the staff overall, forgetting creative arts for the moment, you will not find any large departments. I think this is a conscious effort on the part of the Head to break down influential bodies on the staff. Certainly maths has no influence. (Quoted on p. 39)

The head of languages takes up the point:

> Look at Science, you have specialists there, it is probably the largest department in the school. The last Head of Department

was very strong, utterly ruthless, out for what he could get for his department. Science was a potent influence in the school. I don't think the Head liked it. Look at the new appointment, he's wet, the exact opposite. The result is science now is not an influential body. (Quoted on p. 40)

Two major themes of the analysis re-emerge here. One is the role of influence; here we see the problematic nature of *too much* influence, at least as far as the head is concerned. The other is the crucial importance of control of appointments and promotions; heads can do a great deal to bolster their position politically by the appointments that they make. However, it should not be assumed that it is the headteacher who is always successful in power struggles with departments. Latus offers the following account of ground gained by a head of department against opposition from 'the hierarchy':

The English department is led by an academically strong Head of Department who in addition to taking over in difficult circumstances also had to assert his authority over his own specialism. This involved challenging the deputy headmaster, a member of the department, who was exercising positional power and thus depriving Mr Jenks [the HOD] of authority and status. In ousting his rival Mr Jenks also secured hitherto unknown autonomy for the department and this in turn led to gains on other fronts e.g. the right to be present at departmental appointments, and also a policy change: English specialists are appointed rather than general subject teachers offering some English. (1977, p. 36)

Here the head of department gained ground in exactly those areas which proved so intractable for the head of English at Oak Farm.

The political role of the head of department is clearly significant not only in relations with the head but also in dealings with their own department members. If the heads of department are unable to produce and maintain at least an outward display of unity and coherence within their departments, then it becomes extremely difficult to mount a convincing case for new initiatives, additional resources or changes to the timetable. Both ideological and inter-personal tensions can arise to undermine the unity of a department, and heads of department find themselves more or less able to deal with the difficulties which ensue. (See Jago, 1983, Ch. 8, for a disussion of leadership problems in subject departments.) If strong heads of department can create problems, so too can weak ones. If matters threaten major disruption, then the headteacher may step in.

Meadows (1981) describes a situation at Millrace Comprehensive where an existing head of department is eased out of her position and replaced, through a series of manoeuvres carefully managed by members of the department and the headteacher. Clearly, the head of department was not well regarded by her colleagues:

> Mary Standen gave the impression of perpetual bewilderment. She had a narrow, Scots', rigorous view ... but she was out of her depth. Her qualities just weren't right. ... The department was put in charge of an incompetent. (Colleague 1, quoted on p. 14)

> At the interview some were even worse and so she got the job. She was administratively conscientious, but never well organized. She tended to listen to the last person, therefore the department's autonomy went. (Colleague 2, quoted on p. 14)

The members of department attempted their own solution to the problems created for them. Informal arrangements, a negotiated order of sorts, were brought into play to fill and to circumvent the formal vacuum:

> things tended to get done via the back door ... she was prepared to let me get on, but I was a senior teacher in her eyes. She was very conscious of protocol. But she wouldn't give Victor responsibility for the middle school course. So, last year, the conspirators explored ways of moving things along. Victor produced a job description. It accepted Mary's nominal control, but the responsibility for English was split between different people. The head accepted the job description. (Colleague 1, quoted on pp. 14–15)

With the retirement of the school librarian, despite the appointment of a temporary replacement, the head saw a solution to the English department difficulties:

> He saw the situation and worked out a way of getting a new

head of department. He created a department – Library and Resources – and moved Mary Standen into it. (Colleague 3, quoted on p. 16)

The temporary incumbent was understandably not pleased; she had believed that the head had promised the permanent library post to her.

> Abruptly he pushed Mary Standen sideways into my job. He took five minutes to tell me. I was shocked but I went back and argued with him for half-an-hour. I told him he was unfair. He is incapable of running a school. He has no feelings. He will walk over people. (Colleague 4, quoted on p. 16)

Once again the interplay between institutional politics and individual careers is in evidence. Political solutions tend to dispense advantage to some and disadvantage to others.

What I have been attempting here is to establish some of those factors which enter into the making and breaking of departmental reputations and subject status, concentrating on the degree of influence that may be available to a department in varying circumstances. Certainly, however, as the case of classics illustrates, there are a number of objective indicators which enter into the appraisal of any department. The inability to attract option choices, a poor teaching or disiplinary record and poor examination results will, over time, undermine the position of even the most well entrenched subject. This is evident in the following interview extract where a headteacher explains his view of the mathematics department in his school:

> Their track record now is one which says 'No I'm not going to do this'. In the summer they wanted to have single-sex maths. Well, I said no to that. I had already given them £2000 above their normal capitation to invest in SMILE. So they had this heavy investment in SMILE and immediately, within one year, they wanted to move on to something else. The difficult thing is why is it that the English results are good and the maths results are so appalling. Its roughly 10 per cent O-level in mathematics and 58 per cent in English, across the fifth-year group. It must be to do with the teaching, and with the organization. Now, the maths department has a problem because of the head of maths.

In the contemporary jargon, heads of departments are 'middle managers', with all the implications of 'line' responsibility that that suggests. It may be that baronial politics and the feudal relationships through which they currently work will be replaced by the bureaucratic procedures and relationships of management theory. On the other hand, the pristine language of management may only serve to obscure the real struggles over policy and budgets – who gets what, when and how?

Hidden agendas and sub-texts: the politics of meetings and committees

A great deal of 'apparent' decision-making and policy-making in organizations is focused on official 'moments', like meetings and committees. However, I hope by now to have firmly established the point that the understanding of 'real' decision-making is not as simple as recording the public discussions which take place at such 'moments'. Decision-making is a micro-political process which embraces a whole set of formal and informal arenas of interaction, confrontation and negotiation. To a great extent the official 'moments', the committees and meetings, have only a symbolic role; they celebrate an ideology of participation and collective affirmation. They are more pertinent analytically as symbolic vehicles for performances of power and control than for the content of their deliberations. Here we enter again the realm of political talk introduced in Chapter 5. To paraphrase Bernstein, schools are places organized around talk. The work of teaching is, to a great extent, accomplished via talk and the accomplishment of organization also relies heavily on the verbal medium. As suggested in Chapter 5, particular definitions of the school are established and maintained through talk. I shall look at two main kinds of talk event in school organization: meetings, like staff or departmental meetings; and committees, like the pastoral board or senior management committee. However, this distinction is not intended to be very precise.

School meetings signify a degree of openness and involvement. An opportunity is created for lower participants to express their views; there is the possibility of an articulation of dissatisfaction, of initiatives for change, of challenge to prevailing perspectives. In reality such occurrences seem rare. The appearance of openness is in effect a moment of closure. The degree of formality which surrounds these events, the situational constraints entered into, and the ritual re-enactments of hierarchy that they display normally provide for a pre-emption of available forms and topics of talk. In the classroom it is the teacher who asserts 'ownership' of the talk (Sacks, Schegloff and Jefferson, 1974). Verbal exchanges are typically reduced to a two-party structure, moving between the teacher and the pupils. Pupil contributions are monitored and framed by the teacher's initiations, evaluations and commentary (Ball, 1983; Stubbs, 1983). So it is in the staff meeting: discussions are typically initiated and controlled by the headteacher, the staff more often than not finding themselves in a passive role. They become recipients of information rather than participants in discussion. What passes for discussion is in fact a linear structure of one-to-one exchanges between the head and individual teacher contributors. Jago makes the following comment on the staff meetings she observed at Millrace Comprehensive, and she highlights the sense of hierarchy that is embedded in the conduct of these meetings:

> while the Head did not in fact monopolise the meeting, even his delegation of roles in it to others tended to sound, as it were, rehearsed. I could not see that this was escapable, since to conjure the illusion of sponteneity in such a meeting would be to move yet further from reality; but sitting on the other side of the divide between Hierarchy and Staff I felt something of the alienating effect produced. To return to Harris' (1973) image: the public arena of the Staff Meeting in itself virtually forces Head and Staff into their relative roles as Parent and Child. (1983, p. 189)

Gronn's recordings in staff meetings in Australian high schools reveal the same pattern:

> What the transcripts disclose is standard, unspectacular, and mundane, and replicated in hundreds of staffrooms across the state school system. An administrator has directed his staff to see part of the organizational world in his terms. He has defined the situation and they are expected to fall in line with that view. (1983, p. 12)

The sense of alienation mentioned by Jago, above, is not infrequently expressed by teachers themselves in their responses to meetings. Evans gives two examples in his study of Sageton Comprehensive:

> The number of meetings we have to attend here is just ridiculous. How many of these items could he have dealt with on his desk? There was no decision made. I'm sure he's becoming incapable of making a decision. He keeps putting it off. I don't think we can let him move S, that ought to go round the table. I'm sure everybody would want her to stay in that room. He says management is important, so we ought to take a decision on it, but we don't. It's all decided in his room. If he says something like that . . . I'm sure that's what he'll do. (Quoted in Evans, 1985, p. 21)

There are two interesting and relevant paradoxes in this last comment. First, the teacher seems to be complaining about the number of meetings, but this complaint is embedded in a dissatisfaction with what is achieved at the meetings – nothing, in his view. Second, he appears to criticize the head for not taking decisions, but again this is in fact pointing to a failure to allow, or determination not to allow, decisions to be taken in meetings, collectively. Decisions are made but they are made elsewhere, in the head's office. The meetings are for other purposes clearly. This illustrates again the powerful distinction heads seek to maintain between consultation and decision-making. These concerns were echoed by a junior member of the Sageton staff:

> It's a problem of the quality of the meeting not the quantity. We could triple the meetings and not make things better. We are talking about waste of ideas. There's a frustration at not being allowed to speak. People feel abandoned. (Quoted on p. 21)

Swidler (1979) offers an account of the exact reverse of this situation. In a democratically run 'free school' meetings were long and exhausting opportunities to reaffirm collective solidarity and examine basic ideological positions: 'teachers took every opportunity to prolong discussion, suggest new complications, and turn practical decisions into occasions for exploring basic values, goals and commitments' (Swidler, 1979, p. 84). In contrast, in most state schools the staff meeting is typically an opportunity for the official definition of the school to be rehearsed and re-enacted. The teachers are cast in the position of audience. The teachers are not so much

participants in, as subjects of the meeting. The meeting is a camouflage, a diversion. The ritual of information-giving and consultation
is asserted over any substantive involvement in decision-making.
Talk in these circumstances is talk about control and 'is about being
in authority. This talk is disputation about authorative action as such,
rather than disputation on the particular topic in hand which is what
the talk comprises of' (Gronn, 1983, p. 12). In Hargreaves's (1981)
terms, interactional and institutional power are closely interwoven
here. The interactional structure of the event represents the institutional structure of the organization. Furthermore, given this
structure, the headteacher has certain advantages and possibilities
which may be deployed tactically to quell or avert potential challenges on matters of substance. Most commonly such challenges
may be treated as disruptions to the orderly conduct of the meeting
or as beyond the scope of the agenda. In the former case the
problems of organizing talk for sixty or more persons may be
invoked. This provides an opportunity to assert means, the conduct
of the meeting, over ends, the matters for discussion. Goffman also
makes this point:

> When, during a conversation, communication or social propriety
> suddenly breaks down, pointed effort will follow to set matters
> right. At such moments what ordinarily functions as mere con-
> straints upon action become the ends of action itself. (1981,
> p. 26)

Here it is what Goffman calls the 'custard of interaction' that
becomes important; substance is disregarded. The medium is used
to assert control and override the possibility of dissent: 'what is
orderliness from the superior's position may be excommunication
from the inferior's' (Goffman, 1981, p. 25).

Pushed to its ultimate conclusion such a strategy requires the
overt recognition of the unequal distribution of power in the event.
Persistence by the inferior, the teacher, on a matter of substance,
is treated directly as a more profound challenge to the Head's
'authority'. Form takes precedence over content. In these circumstances escalation is a powerful deterrent. By upping the stakes the
headteacher can make the game not worth playing. For in practice,
attempts to challenge the established definition of the situation
normally extend only to particular substantive issues and are only

more rarely aimed at structures, at toppling the regime. Further-more, the 'available language' for discussion is itself a constraint, 'a verbalized texture of facts, values, roles and so on' (Pocock, 1981, p. 963). The interlocutors in staffroom discussion and debate 'are ruling and being ruled' by the structure of norms and conventions embodied in the 'available language'. There are ways of talking, forms of speech, turns of phrases and idioms that are avoided and subject to sanction in these contexts. 'Discussion' is locked within the conventions of social propriety and the prescribed limits of 'available' time; timing is often crucial and invariably controlled from the chair.

Finally, Hargreaves points to the use by those holding institu-tional power of tactics of limitation, for example the use of what he calls 'contrastive rhetoric'; that is, presenting 'stylized and trivial-ized images of alternative practices, characterizing them as un-acceptable extremes and thereby implicitly drawing the boundaries around the permissible range of present practice' (1981, p. 314). Here we shift from structure to content – the use of counterpoint, of absurdity, to define possibility. Again, we return to the issues of closure and control. The use of meetings to maintain the status quo while at the same time achieving a semblance of participation. Grievances can be aired, the disgruntled can let off steam, infor-mation is disseminated and laggardliness chastized. Meetings have many purposes, they may even serve to reinforce teachers' sense of professional identity, but their significance as arenas of decision-making should not be overestimated.

None the less, as indicated in Chapters 4 and 5, the accomplish-ment of control has its pitfalls; not all heads are successful in this regard. Not all meetings can be maintained at the mundane level; not all challenges can be diverted or ruled out of court. On occasion, meetings can become moments when diversity and lack of con-sensus are exposed. Jago, again discussing the meetings, observed:

> Almost without exception interaction was through the Head, and each comment from the floor occasioned some kind of response from him. I only remember three exceptions during the period of the research (I attended all but one Staff Meeting), all concerning issues where strong feelings were aroused. One was the proposed closure of toilets in some of the blocks as a consequence of and reprimand for vandalism. This occasioned a lengthy and very

heated debate and exposed major divisions among the staff on the principle of children's rights. (1983, pp. 186–7)

Such occasions may be rare (compared with Swidler's free school) but they are revealing. Burke (1986) provides another example in his ethnography of a sixth-form college. In this case a discussion developed around the issues of requirements for entry and the priority given to A-level teaching. As Burke comments, the meeting revealed:

> a basic clash of opinion that divided the College in a way that shook many members of staff who had previously pointed to the broad consensus of opinion which existed among the teachers and who had congratulated themselves on the successful transition from Grammar school to Sixth Form College. (1986, p. 56)

The staff clearly recognized that something out of the ordinary had occurred. Burke goes on to note that 'several teachers approached me afterwards. Some of them felt quite heated, some were elated, one member was plainly embarrassed that a rift should have occurred' (p. 56). What lay at the core of the disagreements thrown up were basic differences of perspective over the identity, definition and purposes of the institution. Several staff were suggesting that little progress had been made in shuffling off the ethos, image and sense of priorities embedded in the college's previous incarnation as a grammar school. An art teacher made the key contribution:

> I'm not sure we have got the atmosphere right. We ought to try and help the evolution along a bit. It used to be a sixth form but it is not yet a sixth form college. Something that would involve students and staff together. . . . There is still the grammar school image. It is not a sixth form college. (Quoted on p. 59)

Chords were struck, hackles rose. Subterranean differences surfaced. Suddenly, almost out of nowhere, an alternative, assertive definition of the college was being articulated over and against the dominant definition. Following a few more hectic contributions, Burke records that 'The meeting which was already running late was brought to an abrupt close as the principal concluded "I disagree with the view but I agree that there should be a discussion on the ethos"' (p. 59) (critical control of timing). The potentially damaging outburst was quickly closed down and rechannelled into an official 'discussion'. A member of staff was asked to prepare a paper. Again, form is asserted over content. Interestingly, this official discussion was planned but never held; quite soon after the meeting the principal announced his intention to retire and he pronounced it inappropriate for such an important discussion to be held prior to the arrival of his successor.

The committee

> A committee is a cul-de-sac down which ideas are lured and then quietly strangled. (Anon)

As suggested already, the distinction between meetings and committees is not an easy one to maintain. However, there are two points of difference between them. First, while the meeting is relatively public and inclusive, membership being defined in terms of a whole population, the committee is relatively private and exclusive, membership being selected or elected from a wider population. Second, while the meeting is relatively loosely and informally governed by rules of procedure, the committee is relatively tightly and formally governed by such rules. Having said that, it is not difficult to find examples in schools of meetings conducted like committees and *vice versa*.

These differences in the type of social arena are, according to Bailey, linked to micro-political differences. The public arena:

> is the place where principles and policies are announced, where issues are simplified down to the point of caricature and slogan, and where a discourse about persons (except when they are used to symbolise a principle) is not acceptable. By contrast the private arena is unprincipled: a place for enlisting the support of individuals by striking individual bargains (by trading off a little of one ideology against another or in more material ways); a place for mediation, where rivals try to escape the heavy costs of outright conflict by reaching compromise. (Bailey, 1977, p. 159)

The committee in school is much more clearly the arena of baronial politics, a matter of 'competition between strongmen' (Bailey, 1977, p. 88). It is here where we find set pieces and prepared presentations, where arrangements discussed in advance (see Ch. 5 above) are presented, where deadly rivals clash, where the language of politics is to the fore. Good committee conduct and understanding are acquired skills which some develop to a high degree: to know when to intervene and when to remain silent, to know who to oppose, what issues to leave alone, to recognize when someone is ill-prepared, to be able to handle the unexpected question, to be able to formulate a compromise statement in the heat of discussion, to know when a show of emotion may be effective, when not, to be aware of the tactics which will ensure that an item is deferred, a decision referred back, a potential clash avoided. Again, Bailey suggests that 'the backstage of politics is played out in a language of great subtlety which is often beyond the reach of those who are not native speakers' (1977, p. 104).

Committees at Casterbridge High (Ball, 1985) proved to be an effective arena for ex-grammar-school teachers who wished to oppose 'comprehensive' innovations. They quickly mastered a whole set of delaying tactics which served to severely inhibit the pace of change. Matters of principle were rarely raised, minor difficulties, worries, uncertainties and lack of clear understanding were much more subtle and effective in producing obstacles than was overt opposition. The result was an absence of decisions. Careful, small-scale experiments were suggested in lieu of full-scale adoption. Concern about the public image of the school was voiced. The problem of inadequate financing and lack of staff commitment and expertise were deployed. Ideologies were rarely to the fore, an institutional façade of community was tenuously maintained, while no one was really fooled. An appreciation of committee behaviour at Casterbridge ultimately lay in the history of the institution and the micro-political struggles arising from that history. However, the reading of history in and through the processes of the present is never straightforward; in one sense the significance of the committees lay in what was not said rather than what was.

To a great extent this is typical of the processes of micro-politics – a certain elusiveness and invisibility. Committees and meetings are but fleeting iceberg tips which mark the passing of business but reveal little of the ongoing processes of governance and control. It is only on rare occasions that the façade is broken and the messy, confused underlife, the tendons of power, the veins of influence, are exposed to view. An understanding of political process can begin in the committee room or the staff meeting but should by no means be sought only there. Committees are typically the site of piecemeal discussion; they pick up on the bits and pieces of institutional life. The process of working through the agenda normally produces a set of skirmishes rather than decisive battles of overall significance to the conduct of the organization. Points scored in argument, votes won, are more often symbolically important than of vital concrete effect. They indicate the current weight of opinion, the way the wind is blowing, which coalition is in the ascendant. In this respect the terms of reference of a particular committee are important. Bailey makes the useful distinction between 'élite' and 'arena' committees: 'in the former, members perceive themselves as guardians of the institution and its values, godlike in their responsibilities' (1977, p. 71). It is in the élite committees that critical discussions are held and decisions lodged, for example concerning the budget. The majority of the members of the organization find themselves confronted with the outcomes of such 'élite' decision-making; they are audience rather than participants – although by lobbying or otherwise seeking to influence committee members it is possible for groups or individuals to make their views known, their concerns felt. Taking this into account, committees and meetings themselves reveal little of the ongoing processes of governance, conflict and compromise. An understanding of political processes can begin in the committee room or the staff meeting but should by no means only be sought there. Corridors (Gronn, 1983), offices and staff-room corners are also sites where significant decisions are arrived at, compromises arranged, appointments agreed, promotions blocked or made. Micro-politics does not finish at the end of the agenda, it does not stop at the committee room door; it is an on-going dynamic process. It is multifaceted, indexical and obscure. It intervenes when least expected, it underpins the fleeting encounter, the innocent-sounding memo, the offhand comment. It is about relationships not structures, knowledge rather than information, talk rather than paper. Even then is it rarely spoken of directly. The hint, the guarded reference, the euphemism are the lexicon of politics. It is the stuff of mutual understanding and misunderstanding, of later denial, of informed sources and second-hand accounts. It deals in short-term gains, expediency and pragmatism rather than long-term goals, principles and ideals. Politics is a way for the dominant to get by and the assertive to deride. It is to be found in casual sniping as well as stated positions, in unexpected praise as well as undeserved blame, in gender and age and race relations as well as departmental structures. It brings together enemies and divides friends. It is the nexus where the formal structure of roles interpenetrates with the informal pattern of influence. It is a skill of judgement and coalition-building rather than a matter of position. Thus power is a goal, an outcome, rather than a precondition of political process. It is also a career, a vehicle, a channel, for some it is a way of life, an end in itself. It is what they do. 'An understanding of political events is a tool for living, an instrument whereby other goals are achieved' (Lane, 1959, p. 111). Reputations are won and lost in the micro-political arena, although reputation is a key resource as well as an outcome. It is perhaps a macho, masculine preoccupation, 'boys games'. As an epithet, 'political' occupies a fine line between insult and praise. The political person is both admired and distrusted. To make one's life by politics is to be tainted by it. It can account for the meteoric rise and the precipitate fall. To be political often means to be underhand. It is by and through politics that ascendancy is achieved, policies pushed through, budgets secured.

Little progress will be made in the field of school organization until we recognize and begin to analyse the processes of micro-politics. There is a need to take the work of armchair theorists less seriously and the folk knowledge of teachers much more so.

10
Inside/out: the school in political context

Confound their politics,
Frustrate their knavish tricks.   (Henry Carey)

One of the key questions which must be raised in any micro-political
analysis is the extent to which the internal dynamics of an organization are independent of, conditioned by or determined by,
outside forces. In other words, how autonomous is the organization
and its actors from its clients, publics, superiors and audiences or
the basic social and economic structures of the society? In this case
the answer has to be couched in terms of that most convenient of
sociological concepts – relative autonomy. As systems theorists
were quick to point out, organizations are not independent or self-
sufficient phenomena. However, the emphasis within the system's
perspective has been straightforwardly upon the adaptation of the
organization to its environment; interactive and dialectical relationships have not been widely considered (Clegg and Dunkerley, 1980,
p. 399). Here I shall begin on the basis of two premises: first, that
schools as organizations cannot be conceived of as independent
from the environment; second, that they cannot be analysed simply
in terms of adaptation to that environment. The national and local
state may operate to limit the range of possibilities available to
teachers, but at the present time at least, they certainly do not
exercise absolute control within that range. As we shall see, in
relation to these issues, the 1985–6 teachers' action may be interpreted as a struggle over where ultimate control over schools is to

lie. However, it can be argued that events over the past ten years have already significantly changed the nature of the autonomy available to schools. Beginning with the publication of the first of the so-called Black Papers on education in 1969, teachers have become the butt of powerful criticisms, from all parts of the political spectrum. The Black Papers to a great extent succeeded in establishing a publicly accepted view of teachers as responsible for declining academic standards and large-scale illiteracy and increasing violence and indiscipline among school pupils. Further, they conjured up an impression of large numbers of 'left wing' teachers working in schools and concerned solely with the political indoctrination of pupils. In addition, schools were accused of holding on to an academic curriculum ill-suited to modern technological and industrial needs and for generally fostering an anti-industrial ethos among pupils. In other words, schools and teachers were failing the nation. Indeed, for some commentators it was necessary to look no further for the causes of Britain's economic recession, notwithstanding the oil crisis – schools were to blame. In several senses these criticisms are patently ridiculous and internally contradictory, but none the less effective and damning. In effect, teachers were condemned both for hanging on stubbornly to outdated curricula and methods and succumbing to the superficial attractions of 'progressive' theories and thus abandoning traditional and well-tried curricula and methods. What these criticisms indicate perhaps is the profound tension which is built into parental, societal and political expectations of the role and purpose of schooling. The tension between the moral and the cognitive, or integrative and economic, aspects of schooling. Schools are expected to produce well-behaved and well-adjusted citizens and at the same time select and train those citizens to take up different roles and statuses within the labour force. The increase in school violence and the general level of crime in society is taken as a mark of failure on the first count and is identified with the move away from traditional practices. The decline in British industry in the face of international competition is regarded as an indication of failure on the second count and is identified with schools' slowness to adapt to technological change. School-leavers neither have the right skills for work nor the right attitudes. Teachers find themselves damned if they do change and damned if they do not.

All of this criticism and the national moral panic about education

which ensued has provided massive legitimation for greater school
and teacher *accountability*. This has become a major watchword for
education in the 1980s. The 'failings' of teachers have provided
justification for much greater direct intervention into school processes by LEAs, the DES, HMI, the Secretary of State for Education, and other agencies like the MSC. Arguably, the education
service has begun to move back towards the form of centralized
control which existed until the late 1920s. Dale conceptualizes this
move in terms of a shift in the relative autonomy of schools from
'licensed autonomy' to 'regulated autonomy'. In the first:

> An implicit licence was granted to the education system, which
> was renewable on the meeting of certain conditions. Just how
> those conditions could be met was again subject to certain broad
> limitations. ... The educational expansion of the decade from
> the early sixties to the early seventies stretched the terms of the
> education system's licence to new limits. (Dale, p. 100)

> The major source of teachers' authority was that they could
> expect to be backed up by their employers and their representa-
> tives as long as they stayed within certain implicit boundaries of
> curriculum, pedagogy, and evaluation. (p. 105)

As for regulated autonomy:

> Control over the education system is to become tighter, largely
> through the codification and monitoring processes and practices
> previously left to teachers' professional judgement, taken on
> trust or hallowed by tradition. (p. 104)

In other words, the freedom of manoeuvre available to teachers is
reduced. Choices have been removed or pre-empted and certain
functions have been withdrawn. In effect, the lines of control are
now visible rather than invisible, direct rather than indirect, explicit
rather than implicit. Significantly, Dale is not suggesting that autonomy has disappeared; it has been reduced, circumscribed. As we
shall see later, intervention and monitoring are making an impact
upon the micro-politics of schools, the rules of the game *are*
changing, but they have not as yet resulted in a wholesale routiniza-
tion and homogenization of the system. Schools are responding
differently to their changing conditions of work. Very briefly I will

examine a range of school–environmental relationships, to include parents, the media, LEAs and local politicians, the DES and other national agencies. This examination will emphasize the articulation of internal micro-politics with outside audiences. Forms of conflict, accommodation and domination will be considered.

While it may be easy to underestimate the degree of licence still available to schools, it is also easy to underestimate the degree of regulation previously imposed. It is instructive in this respect to examine particular cases where the limits of autonomy were apparently exceeded and sanctions brought to bear. The case studies analysed by Fletcher, Caren and Williams (1985), though admittedly based on partisan accounts, are helpful here. They record the experience of four 'high-profile innovative' comprehensives – Risinghill, Summerhill Academy, Countesthorpe and Sutton Centre – which found themselves on public 'trial' for apparently moving beyond the existing bounds of educational acceptability. In particular, the case studies highlight the articulation of internal micro-politics, what Fletcher, Caren and Williams call 'politics with a small p', and external interinstitutional political relationships, involving the LEAs, key figures or groups in the community and the local press.

In each case the events leading up to 'the trial' were triggered off by some particular controversial happening in the school:

> Each had an event, a cause célèbre, which could stick in the public eye like a piece of grit. Each, too, had rumblings of deep issues of principle, conflicts over pedagogy, which had divided the protagonists since the day the school opened.

School	Event	Deeper issues
Risinghill (1961)	Survey on racialism	Sex education
Summerhill (1968)	Pupil's knife threat	Corporal punishment
Countesthorpe (1973)	Library thefts	Independent learning
Sutton Centre (1979)	Swearing lesson	CSE for all 16+ pupils

If one considers the dates of the trials they seem to be marking the boundaries to development of each of the deeper principles. These schools were amongst the first to publicly stake a claim for their innovations. Their claims were quickly denied by their employers. Other secondary schools might follow their example

but do so later, more quietly and in a more piecemeal way.
(Fletcher, Caren and Williams, 1985, pp. 123–4)

Several points should be noted here. First, it is suggested that the
practical problems which initiated the public response were underpinned by significant ideological issues about education. Indeed, it
can be said that what is going on is conflict over the definition of the
schools, what kind of schools they are to be, and struggle over who
is to control these definitions, over the locus of the power to define.
This articulates well within the previous analysis. Second, it is
suggested that the issues of dispute are long-standing and represent
major splits between the schools and their various audiences, as
well as splits among the teachers in the schools. This links to a third
point, that it is the public realization of these disputes that leads to
reaction and escalation, not simply the content of the innovations
themselves. In effect the schools had failed to maintain a public
façade of unanimity. The collective presentation of self of the
schools, their institutional 'front', had cracked and been pene-
trated. Perhaps also the headteachers had failed to maintain the
institutional balance between domination and integration. In
Goffman's (1971) terms, one contributory factor, particularly in
evidence at Risinghill and Summerhill, was a breakdown in 'teamwork' among the teachers. Internal differences in ideology became
more important than the possibility of maintaining or achieving a
sense of shared institutional reality. 'It seems to be generally felt
that public disagreement among members of the team not only
incapacitates them for united action but also embarrasses the reality
sponsored by the team' (Goffman, 1971, p. 91). Once issues have
gone public, there is a loss of control by members of the team and
their leader, the head. In effect, other interested parties are invited
to contribute to the debate and align themselves with one side or the
other. Alliances and coalitions, real or by implication, are formed
between groups of insiders and groups of outsiders. The LEA
advisers or inspectors and the director of education may or may
not support the head. The local press or council members may or
may not sympathize with discontented teachers. Parents, or more
accurately certain articulate and influential parents, may mobil-
ize support for one side or the other. Occasionally, like at Croxeth
Comprehensive, mass parental support may be achieved (Carspecken and Miller, 1983). At other times, as at William Tyndale

(Gretten and Jackson, 1976) or Drummond Middle School in Bradford, the parents are divided themselves. There are in fact two sorts of sanctions which may result from this making public of institutional controversies. The first is substantive and results from direct response to the matters of concern. The second is more basic and comes from a sense of larger-scale teamwork having been spoiled. The education system of the LEA is in a sense a team of schools. Terry Ellis, the head of William Tyndale, recognized this when he commented: 'Schools that create adverse publicity are bad and receive bad inspection reports: those that "don't make waves" wallow on' (Ellis *et al.*, 1976, p.141). Fletcher, Caren and Williams pick up these points:

> The case studies are critical incidents which expose the political tensions that every school is constrained by and can contribute to. The case studies also suggest links between everyday politics and major political movements. At the very least political features suggestive of wider political issues and conflicts may be identified.
>
> * opposition to the head from 'a passing coalition of malcontents' – of staff (Duane and Makenzie) of parents (McCullen and Wilson)
>
> * an authority's inspectorate in disagreement with the school (Risinghill and Countesthorpe)
>
> * high status local people against 'modern education' (Summerhill, Countesthorpe and Sutton)
>
> * politicians who can neutralise the Director of Education and pursue a policy of attrition to the end (all four)
>
> * media which will both bias and keep the balance of forces in tension so that the trigger event, main personalities and inevitability of a show trial are the main news items (all four).

Against this formidable array of political constraints is the strength and unity of purpose shared by the head, staff, teachers' unions, governing body, parents and pupils. The more divided these groups are – within and between themselves – the less chance there is of altering the trial process. It is plain, too, that the heads 'failed' to stay out of the local press. When they thought they were communicating with the host community they were antagonising its more discreet influentials. (1985, p.135)

Hannan (1980) recognized similar potential difficulties in his case study of Redmond College, another innovative school:

> For the conflicts within the school to have reached the point where they endangered the school's existence, it would have been necessary for outside forces to penetrate the exterior boundary of the school which was publicly managed by the Principal. (1980, p.162)

So two aspects of micro-political relations emerge as crucial. One concerns the containment of internal conflicts; the other is the management of relationships with external audiences. The head-teacher is the crucial figure in both. The first was explored at some length in Chapters 4, 5 and 6.

Public relations

As we saw in Chapter 6, different heads tend to invest different amounts of time and effort in monitoring and massaging internal relations as against the external relations. Some heads save their best performances for outside audiences and clearly see their prime function as public-relations officer for their school; that is, defending and advocating the image and material interests of the school against competing institutions and threats to its well-being in the form of financial or resource reductions. At the present time of falling rolls, when schools in many areas are in effective competition for declining numbers of potential pupils, the head's role as maker and maintainer of a public 'front' is all the more crucial. As Levine argues, 'maintenance and survival, are political matters calling for the application of the most sophisticated attack or survival tactics in the arsenal of the skilled bureaucrat-politician' (1978, p.318). The demands made by different audiences may be diverse, even contradictory, as we have seen. The successful head may be the one who is able to present different versions of their school to different audiences. As a public-relations officer the head must make best use of public events and maintain a flow of good publicity in the local press while still being able to respond to diverse pressures from interest-groups campaigning from within. Fletcher, Caren and Williams certainly see such skills as essential, particularly if the head is also concerned to sponsor innovative curricula or pedagogy in their school:

Political skills ask for an honest and unneurotic relationship with the core groups of 'politics with a small p' which need to be with and in support of the school, as well as a cautious exchange with peripheral groups who will mount wave after wave of invasion once they have a trigger event to latch on to. Political skills thus chart a middle way between passivity and high-profile innovation, between anonimity and annoying announcements. (1985, p. 143)

This sense of maintaining a middle way was clearly appreciated by the headteacher at Beachside Comprehensive (Ball, 1981a). The introduction of mixed-ability grouping in the school was managed without drawing unnecessary attention to the school, despite LEA opposition to the scheme. The presentation of the innovation to parents was carefully managed to minimize the degree of radicalness attached to the changes involved. It was not until the third year of the change that the PTA requested an open meeting on the issue. Supporters and opponents from within the school were mustered to speak to the parents (including the author) and the emphasis was clearly upon the presentation of a united front and a message saying all is well. Despite some scepticism from one or two articulate parents, who were able to recount 'horror stories' about mixed-ability, the message was accepted and the inchoate opposition among the parents was dissipated, although clearly part of the 'success' of this exercise lay in the head's self-imposed sense of what would be tolerated by parents. He was aware of how far he could go before the response would become unmanageable. He explained:

We cannot take up the possibilities of mixed-ability at this stage because we would be doing a disservice to the kids and have their parents in uproar because they are not doing exams, we cannot do that locally until the system of 16+ examinations changes nationally.

Here is one of the most important mechanisms in the operation of licensed autonomy. The constraints that schools impose upon themselves as regards what is and what is not possible at any point in time in a particular context.

When self-regulation is delayed or inadvertently set aside, difficulties can arise. The examination of the campaign of criticism mounted against William Tyndale School (Gretton and Jackson,

1976) certainly indicates the effect of a small group of disaffected or well-connected middle-class parents. The use of the media was a key strategy employed by this group to put pressure on the ILEA to 'do something' about the school:

> How did this domestic row, which by June 1975 had been bubbling on for well over a year, suddenly turn into 'news'? Why, at this time, did it become something the newspaper reading public would read about? Part of the answer is made clear in paragraphs 740–744 of the Auld Report. The press was actually invited to write unfavourably about the school by one of the parties in the dispute – the school managers. It was a deliberate tactic in their battle with the teachers. (Holland, 1976, p. 22)

The local press can clearly work for or against the reputation of a particular school. Headteachers are usually eager to maintain good relations with the local editor and attract coverage of events which show the school in a good light. However, it is not unknown for local newspapers to play a leading role in campaigns of criticism against particular schools. In the case of Countesthorpe College, *The Leicester Mercury* has mounted a number of scathing attacks upon the school and its teachers and pupils:

> In a long interview with the News Editor of *The Mercury*, it appeared that the newspaper criticisms were stemming from a conservative stance against comprehensive education as well as from the sincere concerns of parents. Mr Simkins of *The Mercury* felt that the school was particularly weak in its public relations efforts and had made virtually no effective contact with the public concerning the objectives and strategies used in the programme at the school. (Quoted in Norris, 1976)

Hannan (1980) reports the presence of the same newspaper as an ever-present consideration in the mind of the principal of Redmond College. The principal took great pains to maintain integration and not allow the college to display damaging disharmony:

> All this was in pursuit of the Principal's aim to preserve 'one community'; an important aim in light of potential opposition from outsiders such as the *Leicester Mercury* during the period of local authority reorganization. (p. 153)

Typically, it is difficult for parents as a group, or even sub-groups of parents, to constitute themselves as a coalition within the micro-politics of the institution. They lack credibility, organization and information, all this despite the attempts on the part of successive governments to enfranchise parents. One problem is that parental representatives on governing bodies rarely *represent* in any real sense:

> The idea of this school being an open institution is a joke. We have 134 adult students coming in. But they come in the same sense that they go to the local supermarket. They come, buy their loaf of bead, buy their lesson of English, and go. They don't infuse the institution, they don't participate in terms of setting a different agenda for the place. They have no way that they collectively get together. (Headmaster, a Midlands community comprehensive)

None the less, Hatton (1985) in Australia and Arfwedson (1979) in Sweden offer examples which indicate that influential, high-status parents can and do intervene in the pedagogical practices of their children's schools and can, partially at least, determine the occupational socialization of teachers in these schools. Arfwedson's research suggests the emergence of a 'steering group' of active and influential high-status parents in middle- and upper-class schools who are able to effect the teachers' definition of their work either by the use of 'pressure' or the establishment of mutual understanding. This steering group is able to 'cultivate and ferment' (Arfwedson, 1979, p. 35) the teachers' perceptions of their work in order to maintain the established, and approved of, teaching methods and curriculum of the school. The goals of the school become over time closely adapted to the higher social strata of the local community. It was just this group who were attempting to put pressure on the William Tyndale teachers, to achieve this kind of adaptation. Hatton's study demonstrates the considerable potential power of one particular such group, the Parents and Citizens Committee of Riverton School. This committee was over time able to fend off attempts by 'new' teachers in the school, and the education authorities, to introduce team-teaching and open-plan classrooms. They were able to intervene in staffing matters by harassing 'weak' or 'avant-garde' teachers and supporting the work of 'traditionalists'.

The use of local political networks and contacts allowed this steering group access to appointment decision-making at the regional office. Indeed, a coalition was established between the committee and the long-serving 'old guard' teachers at Riverton which acted to confound the innovations attempted by successive principals. In this sense these particular parents were constituted as part of the micro-political system of the school.

Various writers have argued that it is possible to conceive of any school as working within a particular set of community parameters. This is what Charters (1953) called the 'margin of tolerance', or McGiveney and Moynihan the 'zone of tolerance' – 'the latitude or area of manoeuvrability granted or [yielded] to the leadership of the schools by the local community' (McGiveney and Moynihan, 1972, p.221). This parallels Dale's concept of licensed autonomy. In most cases, in Britain and America, it would seem that schools operate well within this limited 'zone' and that overt reaction from the community is rare. Furthermore, American evidence suggests that the restraint involved in keeping within acceptable limits does come from the schools themselves:

> There is evidence to suggest that the ongoing community influence is such that in many, perhaps even most, school districts the superintendents (and their School Boards as well) usually attempt to act in harmony with what they perceive as the predominant community values and expectations concerning schools. (Boyd, 1976, p. 551)

Nevertheless, these community expectations are neither always clear nor are they held in common across the whole clientele of the school. The more diverse the community, the more difficult it will be for any school to respond to all expectations. The dilemmas thrown up here are often most acute when the school intake is multi-ethnic or consists of a wide spectrum of social-class backgrounds. It would also be misleading to present a picture of schools as always passive as regards their community. It may be that active public relations can reshape predominate expectations. Indeed, 'an important part of politics revolves around attempts to define issues in terms favourable to the interests of particular participants' (Boyd, 1976, p. 566). The more active and 'interested' groups within the community are most likely to be attended to but are also most likely to be the target for redefinition. In some cases the alliances established between a school and elements in the community may be of considerable advantage to the school in putting on pressure for additional resources or making good shortfalls in local-government financing. Thus covenanting is an increasingly important source of income for state schools, parents are taking responsibility for the repair and redecoration of buildings and raising funds for school trips, new equipment and basic materials (Pring, 1986). A school may lag behind local opinion (failing to introduce computer-related courses) or may lead it (by introducing mixed-ability grouping or modern mathematics). It is also important to pay some attention to the types of changes embarked upon by schools as well as the general quality of their relationships with the community. Lowi (1964) suggests that problems are most likely to occur, tolerance breached that is, when redistributive policies are proposed or implemented. Such policies challenge the established pattern of advantage, and those groups who see themselves as losers under the new arrangements are likely to react strongly (Peterson, 1972). This would certainly apply in the William Tyndale case, perhaps also to Countesthorpe, and to a lesser degree to the introduction of mixed-ability at Beachside. In the latter case the worries of the PTA were concerned almost exclusively with the effects of mixed-ability grouping on the work of the most able pupils. Redistributive policies bring 'class politics' into play: 'The categories of impact are much broader, approaching social classes. They are crudely speaking, haves and have-nots, bigness and smallness, bourgeoisie and proletariat' (Lowi, 1964, p. 690).

The local education authority

Boyd (1976) argues that the acrimony involved in conflicts over redistribution often brings public officials into the fray. Both in attending to their school's public image and their own freedom of action, headteachers must also always look carefully to their relationships with the local education authority (LEA), both officials and council members. However, while good relationships with officials may be necessary, they are insufficient to ensure that a school maintains a good 'front' and continued access to finance and other resources. Fletcher, Caren and Williams record that:

> All four heads had special relationships with their directors of education. They were hand-picked and initially strongly sup-

ported by their directors. The directors were fully aware of the principles the heads intended to put into practice. (1985, p. 125)

Ultimately these special relationships were strained by the course of events and proved inadequate as a source of support for the heads. None the less, much can be achieved through such personal relationships. Discussions on the golf course or over a dinner table can achieve far more on occasion than a more formal approach. Shared allegiance may also lead to preferment for particular institutions. Freemasonry is often suggested as a network of informal influence and communication available to some heads (Burke, 1986). It is difficult to prove, but often stated, that LEAs tend to deliberately favour some schools and neglect others. Fashionable or politically nimble heads may attract special projects or additional funding for their school: 'Some schools were allowed to bloom, others were allowed to wither away. The competition between the schools was a negation of comprehensive education' (a London comprehensive headteacher). However, recent developments in local authority organization suggest that the general movement in relations between the schools and LEA officials may be towards greater formality, as systems of corporate management are introduced (Cockburn, 1978). Wallace, Miller and Ginsburg certainly found this to be the case in the authority they studied:

> Administrative changes under corporate management had wide implications for negotiative procedures, fragmenting educational interests which were once under the direct control of the Local Education Committee and significantly undermining informal interactions. In the County studied, crucial economic decisions were vested in the powerful Policy, Resources and Finance Committee. Educational buildings became the concern of the property committee and teachers' interests were made part of the task of the Personnel Committee. These shifts in the loci of the decision-making have tended to elevate financial considerations, including such matters as the possible financial return on the sale of school buildings, and to devalue the influence of social and educational criteria in policy deliberations about local schools. (1983, p. 114)

Such changes are perhaps indicative of the shift from licence to regulation at the local level. In addition, when headteachers come incorporated into local-authority management structures, which involve 'The placing of administrative responsibility upon heads for carrying out policies made outside of school' (Wallace, Miller and Ginsburg, 1983, p. 130), then changes are also inevitable in institutional relationships. In this situation the headteacher's role as leading professional is superseded by that as manager. The gap between management and workforce is made yet more decisive.

Intervention and the politics of response

Two sets of factors have decisively changed school–LEA relations in the 1980s. First, the financial cuts imposed first by the Labour and then the Conservative governments (between 1976 and 1985), and the effects of falling rolls, have led to greater emphasis being placed upon planning decisions at LEA level. Levels of staffing and minimum curricula provisions are now commonly set by the LEA. Hewton argues that 'the need for resolute action in the face of uncertainty and confusion causes a shift in the locus of power. . . . Crises thus tend to lead towards the centralization of power and autocratic styles of leadership' (1986, p. 49). In 'Shire' County studied by Hewton the response to falling rolls and financial cuts was the working out of a basic 'curriculum model': 'The curriculum model was drawn up by officers but was carefully worked out in detail with heads and unions and was painstakingly explained to councillors' (p. 66). In other words, crucial decisions concerning curriculum planning were now being taken outside the schools. This also relates to the second area of change in school–LEA relations, for LEAs have been encouraged and empowered by central government to take a more interventionist stance towards the school curriculum, albeit within an increasingly tight framework of control based in the DES. Indeed, following the publication of the government's Green Paper *Influence at School* (DES, 1984), Bennett suggests the following vision of the future of curriculum planning:

> the centre-periphery concept of curriculum creation is articulated in terms of leaving to professionals the task of deciding how to organize and deliver what is required. Curriculum development can therefore be argued to remain in qualified hands. However, the governing body is to define the school's curricular aims and objectives, working within the policy statements of the LEA

and therefore the national statements within which those are themselves contained. (Bennett, 1984, p. 160)

All of this suggests that a comprehensive model of school micro-politics should incorporate both the role of the governing body and LEA. Certainly both need to be taken into account in understanding the constraints within which school-based decision-making is set. However, the data employed in this analysis do not indicate any drastic curtailment of internecine dispute as a result of pre-emption. From the point of view of a theory of school organization, increased environmental constraints on the school and direct intervention by outside agencies must be viewed in two ways: first, as factors that enter into and become part of the existing micro-politics of the institution – these constraints and interventions become subjects of micro-political struggle; their effects are indirect and mediated through existing micro-political relations; second, as factors that change the structure and nature of micro-political relations in the institution – their effects being direct; for example, in shifting the balance of power between headteacher and staff. No particular new constraint or intervention can necessarily be analysed exclusively in terms of the first or second type of impact but the emphasis may be different. For the purposes of exposition I shall explore these different types of impact in relation to two areas of ongoing change in schools: first, the constraints arising from what Hewton (1986) calls 'the crisis of cuts', and the interventions resulting from the introduction of new curricula and examinations (e.g. TVEI, CPVE, and GCSE); second, the effects, general and specific, of the 1985–6 teachers' pay dispute. In effect, these two areas of activity will provide case studies of the impact of intervention upon school organization and micro-politics.

SURVIVAL AND CHANGE

The changing articulation of internal and external politics as financial crisis begins to bite is neatly captured by Pettigrew:

The result is the appearance of the rhetoric of finance, economics and accounting linked to strongly articulated values about efficiency, and all of these harnessed to the new preoccupation of resource management. The old deity of growth has been

superseded by the new deity of survival. The language of survival
becomes the central legitimating force for action. .... The new
concern with control puts the spotlight on who governs the
system, the new concern with resources releases new energy
into the organization's internal and external political processes,
as empires created in the rich times are asked to reconsider
their role, purpose and share of a shrinking organizational cake.
(1982, p. 3)

Thus two somewhat contradictory effects are produced by the onset
of financial crisis. One is a pressure for greater centralization, the
other is the stimulation of conflict. The first effect is noted by
Hewton (1986) in his LEA case study, a reassertion of central
control, behind closed doors. Greenwood (1983) studied several
local authorities and the procedures which they followed during a
period of severe financial constraint and he likens the situation to a
form of 'Spanish Inquisition' which relies upon private meetings of
the powerful figures outside the committee system (Hewton, 1986,
p. 50). The receding locus of control is reflected in the comments of
those teachers who find themselves subject to procedures leading to
redeployment or redundancy (see Ch. 7 above). There is a strong
sense of powerlessness, of decisions being made elsewhere, of unknown or unclear criteria being used. One thing that is heightened
in this sort of situation, literally, is the sense of them and us. 'They'
make the decisions and 'we' have to put up with them. As one of the
interviewed heads put it, 'When the chips are down all decisions are
made from top management in a school, we pretend very often that
we've done it democratically but in the long run decisions are made
finally by people in top management positions'.

As organizational 'slack' (Cyert and March, 1963) is wiped out
and then core funding reduced, competing demands can no longer
be satisfied. The micro-politicial emphasis is upon survival of the
sub-units of the organization; tension increases as some of the
competitors lose out in the allocation of reduced monies, posts or
resources. Value differences and competing material interests will
be directly exposed.

The general effects of cuts on the curricula provision of schools
has been monitored since 1978 by annual HMI Inspectorate reports. These reports give some impression of the potential for and
outcomes of conflicts in schools. In particular, they note 'an increas-

ing mismatch between the qualifications and experience of teachers and their teaching commitments' and 'the loss of individual subjects' included among which are craft, design and technology, modern languages, general studies, aspects of physical education and music, geology and photography, and remedial provision. In particular institutions these are the empires or parts of empires which have been lost. However, set against these losses, the effects of cuts, there are new 'initiatives' which open up possibilities for some individuals or groups of teachers to gain greater influence than previously, to develop their careers, enhance their status or make new claims for resources. Proposals like CPVE, TVEI, GCSE or school self-evaluation or school-based in-service work are both subject to and become part of the micro-political arena of the school. Simply because they eminate from outside the school, they do not automatically nullify, negate or eliminate micro-political struggle. Such initiatives, their acceptance, their implementation, become the site as well as the stake of internal dispute. New territories may be staked out, monies earmarked, appointments captured and policies defined. The initiatives themselves may be captured and redefined by particular interests or coalitions, *in* their interest. They are a beginning not the end of conflict inside the school.

The changing political and educational rhetorics which are addressed to and in which schooling is embedded can provide new and powerful vocabularies of motives and structures of legitimation for interest groups in the micro-political arena. The advancement of the 'pastoral curriculum' is a case in point. In a broad context of youth unemployment, the restructuring of school-work relationships and a 'moral panic' concerning rising crime and 'youth on the streets', schools are expected to 'take the blame' and 'mend their ways'. The 'educational' responses to these issues are a basis for a change in the distribution of influence inside schools. The emphasis on preparation for work (or employment) and/or adult life has given impetus to pre-vocational courses, and to courses on 'life-skills' and 'personal and social education'. The concomitant changes in forms of assessment – profiling, records of achievement, and graded testing – have created new areas of responsibility and specialist knowledge for the teachers involved, usually pastoral-care staff. Such developments may be seen as contributing, on the one hand, to the overall professionalization of pastoral care and, on the other, they have created a focus for renewed struggle between academic and pastoral interests in schools. Both social education and assessment and guidance offer areas of specialism and esoteric knowledge to pastoral-care teachers. Both enable claims to be made for more timetabled time and more non-timetabled time (free periods) for pastoral work. Both types of time are scarce and critical resources. Furthermore, as new or different skills are legitimated for and demanded of teachers then the system of status and reward begins to change. The introduction of vocationally orientated courses can bring about 'status reversal', moving the marginal 'practical' subjects onto centre stage and reducing the importance of the purely 'academic'. However, the 'initiatives' themselves are not necessarily mutually compatible or coherent. There are choices to be made and emphases to be given. For instance, work on GCSE, with its re-emphasizing of subject specialist teaching, is in direct contradiction to the integration of subjects required in CPVE courses. In ILEA schools developments related to Improving Secondary Schools (ILEA, 1984), like Records of Achievement and modular credits, have to be weighed against GCSE and the ILEA's initiatives on social class, race and gender. In each case there is a potential for conflict, the definition of the school is at stake as certain programmes are prioritized and budgets redistributed. The ideological and the material are again intertwined.

Clearly, the changing context and specific interventions can act to significantly disrupt established institutional ideologies and patterns of preferment. The following teacher, in a sixth-form college, is describing the impact of CPVE work:

> the more we get into integrated and thematic work, the less our subject departments are going to be relevant and I think there is going to be a lot of resistance to the old-style grammar-school teacher (of which we still have many). They are going to find attitude change a difficult one to make. Not too devastating for me because I was primary trained – it does make a difference. And my own degree was an OU degree, so I did eleven subjects over four years, so I'm more used to the integrated approach. But for most of them its 'I'm a chemist and a chemist I will be and this is my department'. So I think there are going to be questions asked about the entire structure of the college when we really get moving.

Here a teacher finds her atypical background and training being validated by new developments, and entrenched positions are being challenged even within the bastion of A-level teaching. A similar point is made by the following teacher in another sixth-form college:

> I can meet those core and option requirements in terms of the thinking that is required to go into them because I have myself, prior to working in a sixth-form college, worked in FE and at a technical college and I therefore have some experience of, for instance, the BTEC and BEC type of structure which is essentially core and option module based and within my own experience therefore I've got past knowledge to rely on.

For teachers like these, prevocational courses open up new avenues of career development and status enhancement. Their skills and experience are in demand. They are advocates of change; they see new developments as worthwhile and as better serving the needs of pupils. They invest their time, energy and beliefs into the construction of new courses. They present a challenge to the established definition of the school.

These sorts of interventions represent radical redefinitions of the nature and purposes of schooling sponsored by external groups and coalitions. They carry within them expectations of thorough-going change. Yet one of the apparent mysteries of the 1980s as far as education is concerned is that the most hectic period of state-initiated change since the 1940s is also a period of massive reductions in school financing and one of acrimonious dispute between teachers and their employers. Change is being promoted in what would seem at first sight to be the most improbable and least conducive economic and political conditions imaginable. The mystery is solved, however, if the terms of the analysis are changed. Both the curricular interventions and the development of the teachers' pay dispute can be reduced to a single issue – control. The interventions represent dramatic examples of an overall attempt by the government both to change the 'ethic' of the school curriculum and to alter the balance of control over the teaching process and the curriculum. The 'conditions' attached by Sir Keith Joseph to the settlement of the teachers' pay dispute is part of a general strategy aimed at asserting greater control over teachers themselves. In general terms this strategy involves extension of the popular notion of 'accountability' towards the direct monitoring and appraisal of the work of individual teachers. At the end of a fifteen-year period during which successive governments have been attempting to convince parents and employers that they should believe in education but should not trust schools, the campaign for 'teacher appraisal' commands considerable support:

> At the heart of the teachers' dispute is not money but management. . . . This dispute is about resistance to change in working practices. The essence of education is discipline. . . . By resisting the discipline of assessment of their own performance, the teachers stand opposed to the renovation of Britain. That is why in this dispute management must win – and there is the beginning and end of the lazy comparison that some people have been tempted to make with the coal strike. (*The Times'* leader, 19 March 1985)

The introduction of an appraisal system would, it is argued, put teachers on a par with other groups of professional employees:

> The employing authority can only be satisified that each school is properly staffed if it knows enough about the skills and competencies of individual teachers. Such knowledge can only come from some form of appraisal system. An appraisal system is also needed for the professional enhancement of the individual teacher. Other professions – and some schools – have found that appraisal interviews provide an opportunity to identify individual and collective training needs. To be fully effective an appraisal system would have to be complemented by better arrangements for the individual teachers' career development – including induction, in-service training, guidance on possible teaching posts and promotion. When I refer to the management of the teaching force I have this whole range of positive activity in mind. I am frequently misquoted in terms that suggest that I am only concerned with the need to dismiss the very small number of incompetent teachers who cannot be restored to adequate effectiveness. That is not the case, I am concerned with the whole range of positive advantages that would flow from applying to the teacher force standards of management which have become

common elsewhere. (Speech by Sir Keith Joseph, North of England Education Conference, 4 January 1985)

The key word in both these extracts is 'management'. In effect, control is to be exerted over teacher's work by the use of techniques of management. In general terms the task of schooling is increasingly subject to the logics of industrial production and market competition. Teachers are increasingly becoming drawn into systems of administrative rationality which exclude them from an effective say in the kind of substantive decision-making that could equally well be determined collectively. As Habermas (1984) suggests, this is a process whereby sub-systems of purposive-rational action encroach upon structures of intersubjectivity. Political, ideologically loaded decisions are choked by bureaucratic-administrative systems and attempts are made to displace issues of moral and cultural identity with the imperatives of administrative efficacy. In other words, pragmatism and technologies of control replace ideological dispute. The definition of the school is removed entirely from the hands of teachers. In all this the work of teaching is being proletarianized. The work experience of the teacher is undergoing a significant shift from that of respected professional towards that of beleaguered labourer. The overall effect is a reconstruction of teachers' relationships to their work and their sense of themselves as workers. If such interpretational changes are long-lasting, then the nature of school micro-politics may also shift further towards an industrial-relations/worker-versus-management paradigm. What is being promoted is a shift from the *formal* to the *real* subordination of teachers' work (Braverman, 1974). The conceptual significance of this shift, in its relation to schools, is the appropriation by management of the subjective elements of labour. The worker is reduced 'to a "living appendage" of the production process (instead of being its subject and author)'. The space, the freedom of manoeuvre available for the worker to influence or control production, is closed down. Conception, design and ordering is removed to the responsibility of management 'leaving to the worker only the execution of a pre-set task' (Cressey and MacInnes, 1980, p. 7). To a great extent schools have already succumbed to the ideology of management, as being the one good way to run the organization. The infrastructure of 'real' subordination is already in place in many cases:

> The establishment of management as a separate function . . . with unique expertise and responsibilities, and with major and critical claims to authority . . . upon which the efficiency of the whole enterprise depends . . . is a crucial first step to control over the workforce . . . because once this conception of management has been accepted by workers, they have, in effect, abdicated from any question of, or resistance to, many aspects of their domination. (Littler and Salaman, 1982, p. 259)

I am not here suggesting some kind of complex conspiracy against teachers but rather taking account of the overall effect of the concatenation of initiatives, constraints, changes in control and decision-making, and changes in conditions of work which are having their impact on teachers' daily lives.

However, as was the case with previous elements in this analysis, these developments are not without their own internal contradictions. The pressure towards greater control over teachers' work and increases in direct intervention into curriculum matters are accompanied by pressures upon schools and individual teachers to introduce new curricula, new pedagogies and new forms of assessment. On the one hand, direct intervention and prescription of curricula alongside overall reductions in funding are reducing the possibility of 'initiatory influences' (Offe, 1976) of teachers. On the other hand, teachers are expected to develop new skills, new ways of working, new kinds of teacher–pupil relationship. The 'successful' implementation of externally sponsored curricular changes are making considerable demands upon teachers' innovatory skills. In this situation the strategy of 'omissive action' (like non-co-operation with GCSE) is becoming an increasingly powerful weapon in teachers' political and union struggles.

It also needs to be recognized that these 'interventionary' innovations are being sponsored by a range of disparate agencies, whose modes of operation and interorganizational relationships differ considerably (e.g. TVEI schools are required to enter into contractual relationships with the MSC). Schools are faced with considerable 'innovation incoherence' and in many cases 'innovation overload'. The messages from different agencies are often contradictory, schemes are changed during their implementation, documents fail to appear, key personnel move on suddenly. Speed is of the essence in many of these schemes; the required pace of change is quite at odds with the gradualism typically preferred by teachers when grappling with change. However, schools are set in a 'turbulent environment' where, increasingly, change is associated with survival. In situations of falling rolls, schools must compete for pupils. Services must be 'sold' to potential clients. Curriculum innovations can be crucial factors in the market place. As a result, teachers are caught between incompatible interpretations of their own self-interest. Should they resist loss of autonomy and refuse to engage with new 'initiatives' or underwrite the future security of their job by making a success of these initiatives? As we have noted individual careers can be made and assured by commitment to innovation.

Innovation overload as it affects teachers' working conditions is also an aspect of what Apple (1983) calls 'intensification'. Teachers are confronted by increasing and increasingly diverse workloads which destroy sociability and reduce leisure and self-direction. The range of skills required of them may increase, but time and interaction are also under increasing pressure. 'Getting done becomes more important than what was done or how one got there' (Apple, 1983, p. 59). In several aspects, especially with regard to new assessment procedures, graded-testing, records of achievement, profiling, the new skills being acquired are essentially technical and administrative in character rather than educational. Time spent with pupils and on preparing lesson materials may actually be reduced even though total working hours increase. Apple also points out that the effects of intensification may be contradictory and mystifying 'since teachers thought of themselves as being more professional to the extent that they employed technical criteria and tests, they also basically accepted the longer hours and intensification of work that accompanied the program' (p. 61). What appears in one respect to be professional enhancement may actually serve to obscure a general worsening of working conditions. As new initiatives in assessment combine with curricular change, the introduction of equal opportunity programmes and greater public involvement in educational debate, many schools have developed a kind of siege mentality, and the pressures involved in coping with conflict and change are beginning to take their toll on the health and tolerance of individual practitioners:

It's becoming more difficult to do the job. The amount of pressure building up from the LEA, and other groups, over things like the daily act of worship, the ILEA equality initiatives, is enormous. And I'm spending more and more time doing things I don't think I should be doing. The time will come – especially in relation to the amount of work created by the politically committed authority like ours – when we will need a teaching head and an administrative head. I've only been in the job for two and a half years and its become worse in that time. I know colleagues who have been heads for ten or fifteen years who find it intolerable and are getting out. (London infant-school headteacher)

The micro-politics of industrial action

Once again it is important to emphasize the variability of responses to change in different organizations, different schools. While it may be the case that there is a general process of the restructuring of teachers' professional identity and their working conditions, neither the direct effects of these changes nor of the industrial action itself are uniform. The established pattern of micro-political relations, the institutional history of those relations and the perception and identification by participants of their interests (ideological, self and material) all have a direct bearing. It is the articulation of micro-politics with constraints and wider issues that accounts for much of the substance of political contention (or absence of it) within schools (this was the point made in Chapter 1, p. 24).

Again, briefly, I will consider some of the issues raised in teachers' accounts of the effects of the 1985–6 period of industrial dispute in their schools.

The notion of 'dispute' must be recognized in two senses: first, the formal industrial dispute between the teacher unions and their employers; second, the concomitant disputes which have arisen between teachers themselves as a result of the action. Conflicts can emerge in the interpersonal relations of teachers in one school, in the relations between members of different teacher unions, between teachers and their management, particularly the head, and between teachers and the LEA. Which, if any, of these conflicts develop seems to depend to a great extent on (1) the constitution of the staff, particularly the mix and strength of unions represented, and (2) the history of previous micro-political relations in the school. Small schools – infant, junior and nursery schools in particular – seem most likely to achieve unanimity among the staff as a whole:

> Our school is unusual for a primary school. We have 100 per cent union membership and all of those are in the NUT. So if there's a strike nobody's left, so to speak. And membership also includes the headteacher. So if we make a decision that's 100 per cent, the school is automatically closed down and there are no grey areas and that makes it simpler. (Class teacher, a London primary)

> It's put strains on parent–teacher relationships but it hasn't put any strain on staff relationships because we all agree with the action 100 per cent. And it's put no strain on the staff at all because we've all co-operated with each other and been pleased to co-operate with each other and the nursery nurses who haven't been on strike have understood why we've been on strike and they have found other things to do. (Headteacher, a London nursery)

In some cases the action has actually been seen to have a positive effect on staff morale and relationships, forging great solidarity and improving morale:

> The NAS chap has always been a militant and he's had us pretty well organized even before the action started, so in fact the head has gone along pretty much in the same way as he always did really, negotiating with us. So it didn't really have that much impact. The solidarity amongst the staff grew. (Sociology teacher, a Midlands comprehensive)

> I think staff morale is pretty low anyway. It's abysmally low. I think in fact if anything it has boosted them up because it makes us all feel that we're all doing something worthwhile in a positive way to bring about some sort of change and it's brought people together much more and there's a much stronger feeling of pulling together, of doing something as a unit and taking people on, whoever it is, which is a good feeling, which has been lacking up to now. (Head of PE, a London comprehensive)

The style and stance of the headteacher clearly emerges as a significant factor in the conduct of the dispute. This is one way in which the existing micro-politics of the institution mediates the meaning and practical realization of the dispute for those involved:

> The head refuses point blank to close the school even when on days such as today there were perhaps only 100 children, out of 900, present in the school. He still insists on lessons continuing and this has led to a number of discipline problems. ... He's persuaded other members of the teaching staff to break with unions and to support him over supervision of lunches and support him in other ways. He has very obviously rewarded one of these people and that was done very quickly. An interview was set up where this chap was the only candidate and that sort of attitude from the head has caused a lot of bitterness, though he was never popular, he's even less so now and it's just got worse. He's extremely embarrassed to walk into the staffroom. Nobody talks to him. If he sits at a table where staff are sitting, they get up and move away. (Head of drama, a London comprehensive)

One effect of such antipathy and polarization is the increased feelings of 'them and us' among the staff – the more developed sense of employer–employee type relationships between school management and teachers. The sense of a professional relationship betwen staff and headteacher is drastically eroded. Furthermore, as the extract indicates, positions adopted in the dispute can have direct career implications. Teachers may find their career prospects damaged or, as here, enhanced by their stance in the dispute. Another respondent suggested also that the list of teachers who withdrew labour, which was required by the local authority, would be used as a blacklist when future promotions or appointments were being made. 'If the list is sent someone will read it ... and it's a good way of cutting down the problem of 120–150 applicants for a job' (Head of geography, a south-eastern secondary modern).

> I saw the head this morning. He said everyone seems to be headmaster bashing these days, the teacher representatives on the governing body apparently really had a go at him. ... I don't know if I can say anything about our head, basically he is a bully

and he'll get what he can by bullying people but I think this has sort of shut him up a bit and he realizes that he's taking on something quite powerful. Given that he was covering, he and his deputies were covering as hard as they could to slow down the action. (Head of PE, an outer London comprehensive)

Certainly these data from the dispute highlight once again the contradictions built into the position of headship and particularly the lack of clarity as to where the loyalty as against the responsibility of the head lies. Again the point needs to be made that heads interpret their position differently and work out their handling of dilemmas thrown up by the dispute in different ways.

if you went to her and said such and such is happening – the NUT has decided X, Y and Z – then her response was, 'OK. Well, if that is the situation I can't operate the school'. She's not the sort of person who would stand at the gates saying, 'I'll run the damn place on my own'. Most provocations arose with the deputy head, who of course was the person more involved in the minutiae of running cover, and that was a major area of confrontation . . . he would do things he should have known would make people angry. (Head of careers, a London comprehensive)

The head's in a difficult position because he's a committed Labour supporter. Secondly, he's about to leave to take up another post. And thirdly, he's got to be seen to be backing the system. So he's in a difficult situation, while understanding the feelings of the lower paid down the scales, of lack of career prospects, stagnation. He's also got to present the front of the school as still operating. (Head of geography, a south-eastern secondary modern)

Certainly, though, many teachers also experience dilemmas in their feelings about and involvement in the industrial action. The action has implications for the sense of identity of the teacher. This often comes into play in interpretations of the purpose of the actions. That is the question of what the dispute is really about (discussed more fully below).

There have been moments and times of conflict and there were certainly individual issues that arose which caused problems and people have been put under a certain amount of stress in terms of their trade union loyalties versus what they saw as a kind of professional responsibility and the fact that the action, a lot of people felt anyway, the action in one sense is hurting us and so there was a strong element of self-sacrifice in what we were doing. (Head of drama, a London comprehensive)

It's on issues of education under attack, and in that sense it still falls within what I would call the long history of professional sort of actions that teachers take. And teachers have always felt very guilty about striking for pay, about their own conditions. Half the time they feel embarrassed about it. (Head of careers, a London comprehensive)

Teachers' views and definitions of professionalism and unionism vary considerably (Ginsburg, Meyenn and Miller, 1980). As contrasting ideologies and self-images they can be used to justify all kinds of work-related stances, and they are often a basis for conflict among teachers. This is evident in simple terms in the political standpoints of the different teacher unions; for example, in the case of PAT (the Professional Association of Teachers) strike action is explicitly ruled out by the association's constitution. Union membership can be related to the political affiliations of individual teachers and their views of their own best interests. The unions represent different interests and alliances of interests; they are not necessarily working towards the same ends. Thus, in accounts of the dispute in particular schools, conflicts among the staff were often identified with long-term micro-political divisions *and* different union memberships. The positions articulated by the different unions also reflect different definitions of the school and views of education:

The souring of the relationships has been in my school largely between the Scale 1 and Scale 2 people, who are mainly NUT, and the senior teachers, heads of department and above, who are by and large AMMA and PAT. And the problem has become almost one of us versus them. And the souring of relationships has come in cover, that is the most definite aspect of the dispute at the moment. Lunchtime supervision has caused problems and the walking off of the premises which has been taking place by the

NAS and NUT, who have been walking out at any time. . . . The arguments are not so much open as under the surface, so at potential flashpoints like cover the sores are opened up. (Head of geography, a south-eastern secondary modern)

A variety of issues extant within the institution may be pulled into the dispute. Consciousnesses are raised, disgruntlements focused and old scores settled. Tensions created by issues of race, gender, promotion and patterns of influence are laid bare by the dispute. As with other events (falling rolls, change of head, amalgamation), industrial action embodies the potential for a restructuring of the established patterns of advantage and disadvantage. The pay dispute is neither entirely limited to material concerns nor totally divorced from educational issues. Ideological interests are set against material and self-interests:

I would say that our staff relationships are extremely strained at this present time. Particularly between unions and between the body of the staff and the management, relationships have deteriorated a good deal in the past term. The main reason for this is that we haven't closed yet although both the NUT and NAS have been taking continual union action. They've failed to agree on the type of action and often the actions have been contradictory so that there are inter-union disputes. In fact the two union reps aren't talking to each other so it's the deputies who are doing the organizing and the talking. . . . It's a very high pressure situation, but most people are just totally fed up with what's happening and with what's actually happening to the children. There's a large body of people who wanted the union action to be swift and effective and to get back into a normal routine which we think is the essence of our type of school, but this hasn't been the case and the management hasn't helped so people are just very disenchanted, and there are lots of other factors to do with the management whose policy, as a child-centred school, ethically is very sound but practically it presents some dangers and a lot of concern by the teaching staff. (Head of drama, a London comprehensive)

In most cases teachers interviewed linked the conduct of the dispute and the problems arising from it to the organizational and educational ethos of their school. The primary teachers interviewed also specifically mentioned the effect of the action on their relationships with parents. Their daily routine typically brings them into immediate, face-to-face contact with parents. While this contact can offer a very direct sense of parental concern about the effects of the action on their children – 'their faces dropped and there was a different atmosphere' (nursery teacher) – it also provides a channel for teachers to explain themselves and develop support: 'we can talk to them about the action and the need for it' (primary teacher); 'we talked to them at great length about the reasons why we were doing it . . . they are very co-operative' (nursery head).

However, coherent explanations of the action are not necessarily easy to assemble. The reasons for the action, and for the length and bitterness of the dispute, offered by teachers I interviewed were typically complex and priorities differed from one school to another. The cutting edge of the dispute seemed to be forged by local conditions and experiences rather than by general principles. The concerns of the teachers were often a reflection of institutional priorities as much as national issues. The following comments illustrate the range:

- The dominant issue is pay absolutely, as the battle has gone on and as Sir Keith Joseph has tried to connect it up with teachers' contracts and conditions of service and so on, it has also become something about teachers' conditions of service, perhaps their professionalism.

- I don't honestly believe in our situation in my particular school that it is actually about pay. I think it's about conditions of service, very much so. In fact, in our first union meeting about strike action pay wasn't mentioned. The percentage was something that everyone was happy to leave to the union to negotiate. The actual thought of changing our contract was pretty horrific. I can see that in some ways assessment could be very useful to teachers, if we were to govern it ourselves, but to place the control over salary and control over us firmly in the hands of the DES and the headmaster, who nobody trusts, fills everyone with grim realization that this could be the end of a bad, bad unhappy career.

- I think that pay is important in the fact that it affects everything else. I don't think it's the actual money. I think it's the worth that is put on teachers. I think teachers are getting fed up because they are not thought anything of and they are getting more and more responsibility and more and more stick for everything that happens. The government accuses teachers all the time and parents accuse teachers all the time.

● The most important issue is what constitutes the teachers' contract. What precisely are we being paid for and not being paid for. When they're not getting a decent pay rise it's highlighted that they're doing a whole lot of things that they're getting no recognition for. I think the general attitude is we are doing it now, why don't we get paid for it?

● In our school it's about getting a better working situation for teachers. I think all sorts of things, discipline, it's certainly not just money, there's no question of that . . . it's being used as a vehicle for all sorts of things, the disruptive kid, the truanting kid. It's opened the way for a whole load of other things in our school to be brought up which were sort of bubbling away before . . . people are now making a stand where they have never made a stand before.

● Professionalism, teacher's morale, the quality of education, the fact that there aren't enough nursery teachers in London. Because they can't afford to live in London.

● That's absolutely clear, I mean it's not really just the pay, I mean it's on issues of education under attack . . . you wouldn't get this level of support across the country if it wasn't a general feeling that education, status, their professionalism, their worth, the services themselves, the services to the kids, money for books were not under massive attack. They are fighting a thin-line rearguard action, they're saying this is enough. And certainly the individuals from the school are clearly angry about lots of things. Lots of things get dragged in, redeployment, which is nothing to do with it, the redeployment of teachers within ILEA over falling rolls has been a constant running sore. People have been much more ready to say, 'let's go, let's do it'.

Here again are the mixture of concerns and commitments which have been reiterated throughout this analysis: material interests –

pay and conditions of work and conditions of service, control; self-interests – a sense of worth, status and professional autonomy; ideological interests – educational services, teacher numbers and money for books all under attack. (They provide validation of the initial analytical structure put forward in Ch. 1.) These diverse interests and concerns intersect and link national and local with institutional issues. The micro-politics of the school channel and shape the dispute and the dispute provides an outlet for entrenched grievances. Politics, unionism and micro-politics interplay.

Furthermore, these factors within the dispute, diverse and multifaceted as they are, parallel those factors – wages, conditions, control and status (being indicators of structural contradiction) – identified by Althusser and Balibar (1970) as providing the ingredients, when occurring together, for 'ruptural unity' (and thus as capable of producing radical change). In this sense the teachers' dispute and the form it has taken may be regarded as predictable and inevitable and it is possibly far-reaching in its long-term effects on teachers' work roles and political consciousness. Clearly, for many teachers it is an attempt to resist the changes in their work situation that were outlined above and to ensure that the extent of their professional autonomy, such as it is, and their influence in school policy-making are reduced no further.

Conclusion

The basic message of this attempt to analyse and theorize school organization is in part contradictory. First, I have tried to indicate the *conflictual* basis of the school as an organization. Second, and concomitantly, I have attempted to indicate that the control of school organizations, focused in particular on the position and role of the headteacher, is significantly concerned with *domination* (the elimination or pre-emption of conflict). Thus domination is intended to achieve and maintain particular definitions of the school over and against alternative, assertive definitions. The process which links these two basic facets of organizational life – conflict and domination – is *micro-politics*.

The concepts which have been developed to elaborate and articulate the idea of micro-politics are rooted in data which were drawn from teachers' immediate experiences of organizational life. These are not abstract concepts of prescription, rather they are grounded concepts of meaning, they attempt to explore and explain the organizational and political 'terrain on which men and women move' (Gramsci). They provide ways of understanding the interweaving of personal lives with organizational and social structures, but this is not simply a reversion to the primacy of agency, rather it serves to 'maintain the elements of choice, doubt, strategy, planning, error, transformation' (Connell, 1985, p. 266) that are the stuff of practical politics and ideological struggle. The constraining power of the organization that people confront daily is real. It is embedded in the actions of others with all their ambiguities and complexities.

There is another sense, related to educational change and transformation, in which this analysis contains contradictory messages. Clearly, micro-political processes in the organization operate to inhibit change, to maintain the status quo. Yet attention to micro-political processes also highlights the degree of 'tenuousness, dysfunction, interruption and possibility' that is inherent in educational context (Whitty, 1985, p. 45). Organizational domination is not 'naturally preordained ... [but] something that is won or lost in particular conflicts and struggles' (Apple, 1982, p. 264). Micropolitics recognizes constraint, but it also focuses upon what people do by way of shaping the social relations they live in.

Abstract, functional theories of organization only seem to obscure these lived realities and they portray schools as consensual institutions. In such theories ideologies are treated as irrelevant and conflicts as pathological. Indeed, these theories work ideologically to displace or divert conflict; they represent a 'preferred view' of the organization, a view of management, of domination. None the less, the maintenance of domination in the organization is not unproblematic, nor totally foregone, nor smooth and elegant. The 'structural looseness' of schools is evidence of that. Schools *are* sites of ideological struggle. They are also arenas of competition and contest over material advantage and vested interest. Careers, resources, status and influence are at stake in the conflicts between segments, coalitions and alliances. Teachers' interests, individual and collective, as well as those of students are being advanced and challenged in the micro-politics of the school, ideologies of control over teachers are normally associated with concomitant ideologies concerning the control of students:

But it is precisely because there is room for struggle and con-
testation in schools around cultural and ideological issues that
pedagogies can be developed in the interest of critical thinking
and civic courage. (Aronwitz and Giroux, 1985, p. 133)

Beyond the attempt at theorizing school organization, another
fundamental question is begged. Is the form of organizational life
presented here the only possible form for running schools? The
answer must be 'no', and as I see it the alternative lies in the
direction of *school democracy*. But that, as they say, is another
story.

Notes

Chapter 1

1. The term 'ideology' is used in two distinct senses in this volume. First, and most straightforwardly, it is used to refer to the educational perspectives and commitments of teachers. These are views about classroom practice, teacher–pupil relationships and pupils' learning which often rest upon more fundamental beliefs and ideas about social justice and human rights and the purposes of education in society (see the definition of teaching ideology on p. 14). It is this definition of ideology employed in the concept of ideological interests which is used extensively in the text (see p. 17). Second, 'ideology' is used to refer to ideas which can be shown to conceal or to resolve problematic aspects of social life in an idealistic or imaginary way. In this sense ideological accounts serve to secure the position of dominant groups. Hence, the ideology of management (see p. 5).

Chapter 8

1. While I recognize the weaknesses in the NUT/EOC sample, being self-selected, I quote it none the less as providing important evidence to set against 'men's theories' of women teachers and their careers.

Appendix

A number of specific school case studies are referred to at several points in the text or are discussed in some detail. It may be helpful to the reader to have some general information about the schools concerned.

Alder School: An all-through mixed, primary school with nursery, infant and junior departments, in inner London, sixteen full-time and four part-time staff. Studied by Price (1979).

Beachside Comprehensive: An 11–18 mixed south-coast comprehensive, became comprehensive 1967, previously secondary modern, 1504 pupils, seventy-nine staff. Studied by Ball (1981a).

Bishop McGregor Comprehensive: Purpose-built, mixed, Midlands comprehensive, Roman Catholic, 1269 pupils, seventy-five staff. Studied by Burgess (1983).

Casterbridge High School: An 11–18, mixed, west-country comprehensive, formed 1983 from amalgamation of boys grammar, boys secondary modern and mixed secondary modern, 1300 pupils, eighty-four staff. Studied by Ball (1984, 1985).

Green Hill Comprehensive: An 11–18, mixed, southern comprehensive, reorganized in 1972, having been a secondary modern. Small town and wide rural catchment, 1500 pupils. Studied by Wagstaff (1983).

Inner City Comprehensive: An 11–18, mixed, multi-racial comprehensive in an outer London borough. Formed in 1969 by the amalgamation of a boys secondary modern with a girls secondary modern, 1300+ pupils. Studied by Hanna (1978).

Millrace Comprehensive: An 11–18, mixed, south-coast comprehensive, 12 form entry, 1700+ pupils, ninety-six staff. Studied by Jago (1983) and Meadows (1981).

Nailsea School: An 11–18, mixed, comprehensive, reorganized from a grammar school in 1966. Small dormitory town ten miles from Bristol, 1100 pupils and seventy staff (fifty-eight full-time). Studied by Richardson (1973b).

Phoenix Comprehensive: An 11–18 comprehensive, in 'Wood End' (pop. 30,000), a town on the periphery of a major northern conurbation, 1300 pupils. Studied by Riseborough (1981).

Redmond College: A 14–18, mixed, Midlands comprehensive upper school, reorganized from small county grammar school, 1500 pupils and 100 staff. Studied by Hannan (1980).

Victoria Road Comprehensive: A South Wales boys comprehensive, formed by the amalgamation of a local grammar and a number of secondary moderns. On three sites (lower, middle and upper schools), 2000 pupils. Lower school, 10 form entry, twenty-two staff. Studied by Beynon (1981, 1985).

In other cases where interview data are cited in the text these are labelled according to the respondent's position (e.g. deputy head, head of maths, history teacher) and the general location and type of school (eastern comprehensive, London primary, Midlands secondary modern).

Bibliography

Abrahamson, P. (1974) 'Utbildning och Samhalle: Nogra problemonraden', in *Skolan som arbetsplats*, 9(4), 56–64.

Acker, S. (1980) 'Women, the other academics', *British Journal of Sociology of Education*, 1 (1), 68–80.

Acker, S. (1983) 'Women and teaching: a semi-detached sociology of a semi-profession', in Walker, S. and Barton, L. (eds) *Gender, Class and Education*, Lewes, Falmer Press.

Albrow, M. (1973) 'The study of organizations – objectivity or bias?', in Salaman, G. and Thompson, K. (eds) *People and Organizations*, London, Longman.

Althusser, L. and Balibar, E. (1970) *Reading Capital*, London, New Left Books.

Apple, M.W. (1979) *Ideology and Curriculum*, London, Routledge & Kegan Paul.

Apple, M.W. (1982) *Education and Power*, London, Routledge & Kegan Paul.

Apple, M.W. (1983) 'Work, class and teaching', in Walker, S. and Barton, L. (eds) *Gender, Class and Education*, Lewes, Falmer Press.

Arfwedson, G. (1979) 'Teachers' work', in Lundgren, U.P. and Patterson, S. (eds) *Code, Context and Curriculum Processes*, Stockholm, Gleerup.

Argyris, C. (1975) 'The individual and organization: some problems of mutual adjustment', in Houghton, V. *et al. Management in Education Reader 1*, London, Ward Lock.

Arnot, M. (1983) 'A cloud over co-education: an analysis of the forms of transmission of class and gender relations', in Walker, S. and Barton, L. (eds) *Gender, Class and Education*, Lewes, Falmer Press.

Aronowitz, S. and Giroux, H. (1985) *Education under Siege*, Cambridge, Mass., Bergin and Garvey.

Bacharach, S.B. and Lawler, E.J. (1980) *Power and Politics in Organizations*, San Francisco, Jossey-Bass.

Bachrach, P. and Baratz, M. (1970) *Power and Poverty*, New York, Oxford.

Bacon, W. (1981) 'Professional control and the engineering of client consent', in Dale, R. *et al.* (eds) *Education and the State, Volume 2: Politics, Patriarchy and Practice*, Lewes, Falmer Press.

Bailey, A.J. (1982) 'A question of legitimation: a response to Eric Hoyle', *Educational Management and Administration*, 10, 99–104.

Bailey, F.G. (1977) *Morality and Expediency*, Oxford, Basil Blackwell.

Baldridge, V.J. (1971) *Power and Conflict in the University*, New York, John Wiley.

Baldridge, V.J. *et al.* (1978) *Policy Making and Effective Leadership*, San Francisco, Jossey-Bass.

Ball, D. (1972) 'Self and identity in the context of deviance', in Scott, R.A. and Douglas, J.D. (eds) *Theoretical Perspectives on Deviance*, New York, Basic Books.

Ball, S.J. (1981a) *Beachside Comprehensive*, Cambridge, Cambridge University Press.

Ball, S.J. (1981b) 'The teaching nexus: a case of mixed-ability', in Barton, L. and Walker, S. (eds) *Schools, Teachers and Teaching*, Lewes, Falmer Press.

Ball, S.J. (1983) *Inside the Classroom*, Block 2, Unit 10, Open University Course E205, Conflict and Change in Education, Milton Keynes, Open University Press.

Ball, S.J. (1984) 'Facing up to falling rolls: becoming a comprehensive school', in Ball, S.J. (ed.) *Comprehensive Schooling: A Reader*, Lewes, Falmer Press.

Ball, S.J. (1985) 'School politics, teachers' careers and educational change: a case study of becoming a comprehensive school', in Barton, L. and Walker, S. (eds) *Education and Social Change*, Beckenham, Croom Helm.

Ball, S.J. and Lacey, C. (1980) 'Subject disciplines and the opportunity for group action: a measured critique of subject sub-cultures', in Woods, P.E. (ed.) *Teacher Strategies*, London, Croom Helm.

Banks, O. (1976) *The Sociology of Education*, 3rd edn, London, Batsford.

Barker, R. (1978) *Political Ideas in Modern Britain*, London, Methuen.

Barr-Greenfield, T. (1975) 'Theory about organization: a new perspective and its implications for schools', in Houghton, V.P., McHugh, G.A.R. and Morgan, C. (eds) *Management in Education: Reader 2*, London, Ward Lock/Open University Press.

Beck, R. (1983) 'Recollections and observations on a period of change', unpublished MA project in Education, Education Area, University of Sussex.

Becker, H. (1952) 'The career of the Chicago public school teacher', *American Journal of Sociology*, 57 (March), 470–7.

Becker, H. and Strauss, A. (1956) 'Careers, personality and adult socialization', *American Journal of Sociology*, 62(3), 253–63.

Becker, H. *et al.* (1961) *Boys in White*, Chicago, University of Chicago Press.

Belasco, J.A. and Alutto, J.A. (1975) 'Decisional participation and teacher satisfaction', in Houghton, V. *et al.* (eds) *Management in Education: Reader 1*, London, Ward Lock.

Bell, L.A. (1980) 'The school as an organization: a re-appraisal', *British Journal of Sociology of Education*, 1 (2), 183–92.

Bell, L.A., Pennington, R.C. and Burridge, J.B. (1979) 'Going mixed-ability: some observations on one school's experience', *Forum*, 21 (3), 14–17.

Bennet, C. (1984) 'Paints, pots or promotion', in Ball, S.J. and Goodson, I.F. (eds) *Teachers' Lives and Careers*, Lewes, Falmer Press.

Bennet, S. and Wilkie, R. (1973) 'Structural conflict in school organization', in Fowler, G. *et al.* (eds) *Decision-Making in British Education*, London, Heinemann.

Bennett, N. (1985) 'Central control and parental influence: reconciling the tensions in current proposals for school governance and policy-making', *Educational Management and Administration*, 12 (3), 157–63.

Berlak, A. and Berlak, H. (1981) *The Dilemmas of Schooling*, London, Methuen.

Bernbaum, G. (1976) 'The role of the head', in Peters, R.S. (ed.) *The Role of the Head*, London, Routledge & Kegan Paul.

Bernstein, B. (1971) 'On the classification and framing of educational knowledge', in Young, M.F.D. (ed.) *Knowledge and Control*, London, Collier-Macmillan.

Beynon, J. (1981) 'Poor Miss Floral', paper presented at the OU/SSRC Conference on the Sociology of the Curriculum, St Hilda's College, Oxford.

Beynon, J. (1985) 'Career histories in a comprehensive school', in Ball, S.J. and Goodson, I.F. (eds) *Teachers' Lives and Careers*, Lewes, Falmer Press.

Bidwell, C. (1965) 'The school as a formal organization', in March, J.F. (ed.) *Handbook of Organizations*, Chicago, Rand-McNally.

Bland, L. *et al.* (1978) 'Women "inside and outside" the relations of production', in CCCS (eds) *Women Take Issue*, London, Hutchinson.

Blecher, M.J. and White, G. (1979) *Micropolitics in Contemporary China*, London, Macmillan.

Bloch, M. (1965) *Feudal Society (1) The Growth of Ties of Dependence*, London, Routledge & Kegan Paul.

Blumer, H. (1971) 'Sociological implications of the thought of George Herbert Mead', in Cosin, B.R. *et al.* (eds) *School and Society*, London, Routledge & Kegan Paul/Open University.

Blumer, H. (1976) 'The methodological position of symbolic interactionism', in Hammersley, M. and Woods, P. (eds) *The Process of Schooling*, London, Routledge & Kegan Paul/Open University Press.

Boyd, W.L. (1976) 'The public, the professionals and educational policy-making: who governs?' *Teachers College Record*, 77, 539–77.

Boyd-Barrett, O. (1976) 'The organization as groups in conflict', in *Management in Education*, Unit 18, The Manager and Groups in the Organization, Milton Keynes, Open University Press.

Braverman, H. (1974) *Labour and Monopoly Capital*, New York, Monthly Review Press.

Briault, E. and Smith, F. (1980) *Falling Rolls in Secondary Schools*, Windsor, NFER-Nelson.

Brown, R. (1976) 'Women as employees: some comments on research in industrial sociology', in Allen, S. and Barker, D.L. (eds) *Sexual Divisions and Society: Process and Change*, London, Tavistock.

Buchan, L. (1980) 'Its a good job for a girl (But an awful career for a woman!)', in Spender, D. and Sarah, E. (eds) *Learning to Lose*, London, The Women's Press.

Bucher, R. and Strauss, A. (1961) 'Professions in process', *American Journal of Sociology*, 66 (Jan.), 325–34.

Burgess, R.G. (1983) *Experiencing Comprehensive Education*, London, Methuen.

Burgess, R.G. (1984) 'Headship: freedom or constraint?' in Ball, S.J. (ed.) *Comprehensive Schooling: A Reader*, Lewes, Falmer Press.

Burke, J. (1986) 'Concordia Sixth Form College: a sociological case study based on history and ethnography', unpublished D.Phil. thesis, Educational Area, University of Sussex.

Burns, T. (1955) 'The reference of conduct in small groups: cliques and cabals in occupational milieux', *Human Relations*, 8, 467–86.

Burns, T. and Stalker, G.M. (1961) *The Management of Innovation*, London, Tavistock.

Byrne, E. (1978) *Women and Education*, London, Tavistock.

Callahan, R. (1962) *Education and the Cult of Efficiency*, Chicago, University of Chicago Press.

Campbell, D.T. (1968) 'Ethnocentricism of disciplines and the fish-scale model of omniscience', in Sherif, M. and Sherif, C.W. (eds) *Interdisciplinary Relationships in the Social Sciences*, New York, Aldine.

Carspecken, P. and Miller, H. (1983) 'Teachers in an occupied school', paper presented at the Teachers' Lives and Teachers' Careers Conference, St Hilda's College, Oxford.

Charters, W.W., Jnr (1953) 'Social class analysis and the control of public education', *Harvard Education Review*, 24, 268–83.

Child, J. (1972) 'Organizational structure, environment and performance: the role of strategic choice', *Sociology*, 6, 1–22.

Christie, R. and Geis, F. (1970) *Studies in Machiavellianism*, London, Academic Press.

Clarricoates, K. (1980) 'All in a day's work', in Spender, D. and Sarah, E. (eds) *Learning to Lose: Sexism and Education*, London, The Women's Press.

Clegg, S. and Dunkerley, D. (1980) *Organization, Class and Control*, London, Routledge & Kegan Paul.

Cockburn, C. (1978) *The Local State*, London, Pluto Press.

Cohen, M.D., March, J.G. and Olsen, J.P. (1972) 'A garbage can model of organizational choice', *Administrative Science Quarterly*, 17, 1–25.

Collins, R. (1975) *Conflict Sociology*, New York, Academic Press.

Commission for Racial Equality (1985) *Swann: A Response from the Commission for Racial Equality*, London, CRE.

Connell, R.W. (1985) 'Theorizing gender', *Sociology*, 19 (2), 260–72.

Connell, R.W. *et al.* (1982) *Making the Difference*, Sydney, Allen & Unwin.

Corwin, R.G. (1983) *The Entrepreneurial Bureaucracy*, London, JAI Press.

Cressey, P. and MacInnes, J. (1980) 'Voting for Ford: industrial democracy and the control of labour', *Capital and Class*, 11 (Summer), 5–33.

Cunnison, S. (1985) 'Making it in a man's world: women teachers in a senior high school', University of Hull, Deparment of Sociology and Social Anthropology, Occasional Paper No. 1.

Cyert, R.M. and March, J.G. (1963) *A Behavioural Theory of the Firm*, Englewood Cliffs, NJ, Prentice-Hall.

Dahl, R. (1961) *Who Governs?*, New Haven, Conn., Yale University Press.

Dale, R. (1979) 'The politicisation of school deviance: reactions to William Tyndale', in Barton, L. and Meighan, R. (eds) *Schools, Pupils and Deviance*, Driffield, Nafferton.

David, M. (1980) *The State, the Family and Education*, London, Routledge & Kegan Paul.

Davies, B. (1981) 'Schools as organizations and the organization of schooling', *Educational Analysis*, 3 (1), 47–67.

Day, R. and Day, J.V. (1977) 'A review of the current state of negotiated order theory: an appreciation and a critique', *The Sociological Quarterly*, (Winter), 126–42.

Deem, R. (1978) *Women and Schooling*, London, Routledge & Kegan Paul.

Delamont, S. (1980) *Sex Roles and the School*, London, Methuen.

Delamont, S. (1983) *Interaction in the Classroom*, 2nd edn, London, Methuen.

Denscombe, M. (1980) 'Keeping 'em quiet: the significance of noise for the practical activity of teaching', in Woods, P.E. (ed.) *Teacher Strategies*, London, Croom Helm.

DES (1977) *Education in Schools: A Consultative Document*, Government Green Paper, London, HMSO.

DES (1984) *Influence at School*, Government Green Paper, London, HMSO.

Du Boulay, J. (1974) *Portrait of a Greek Mountain Village*, Oxford, Clarendon Press.

Duverger, M. (1972) *The Study of Politics*, London, Nelson.

Dwyer, D. (1984) 'Leadership succession as explanation of organizational change: necessary but insufficient', a paper presented at the AERA Annual Conference, New Orleans.

Eagleton, T. (1976) *Marxism and Literary Criticism*, London, Methuen.

Edwards, A. and Furlong, V.J. (1976) *The Language of Teaching*, London, Longman.

Ellis, T. *et al.* (1976) *William Tyndale: The Teachers' Story*, London, Writers and Readers Cooperative.

Epstein, C. (1981) *Women in Law*, New York, Basic Books.

Esland, G. (1971) 'Teaching and learning as the organization of knowledge', in Young, M.F.D. (ed.) *Knowledge and Control*, London, Collier-Macmillan.

Esland, G. (1972) *Innovation in the School*, Unit 12 Educational Studies Course E282, School and Society, Milton Keynes, Open University Press.

Evans, J. (1985) *Teaching in Transition*, Milton Keynes, Open University Press.

Everhart, R.B. (1976–7) 'Patterns of becoming; the making of roles in changing schools', *Interchange*, 7 (1), 24–33.

Fleishman, E.A. and Peters, D.A. (1962) 'Interpersonal values, leadership attitudes and managerial success', *Personnel Psychology*, 15, 127–43.

Fletcher, C., Caren, M. and Williams, W. (1985) *Schools on Trial*, Milton Keynes, Open University Press.

Foley, M. (1985) *Institutional Profile*, unpublished MA in Education Project, Education Area, University of Sussex.

Freidson, E. (1970) *Professional Dominance*, Chicago, Aldine.

Freidson, E. (1975) *Doctoring Together: A Study of Professional Social Control*, New York, Elsevier.

Gans, H. (1967) *The Levittowners*, New York, Pantheon.

Gibbes, N. (1980) *West Indian Teachers Speak Out: Their Experiences in Some of London's Schools*, Lewisham Council for Community Relations, Caribbean Teachers' Association.

Ginsburg, M., Meyenn, R. and Miller, H. (1980) 'Teachers' conceptions of professionalism and trades unionism: an ideological analysis', in Woods, P.E. (ed.) *Teacher Strategies*, London, Croom Helm.

Glen, F. (1975) *The Social Psychology of Organizations*, London, Methuen.

Gluckman, M. (1963) 'Gossip and scandal', *Current Anthropology*, 4, 307–16.

Goff, T. (1980) *Marx and Mead*, London, Routledge & Kegan Paul.

Goffman, E. (1971) *The Presentation of Self in Everyday Life*, Harmondsworth, Penguin.

Goffman, E. (1981) *Forms of Talk*, Oxford, Basil Blackwell.

Goodson, I.F. (1983) *School Subjects and Curriculum Change*, Beckenham, Croom Helm.

Goodson, I.F. (1987) *The Making of Curriculum: Essays in the Social History of Education*, Lewes, Falmer Press.

Gouldner, A. (1954) *Wildcat Strike*, Yellow Springs, Ohio, Antioch Press.

Gouldner, A. (1957) 'Cosmopolitans and locals: towards an analysis of latent social roles', *Administrative Science Quarterly*, 2, 281–306.

Gouldner, A. (1959) 'Organizational analysis', in Merton, M.K. (ed.) *Sociology Today*, New York, Basic Books.

Grace, G. (1978) *Teachers, Ideology and Control*, London, Routledge & Kegan Paul.

Gray, H. (1975) 'Exchange and conflict in the school', in Houghton, V., MacHugh, R. and Morgan, C. (eds) *Management in Education: Reader 1*, London, Ward Lock.

Greenfield, W.D. (1984) 'Sociological perspectives for research on educational administrators: the role of the assistant principal', paper presented at the AERA annual meeting in New Orleans, April 23–7.

Greenwood, R. (1983) 'Changing patterns of budgeting in English local government', *Public Administration*, 61 (Summer), 149–68.

Gretten, J. and Jackson, M. (1976) *William Tyndale: Collapse of a School – or a System*, London, Allen & Unwin.

Griffin, C. (1985) *Typical Girls*, London, Routledge & Kegan Paul.

Gronn, P. (1983) 'Talk as the work: the accomplishment of school administration', *Administrative Science Quarterly*, 28, 1–21.

Gross, N., Giaquinta, J.A. and Bernstein, M. (1971) *Implementing Organizational Innovations*, New York, Harper & Row.

Gross, N. and Trask, A.E. (1976) *The Sex Factor and the Management of Schools*, New York, John Wiley.

Guest, R.H. (1962) *Organizational Change: The Effect of Successful Leadership*, London, Tavistock.

Habermas, J. (1984) *The Theory of Communicative Action, Volume 1: Reason and the Rationalization of Society*, London, Heinemann.

Hagen, R.I. and Kahn, A. (1975) 'Discrimination against competent women', *Journal of Applied Social Psychology*, 5, 362–76.

Hall, P.M. (1972) 'A symbolic interactionist analysis of politics', *Sociological Inquiry*, 42 (3–4), 35–75.

Hall, P.M. (1979) 'The presidency and impression management', in Denzin, N.L. (ed.) *Studies in Symbolic Interactionism Volume 2*, Greenwich, Conn., JAI Press.

Hanna, J.P. (1978) 'The study of organizations', unpublished MA project in Education, Institutional Profile, Education Area, University of Sussex.

Hannan, A. (1980) 'Problems, conflicts and school policy: a case study of an innovative comprehensive school, *Collected Original Resources in Education*, 4 (1).

Hargreaves, A. (1981) 'Contrastive rhetoric and extremist talk', in Barton, L. and Walker, S. (ed.) *Schools, Teachers and Teaching*, Lewes, Falmer Press.

Hargreaves, D.H. (1967) *Social Relations in a Secondary School*, London, Routledge & Kegan Paul.

Hargreaves, D.H. (1980) 'The occupational culture of teachers', in Woods, P.E. (ed.) *Teacher Strategies*, London, Croom Helm.

Harris, K. (1982) *Teachers and Classes*, London, Routledge & Kegan Paul.

Harris, T.A. (1973) *I'm OK – You're OK*, London, Pan.

Hatton, E.J. (1985) 'Equality, class and power: a case study', *British Journal of Sociology of Education*, 6 (3), 255–72.

Havelock, R.G. (1973) *The Change Agent's Guide to Innovation in Education*, Englewood Cliffs, NJ, Educational Technology Publications.

Henley, N.M. (1977) *Body Politics: Power, Sex, and Nonverbal Communication*, Englewood Cliffs, NJ, Prentice-Hall.

Hewton, E. (1986) *Education in Recession: Crisis in County Hall and Classroom*, Hemel Hempstead, Allen & Unwin.

Hilsum, S. and Start, K.R. (1974) *Promotion and Careers in Teaching*, Windsor, NFER.

Hindess, B. (1982) 'Power, interests and the outcomes of struggles', *Sociology*, 16 (4), 498–511.

Hirschmann, A.O. (1970) *Exit, Voice and Loyalty*, Cambridge, Mass., Harvard University Press.

Holland, P. (1976) 'Scandal for schools', *Times Educational Supplement*, 17 September.

House, E. (1979) 'Technology versus craft: a ten year perspective on innovation', *Journal of Curriculum Studies*, 11 (1), Jan.–March.

Howell, D. (1976) *British Social Democracy: A Study in Development and Decay*, London, Croom Helm.

Hoyle, E. (1969) *The Role of the Teacher*, London, Routledge & Kegan Paul.

Hoyle, E. (1975) 'The study of schools as organizations', in Houghton, V., MacHugh, R. and Morgan, C. (eds) *Management in Education: Reader 1*, London, Ward Lock.

Hoyle, E. (1982) 'Micropolitics of educational organizations', *Educational Management and Administration*, 10, 87–98.

Hughes, E.C. (1964) *Men and Their Work*, Glencoe, The Free Press.

Hunter, C. (1980) 'The politics of participation, with specific reference to teacher–pupil relationships', in Woods, P.E. (ed.) *Teacher Strategies*, London, Croom Helm.

Hunter, C. and Highway, P. (1980) 'Morale, motivation and management in a middle school', in Bush, T. *et al.* (eds) *Approaches to School Management*, Cambridge, Harper Row.

Inner London Education Authority (1984) *Improving Secondary Schools: Report of the Hargreaves Committee*, London, ILEA.

Isaacs, J. (1981) 'Amalgamation of schools: effects on quality of work', *Educational Administration*, 9 (2) (May), 92–8.

Jago, W. (1983) *Teachers at Work: A Study of Individual and Role in School*, unpublished D.Phil. thesis, Education Area, University of Sussex.

Johnson, T. (1972) *Professions and Power*, London, Macmillan.

Jones, C. (1985) 'Sexual tyranny: male violence in a mixed secondary school' in Weiner, G. (ed.) *Just a Bunch of Girls: Feminist Approaches to Schooling*, Milton Keynes, Open University Press.

Kanter, R.M. (1977) *Men and Women of the Corporation*, New York, Basic Books.

Kelly, A. (1985) 'Traditionalists and trendies: teachers' attitudes to educational issues', *British Educational Research Journal*, 11 (2), 91–112.

Kelly, J. (1969) *Organizational Behaviour*, New York, Irwin-Dorsey.

Kelly, J. (1974) *Organizational Behaviour: An Existential-Systems Approach*, rev. edn, New York, Irwin-Dorsey.

King, R. (1968) 'The head teacher and his authority', in Allen, B. (ed.) *Headship in the 1970s*, Oxford, Basil Blackwell.

King, R. (1978) *All Things Bright and Beautiful? A Sociological Study of Infants' Classrooms*, Chichester, John Wiley.

King, R. (1983) *The Sociology of School Organization*, London, Methuen.

King, R. (1984) 'Educational adminstration and organizational theory', *Educational Management and Administration*, 12, 59–62.

Klein, R. (1967), in a review of Nicholson, M. *The System*, in *The Observer*, 24 September.

Krekel, N.R.A., Van der Woerd, T.G. and Wouterse, J.J. (1967) *Mergers: A European Approach to Technique*, London, Business Books.

Lacey, C. (1970) *Hightown Grammar*, Manchester, Manchester University Press.

Lacey, C. (1974) 'De-Streaming in a pressured academic environment', in Eggleston, J. *Contemporary Research in the Sociology of Education*, London, Methuen.

Lacey, C. (1977) *The Socialization of Teachers*, London, Methuen.

Ladd, E.C. and Lipset, S.M. (1975) *The Divided Academy*, New York, McGraw-Hill.

Lane, R.E. (1959) *Political Life: Why People Get Involved in Politics*, Glencoe, Ill., The Free Press.

Langrish, S.V. (1981) 'Why don't women progress in management jobs?', *Business Graduate*, 11 (1), 7.

Lasswell, H.D. (1951) *The Political Writings of Harold D. Lassell*, Glencoe, Ill., The Free Press.

Latus, E. (1977) 'Seatown High School', unpublished MA project in Education, Education Area, University of Sussex.

Lehmann, E. (1969) 'Toward a macro-sociology of power', *American Sociological Review*, 38, 212–30.

Levine, C.H. (1978) 'Organizational decline and cutback management', *Public Administration Review*, (July/August), 316–25.

Lewin, K. (1943) 'Forces behind food habits and methods of change', *Bulletin of the National Resource Council*, 8, 35–65.

Lewin, K. (1947) 'Group decision and social change', in Newcomb, T. and Hartley, E. (eds) *Readings in Social Psychology*, New York, Holt, Rinehart & Winston.

Lipham, J. (1964) 'Leadership and administration', in Griffith, D. (ed.) *Behavioural Science and Educational Administration, 64th Yearbook of the National Society for the Study of Education*, Chicago, Chicago University Press.

Littler, C. and Salaman, G. (1982) 'Bravermania and beyond: recent theories of the labour process', *Sociology*, 16(2), 251–69.

Lorber, J. (1984) *Women Physicians*, New York, Tavistock.

Lortie, D. (1975) *The School Teacher: A Sociological Study*, Chicago, University of Chicago Press.

Lowi, T.J. (1964) 'American business, public policy, case studies and political theory', *World Politics*, 16 (4) (July), 677–715.

Lukes, S. (1977) *Essays in Social Theory*, London, Macmillan.

Lyons, G. (1981) *Teacher Careers and Career Perceptions*, Windsor, NFER-Nelson.

Macdonald, B. and Walker, R. (1976) *Changing the Curriculum*, London, Open Books.

McGiveney, J.H. and Moynihan, W. (1972) 'School and community', *Teachers College Record*, 74, 209–24.

March, J.G. and Olsen, J.P. (1976) *Ambiguity and Choice in Organization*, Bergen, Universitetslaget.

Marland, M. (1982a) 'The politics of improvement in schools', *Educational Management and Administration*, 10, 122–32.

Marland, M. (1982b) 'Staffing for sexism: educational leadership and role models', *Westminster Studies in Education*, 5, 11–26.

Marshall, J. (1984) *Women Managers: Travellers in a Male World*, Chichester, John Wiley.

Masters, K. (1982) 'Open enrolment – flexible boundaries – closing choice', unpublished MA project in Education, Education Area, University of Sussex.

Meadows, E. (1981) 'Politics and personalities', upublished MA project in Education, Institutional Profile, Education Area, University of Sussex.

Meyer, J.W. and Rowan, B. (1978) 'The structure of educational organiz- ations', in Meyer, M.W. (ed.) *Environments and Organizations*, San Francisco, Jossey-Bass.

Miller, H. (1984) 'The local state and teachers', paper presented at the International Sociology of Education Conference, West Hill College, Birmingham, 2–4 January.

Miskel, C. and Owens, M. (1983) 'Principal succession and changes in school coupling and effectiveness', paper presented at the AERA Annual Conference, Montreal, Canada.

Mitchell, P. (1983) Lecture, University of Sussex.

Morgan, C., Hall, V. and Mackay, H. (1983) *The Selection of Secondary School Heads*, Milton Keynes, Open University Press.

Murgatroyd, S. and Gray, H. (1984) 'Leadership and the effective school', in Harling, P. (ed.) *New Directions in Educational Leadership*, Lewes, Falmer Press.

Musgrove, F. (1971) *Patterns of Power and Authority in English Education*, London, Methuen.

NUT (1980) *Promotion and the Woman Teacher*, London, EOC/NUT.

Nias, J. (1984) 'Definition and maintenance of self in primary teaching', *British Journal of Sociology of Education*, 5 (3), 267–80.

Nias, J. (1985) 'Reference groups in primary teaching: talking, listening and identity', in Ball, S.J. and Goodson, I.F. (eds) *Teachers' Lives and Careers*, Lewes, Falmer Press.

Nicholls, A. (1983) *Managing Educational Innovations*, Hemel Hemp- stead, Allen & Unwin.

Norris, R. (1976) '*Countesthorpe: After Three Years*', E203, Curriculum Design and Development, Case Study 5, Milton Keynes, Open University Press.

Novarra, V. (1980) *Men's Work, Women's Work: The Ambivalence of Equality*, London, Marion Boyars.

Oakeshott, M. (1962) *Rationalism and Politics and Other Essays*, London, Methuen.

Offe, C. (1976) *Industry and Inequality*, London, Edward Arnold.

Open University (1972) *Innovation and Ideology*, Units 11 to 14, E282, School and Society, Milton Keynes, Open University Press.

Ozga, J. and Lawn, M. (1981) *Teachers, Professionalism and Class: Study of Organized Teachers*, Lewes, Falmer Press.

Paine, R. (1967) 'What is gossip about? An alternative hypothesis', *Man*, 2, 278–85.

Paisey, A. (1984) 'Trends in educational leadership thought', in Harling, P. (ed.) *New Directions in Educational Leadership*, Lewes, Falmer Press.

Parsons, T. (1951) *The Social System*, Chicago, The Free Press.

Parsons, T. (1960) *Structure and Process in Modern Societies*, Chicago, The Free Press.

Partridge, J. (1968) *Life in a Secondary Modern School*, Harmondsworth, Penguin.

Peterson, P.E. (1972) 'The school bussing controversy: redistributive or ruralist politics', *Administrators Notebook*, 20 (9), (May).

Peterson, W.A. (1964) 'Age, teachers' role and the institutional setting', in Biddle, B.J. and Elena, W.S. (eds) *Contemporary Research in Teacher Effectiveness*, London, Holt, Rinehart & Winston.

Pettigrew, A.M. (1982) 'Patterns of managerial response as organizations move from rich to poor environments', paper delivered to the British Educational Management and Administration Society, Annual Conference, West Hill College, 17–19 September.

Pfeffer, J. (1978) 'The micropolitics of organizations', in Meyer, M.W. *et al.* (eds) *Environments and Organizations*, San Francisco, Jossey-Bass.

Pfeffer, J. (1981) *Power in Organizations*, Cambridge, Mass., Pitman.

Pocock, J.G.A. (1981) 'The reconstruction of discourse', *Modern Language Notes*, 96, 959–80.

Pratt, S. (1984) 'Subordinates' strategies of interaction in the management of schools', in Harling, P. (ed.) *New Directions in Educational Leadership*, Lewes, Falmer Press.

Price, R. (1979) 'A school in transition: a case study of a primary school in its first 18 months under a new head', unpublished MA dissertation in Education, Education Area, University of Sussex.

Pring, R. (1986) 'The privatization of schooling', in Rogers, R. (ed.) *Education and Social Class*, Lewes, Falmer Press.

Radnor, H. (1983) 'The invisible job: a study of the role of the female deputy head in the comprehensive school', unpublished MA major project, Education Area, University of Sussex.

Raff, M. (1982) 'The NUT and women teachers', *Secondary Education Journal*, 12 (2), 19–20.

Ramazanoglu, C. (1985) 'Sex and violence in academic life or You can keep a good woman down', paper presented at the BSA Annual Conference, War, Violence and Social Change.

Reid, M. *et al.* (1981) *Mixed-Ability Teaching: Problems and Possibilities*, Slough, NFER.

Reid, W.A. (1984) 'Curricular topics as institutional categories: implicaions for theory and research in the history and sociology of school subjects', in Goodson, I.F. and Ball, S.J. (eds) *Defining the Curriculum: Histories and ethnographies*, Lewes, Falmer Press.

Reskin, B.F. (1978) 'Sex differentiation and the social organization of science', in Gaston, J. (ed.) *Sociology of Science*, San Francisco, Jossey-Bass.

Reynolds, D. and Sullivan, M. (1981) 'The comprehensive experience', in Barton, L. and Walker, S. (eds) *Schools, Teachers and Teaching*, Lewes, Falmer Press.

Richardson, E. (1973a) *The Environment of Learning: Conflict and Understanding in the Secondary School*, London, Heinemann.

Richardson, E. (1973b) *The Teacher, the School and the Task of Management*, London, Heinemann.

Rillie, I. (1982) 'Downview: one man's school', unpublished MA project in Education, Education Area, University of Sussex.

Riseborough, G. (1981) 'Teacher careers and comprehensive schooling: an empirical study', *Sociology*, 15 (3), 352–81.

Rogers, E.M. and Shoemaker, F.F. (1971) *Communication of Innovations*, 2nd edn, New York, The Free Press.

Rogers, R. (1981) 'Pioneers in unchartered territory', *Times Educational Supplement*, 3415, 11 December.

Roy, W. (1983) *Teaching Under Attack*, Beckenham, Croom Helm.

Sacks, H., Schegloff, E.A. and Jefferson, G. (1974) 'A simplest systematics for the organization of turn-taking for conversation', *Language*, 50, 696–735.

St John Brooks, C. (1983) 'English: a curriculum for personal development?', in Hammersley, M. and Hargreaves, A. (eds) *Curriculum Practice: Some Sociological Case Studies*, Lewes, Falmer Press.

Salaman, G. (1979) *Work Organizations: Resistance and Control*, London, Longman.

Salaman, G. and Thompson, K. (1973) (eds) *People and Organizations*, London, Longman.

Saunders, P. (1981) *Urban Politics: A Sociological Interpretation*, London, Hutchinson.

Schein, E.H. (1972) *Professional Education: Some New Directions*, New York, McGraw-Hill.

Schutz, A. and Luckmann, T. (1974) *The Structures of the Lifeworld*, London, Heinemann.

Seaman, P. (1972) 'The changing organization of school knowledge', Unit

11, in *Innovation and Ideology*, School and Society E282, Milton Keynes, Open University Press.

Shapiro, H. Svi (1982) 'Education in capitalist society: towards a reconsideration of the state in educational policy', *Teachers College Record*, 83 (4), 515–27.

Sharp, R. (1981) 'Review of Beachside Comprehensive', *British Journal of Sociology of Education*, 2 (3), 278–85.

Sharp, R. (1985) 'Urban education and the current crisis', in Grace, G. (ed.) *Education and the City: Theory, History and Contemporary Practice*, London, Routledge & Kegan Paul.

Sharp, R. and Green, A. (1975) *Education and Social Control*, London, Routledge & Kegan Paul.

Sharpe, S. (1976) *Just Like a Girl*, Harmondsworth, Penguin.

Shibutani, T. (1966) *Improvised News*, Indianapolis, Bobbs-Merril.

Sikes, P. (1985) 'The life cycle of the teacher', in Ball, S.J. and Goodson, I.F. (eds) *Teachers' Lives and Careers*, Lewes, Falmer Press.

Sikes, P., Measor, L. and Woods, P. (1985) *Teacher Careers: Crises and Continuities*, Lewes, Falmer Press.

Silverman, D. (1970) *The Theory of Organizations*, London, Heinemann.

Simmel, G. (1968) *The Conflict in Modern Culture and other Essays*, New York, Teachers' College Press.

Simpson, R.L. and Simpson, I.H. (1969) 'Women and bureaucracy in semi-professions', in Etzioni, A. (ed.) *The Semi-Professions and Their Organization*, New York, The Free Press.

Smetheram, D. (1979) 'Identifying strategies', paper given at SSRC funded conference, Teacher and Pupil Strategies, St Hilda's College, Oxford, 15–17 September.

Smith, D.E. (1975) 'An analysis of ideological structures and how women are excluded: considerations for academic women', *Canadian Review of Sociology and Anthropology*, 12 (4) (Part 1), 353–69.

Smith, D.E. (1978) 'A peculiar eclipsing: women's exclusion from man's culture', *Women's Studies International Quarterly*, (4), 482–96.

Smith, T.J. (1983) 'On being political', *Educational Management and Administration*, 11, 205–8.

Spender, D. (ed.) (1980) *Learning to Lose: Sexism and Education*, London, Women's Press.

Spender, D. (ed.) (1981) *Men's Studies Modified*, Oxford, Pergamon.

Stephenson, R.M. (1951) 'Conflict and control functions of humor', *American Journal of Sociology*, 56, 569–74.

Strauss, A. (1978) *Negotiations: Varieties, Contexts, Processes and Social Order*, San Francisco, Jossey-Bass.

Strauss, A.L. (1959) *Mirrors and Masks: A Search for Identity*, Glencoe, Ill., The Free Press.

Stray, C. (1985) 'From monopoly to marginality: classics in English education since 1800', in Goodson, I.F. (ed.) *Social Histories of the Secondary Curriculum*, Lewes, Falmer Press.

Strodbeck, F.L. and Marm, R.D. (1956) 'Sex role differentiation in jury deliberations', *Sociometry*, 19 (March), 9–10.

Stubbs, M. (1983) *Language, Schools and Classrooms*, 2nd edn, London Methuen.

Sugarman, B. (1967) *The School and Moral Development*, London, Croom Helm.

Swann Report, The : Committee of Inquiry into the Education of Children from Ethnic Minority Groups (1985) *Education for All*, Cmnd 9453, London, HMSO.

Swidler, A. (1979) *Organization Without Authority*, Cambridge, Mass., Harvard University Press.

Taafe, R. (1980) 'Charisma and collegiate: conflict or harmony?', unpublished MA minor project in Education, Education Area, University of Sussex.

Tarn, J. (1984) 'Institutional profile', unpublished MA project in Education, Education Area, University of Sussex.

Turner, C.M. (1968) 'An organizational analysis of a secondary modern school', *Sociological Review*, 17 (1), 67–87.

Turner, G. (1983) *The Social World of the Comprehensive School*, Beckenham, Croom Helm.

Turner, V.W. (1957) *Schism and Continuity in an African Society: A Study of Village Life*, Manchester, Manchester University Press.

Turner, V.W. (1971) 'An anthropological approach to the Icelandic saga', in Beidelman, T.O. (ed.) *The Translation of Culture: Essays to E.E. Evans-Pritchard*, London, Tavistock.

Tyack, D. (1974) *The One Best System: A History of American Urban Education*, Cambridge, Mass., Harvard University Press.

Vidich, A., and Besman, J. (1958) *Small Town in Mass Society*, New York, Anchor Books.

Wagstaff, C. (1983) 'Green Hill School: An Institutional Profile', unpublished MA project in Education, Education Area, Univeristy of Sussex.

Wallace, G., Miller, H. and Ginsburg, M. (1983) 'Teachers' responses to the cuts', in Ahier, J. and Flude, M. (eds) *Contemporary Education Policy*, Beckenham, Croom Helm.

Watts, J. (ed.) (1977) *The Countesthorpe Experience: The First Five Years*, London, Allen & Unwin.

Weber, M. (1948) *From Max Weber: Essays in Sociology*, ed. H.H. Gerth and C. Wright Mills, London, Routledge & Kegan Paul.

Weber, M. (1978) *Ecomomy and Society: An Outline of Interpretive Sociology*, Berkeley and Los Angeles, University of California Press.

Weick, K. (1976) 'Educational organizations as loosely coupled systems', *Administrative Science Quarterly*, 21, 1–9.

West, C. (1974) 'Sexism and Conversation', unpublished MA thesis, Department of Sociology, University of California, Santa Barbara.

Whitbread, A. (1980) 'Female teachers are women first: sexual harassment at work!', in Spender, D. and Sarah, E. (eds) *Learning to Lose: Sexism and Education*, London, The Women's Press.

Whiteside, T. (1978) *The Sociology of Educational Innovation*, London, Methuen.

Whitty, G. (1985) *Sociology and School Knowledge*, London, Methuen.

Whyld, J. (1983) 'School life: organization and control', in Whyld, J. (ed.) *Sexism in the Secondary Curriculum*, Cambridge, Mass., Harper & Row.

Wildavsky, A. (1968) 'Budgeting as a political process', in Sills, D. (ed.) *International Encyclopaedia of the Social Sciences*, 2, 192–9, New York, Cromwell, Collier and Macmillan.

Willis, P. (1977) *Learning to Labour*, Farnborough, Saxon House.

Wilson, B. (1962) 'The teacher's role: a sociological analysis, *British Journal of Sociology*, 3 (1), 15–32.

Winkley, D. (1984) 'Educational management and school leadership', in Harling, P. (ed.) *New Directions in Educational Leadership*, Lewes, Falmer Press.

Wolcott, H.F. (1973) *The Man in the Principal's Office: An Ethnography*, New York, Holt, Rinehart & Winston.

Wolin, S. (1961) *Politics and Vision: Continuity and Innovation in Western Political Thought*, London, Allen & Unwin.

Woods, P.E. (1979) *The Divided School*, London, Routledge & Kegan Paul.

Woods, P.E. (1981) 'Strategies, commitment and identity: making and breaking the teacher role', in Barton, L. and Walker, S. (eds) *Schools, Teachers and Teaching*, Lewes, Falmer.

Woods, P. E. (1983) *Sociology and the School*, London, Routledge & Kegan Paul.

Yeandle, S. (1984) *Women's Working Lives*, London, Tavistock.

Index

Abrahamson, P. 6
absentee heads 160
academic/pastoral conflict 55−9,
    221−2, 263−4
academic subjects 174−7
accountability 249, 266
Acker, S. 73, 75, 77, 191, 197, 207
activists 22, 129, 150
administration 4−5, 101
advantage, patterns of 174−7
adversarial style of headship 87,
    104−8
age, of teachers 60−70
Albrow, M. 1
Alder School 151−6, 282
Althusser, L. 278
amalgamation 178−83
anarchic organization 12−13
'anticipated reactions' 128, 130
apathetics 22−3, 129
Apple, M. W. 15, 269, 279
appraisal schemes 135, 266
'arena' committees 245
arenas 19, 33, 38−9, 212, 221,
    243−4
Arfwedson, G. 256

Argyris, 189−90
Arnot, M. 71
Aronwitz, S. 280
art teachers 174−5
assessment 263, 269
attentives 22, 129, 150
Australia 256
Australian schools 72−3
authoritarian style of headship 87,
    109−16
authority 25, 180
autonomy of schools 249−50, 254
autonomy of teachers 121−3

Bacarach, P. 128
Bacarach, S.B. 54, 63
Baily, A.J. 31, 180, 181, 186
Baily, F.G. 216, 218, 220, 243−4,
    245
Baldridge, V.J. 11, 18, 20, 21−2,
    28, 68, 129, 150, 206, 208
Balibar, E. 278
Ball, S. J. 2, 12, 13, 15, 33, 36, 40,
    48, 54, 144, 168, 178, 183, 231,
    238, 244, 254
Banks, O. 82

Baratz, M. 128
Barker, R. 138
baronial politics 221–30
Barr-Greenfield, T. 2–3, 4–5
Beachside Comprehensive xi, 33, 40, 254, 258
Beck, R. 189, 200
Becker, H. 34, 66, 178
Bell, L. A. 7, 12, 13
Bennet, S. 15, 174, 175
Bennett, N. 260–1
Berlak, A. 157
Berlak, H. 157
Bernbaum, G. 80, 87–8
Berstein, B. 41, 63, 66, 237
Beynon, J. 15, 46–8, 122, 168, 182, 196
Bidwell, C. 6, 11
Bishop McGregor Comprehensive 9, 10, 56–7, 81, 149, 213–14, 282
Black Papers 248
black teachers 209–11
Bland, L. 197, 199
Blecher, M. J. 16, 24
Bloch, M. 89
Blumer, H. 19, 27, 83–4, 155
Boyd, W. L. 257, 258
Boyd-Barrett, O. 19
Braverman, H. 267
Briault, E. 185
Brown, R. 71
Buchan, L. 208
Bucher, R. 224, 227
bureaucracy 99, 101–3
Burgess, R.G. 2, 9, 56, 57, 66, 81, 82, 93, 149, 168, 177, 213, 216–17
Burke, J. 242, 259
Burns, T. 53
Byrne, E. 196, 205

Callahan, R. 6
Campbell, D. T. 41
career: author's concept of 167; and patterns of advantage 174–7; and structural uncertainties 177–8; and subjective/objective interface 186
career 'breaks' 193, 194
career interests 167
career paths 55–6
career strategies 168–7
careerism 166
Caren, M. 250–2, 253, 258
Carey, Henry 247
Carspecken, P. 251
case studies as data xi
Casterbridge High School xi, 48–54, 73–5, 144, 159, 161, 178, 183, 186, 202–3, 244, 282
caucuses 147–8
centralization 262
change: and conflict 18, 28, 78; and environment 38, 265; and group participation 30; and head teacher 78–9; and persuasion 114; 'planned' 30; in policy and practice 40; resistance to 30, 31; speed of 268–9; and survival 259–70; and women in schools 72–3, 78
change-agent 30, 31
charisma 95, 180
Charters, W. W. 257
Child, J. 45
China, Repulic of 24
Christie, R. 109, 111
Clarricoates, K. 198
'class politics' 258
classics 227–9
Clegg, S. 2, 247
'closure principle' 17, 140, 241
coalitions and conflict 54
'coercive collectivist' strategies 43, 48
Cohen, M. D. 12
Collins, R. 8, 18, 19
Columbia University's Teachers College 29
Commission for Racial Equality (CRE) 211
committees 243–8

commitment (integration) 120
communication channels 221
communication patterns 169
'community' 100–1
community expectations 257
comprehensive education:
commitment to 36–7; definitions
of 35, 57
comprehensive schools, and staff
from different traditions 42–3
computer studies 230
conflict: and change 18, 28, 78;
inter-generational 67; and
organizational theory 4; in
schools 17–26, 278
'conflict-avoidance ignorance' 22
conflict perspective, the 18
Connel, R. W. 72, 192, 279
consensus 11
consultation 125–7, 137
'continuance commitment' 62
'contrastive rhetoric' 241
control: and autonomy 122–3;
(domination) 120; and headship
82–3; ideologies of 279; and
intervention 265–8; and
meetings 241; strategies in
schools 8–11
control of information 153, 154
control of work 2
corporate management 24–5, 259
Corwin, R. G. 165
'cosmopolitan' 133
Countesthorpe College 250, 255,
258
Countesthorpe Moot 126
covenanting 258
Cowper, William 166
CPVE 230, 263, 264
Cressey, P. 267
Croxteth Comprehensive 251
Cunnison, S. 168, 199, 202, 204, 206
curriculum intervention 260, 265
'curriculum negotiation' 33
cuts in funding 134–5, 139,
260–70
Cyert, R.M. 12, 18, 19, 135, 213,
262

Dale, R. 249, 257
data: collection and use of by
author x–xiii; and theory 26–7
David, M. 71
Davies, B. 2, 6
Day, J. V. 215
Day, R. 215
decision-making: and autonomy
123; and change 30; and
consultation 137, 239;
ideological 13, 16; and
participation 124; as a political
process 26; and style of headship
92–3, 103, 104, 118–19
decision-making process 237
Deem, R. 191, 193
Delamont, S. 2, 197
Denscombe, M. 122
Department of Education and
Science (DES) 82, 102, 193, 260
departmental power 40–2
diffusion studies 29
discrimination, sexual 194–5
disciplinary perspective 35
discussion, and gender 77–8
dispute, notion of 270
dissensus, and school structure 11
'dominant coalition' 112, 113
domination 120, 278, 279
dress, and career 169
Drummond Middle School 252
Du Boulay, J. 218, 220
Dunkerley, D. 2, 247
Duverger, M. 28, 82
Dwyer, D. 151

Eagleton, T. 5
Education Act (1980) 25, 139
Edwards, A. 2
'egg-crate' conception of teaching
123
elementary school traditions 42–3
'élite' committees 245
Ellis, T. 252
empiricism 138
environment 248
Epstein, C. 195
Esland, G. 32, 222

ethnography 81
European studies 224—9
Evans, J. 2, 239
Everhart, R.B. 31
'Exit, Voice and Loyalty' 62—3, 68
extra-curricular activities 169

falling rolls 139, 178, 183—90, 260
Fayol, Henry 95
feminism, political nature of 75—6
feudalism 89, 170
Fleishman, E.A. 91
Fletcher, C. 250—2, 253, 258
Foley, M. 159
followership 116, 119
'formal' and 'informal' arenas 212, 221
Freemasonry 259
Freidson, E. 136
funding, see cuts in funding
Furlong, V. J. 2, 26

Gans, H. 125
GASing 169—70
gatekeepers 195
GCSE 263, 264, 268
Geis, F. 109, 111
gender, social identity of 71—2
'gender regime' 192
generation conflict 60—70
Gibbes, N. 210
Ginsburg, M. 259, 260, 274
Giroux, H. 280
Glen, F. 155
Gluckman, M. 217
goal diversity 11—17
Goffman, E. 39, 42, 85—7, 240, 251
Goodson, I. F. 176, 224—5, 226
gossip 216—19
Gouldner, A. 69, 71, 133, 146, 151, 153, 161
Grace, G. 141—2
grammer-school staff in comprehensives 42—54, 55, 178—81
Gramsci, A. 279
Gray, H. 22, 122

Green, A. 2, 14
Greenfield, W. D. 81
Green Hill Comprehensive School 69—70, 92, 93, 147, 148, 161, 162, 282
Greenwood, R. 262
Gretten, J. 252, 254
Griffin, C. 2
Gronn, P. 238, 240, 245
Gross, N. 196
group perspectives 34
Guest, R.H. 151

Habermas, J. 267
Hall, P.M. 104, 136, 144, 195
Hall, V. 80, 156, 157
Hanna, J. P. xi, 117, 118, 158, 163
Hannan, A. 4, 19, 20, 29, 36, 64, 78, 253, 255
Hargreaves, A. 39, 240, 241
Hargreaves, D. H. 2, 42—3, 54—5
Harris, K. 177, 204
Harris, T. A. 112
Hatton, E. J. 256
Havelock, R. G. 31
headship: case study of 117—19; and environment 164—5; and physical/personal involvement 160—4; and participation versus control 157—60; studies of 25, 80—1
heads of departments 233—7
headteacher(s): allies 107—8; and challenges 107—8; and conflict of loyalties 135; 'cosmopolitan' 161; as critical reality definers 171—2, 182; and innovation/ change 34, 78—9; leadership style of 83—117, 124—5, 272—3; 'local' 161; male/female styles 195, 196; new 146—7; number of women 200; as officials 22; and opposition 137—8; 'performance' of 85—7; power of 82, 85; relationships of with officials 258; role of as leader 120; role and self-conception of 9—10; role, conflicts in 156; as

'senior professional' 94; and staff promotion 171–4; staffroom grumbling about 185; subject background of 174–5
Hegen, R. L. 207
Henley, N. M. 197
Hewton, E. 260, 261, 262
hierarchic organizations 8–9
Hilsum, S. 174, 175, 192
Hindess, B. 25–6
Hirschmann, A. O. 62, 63, 68
HMI 82, 262
Holland, P. 255
House, E. 29, 30
Howell, D. 138
Hoyle, E. xiii, 4, 7, 18, 22, 193
Hughes, E. C. 167, 181, 186
humour 220–1
Hunter, C. 111, 112–13, 114, 185

idealist perspective 35
ideological interests: and career 167–8; and change 32, 36, 37, 180; defined 17; of women teachers 73
ideologies of control 279
ideology: and decision-making 13–17; use of term 281
ILEA 264
'incorporate collectivist' strategies 43, 48
'indulgency' 146, 153
industrial action 139, 270–8
industrial organizations 12
influence: definition of 22; departmental 231–7; in schools 131–4
Influence at School 260
'informal' arenas, see formal and informal arenas
'informality 88
initiatives 263, 264
'initiatory influences' 268
Inner City Comprehensive 117–19, 282
'innovation incoherence' 268
innovation processes, studies of 29–31

innovative schools 250–3
integration 120
'intensification' 269
interdisciplinarity 226
interests: and career 167; of teachers 16–18; and values 180
interpersonal politics 212
interpersonal style of headship 86, 87, 88–95
intervention 260–1
interview data xi

Jackson, M. 252
Jago, W. 112, 171, 174, 238, 241
Jefferson, G. 238
Johnson, T. 136
joint action 83–4, 86, 160
Jones, C. 196
Joseph, Sir Keith 265, 267

Kahn, A. 207
Kanter, R. M. 206–7, 215
Kelly, J. 78, 83
King, R. 1, 2, 4, 80, 82, 116
King's College London xi
Krekel, N. R. A. 178

Labour Party 138
Lacey, C. 2, 20, 28, 61, 69, 168, 178, 231
Lane, R. E. 17, 22, 140, 246
Langrish, S. V. 198
language of the opposition 143
language of patriarchy 192
Latin 228
Latus, E. 234
Lawler, E. J. 54, 63
leadership functions 83
leadership succession, case study 151–6
legitimation 180–1
Leicester Mercury, The 255
Levine, C. H. 253
Lewin, K. 30
licensed authority 82–6
licensed autonomy 249, 254, 257, 259
'linkage model' of innovation processes 31

Lipham, J. 144
Littler, C. 268
Llangarr Comprehensive 227—9
local education authority 258—60
local education authority officers
195
local government 24—5
'loose-coupling' 12, 15
Lorber, J. 170, 195
Lortie, D. 39, 123, 193
Lowfield Secondary Modern xi,
197
Lowri, T. J. 258
loyalty 143; *see also* 'Exit, Voice
and Loyalty'
Luckmann, T. 41
Lukes, S. 126
Lyons, G. 168—9, 170,
176

Macdonald, B. 32, 33, 38
McGiveney, J. H. 257
Machiavellianism 109, 116
MacInnes, J. 267
Mackay, H. 80, 136, 156, 157, 195
'macro-blindness' 23
male dominance, resistance to
202—4
male takeover of merged single-
sex schools 200—2
management, ideology of 267—8
management techniques 96, 138,
267
management theories 5, 6
management training courses 102
managerial style of headship 87,
95—103
Manpower Services Commission
(MSC) 268
March, J. G. 12, 18, 19, 135, 213,
262
'margin of tolerance' 257
Marland, M. 50, 149, 191
Marm, R. D. 77
married women teachers 198,
203—4
Marshall, J. 192, 195, 196, 199,
208, 215

Masters, K. 90, 146
Meadows, E. xi, 158, 159, 163,
171—2, 235
'meaning structures' 35
Measor, L. 169
meetings, politics of 237—43
membership-controlled
organizations 8—9
mergers 178, 181—2
meso-level, the 3, 23
Meyenn, R. 274
Meyer, J. W. 12
micro-political concepts 8
micro-politics, definitions of
18—19, 278
Miller, A. 25
Miller, H. 251, 259, 260, 274
Millrace Comprehensive 158, 159,
163, 171—4, 238, 282
Miskel, C. 151
Mitchell, P. 94
mixed-ability grouping,
introduction of 33—40, 47, 49,
52—3, 254
'mobilization of bias' 128
Montaigne, Michel de 28
Morgan, C. 80, 136, 156, 157, 195
Mort, Paul 29
Moynihan, W. 257
Murgatroyd, S. 122

Nailsea Comprehensive xi, 206,
223, 283
National Management Training
Centre 102
National Union of Teachers
(NUT) 71, 167, 195
'negative decision-making' 128
'negotiated oreer' 20
network, of social relations 212,
214—15
Newsom teachers 177
New York University 21
Nias, J. 37, 148, 180
Nicholls, A. 78
'non-decision making' 128
Norris, R. 255
Novarra, V. 199

NUT/EOC survey 193−4, 204, 281

Oak Farm Comprehensive 231
Oakeshott, M. 138
occupational cultures of teachers 43
Offe, C. 268
officials 21−2
'old guard' 69−70, 144
Olsen, J. P. 12, 18
'omissive action' 268
opposition 131, 134−48, 150
organization, definition of 2−3
'organizational science' 5, 8
organizational theory 1, 3−6, 18, 95, 279
organizations and individuals 189−90
Owens, M. 151

Paine, R. 218, 219
Paisey, A. 120
parents 251−2, 256, 276
Parsons, T. 4
participation 124−9
participation/control dilemma 157−60
part-time posts 203−4
pastoral and academic systems, conflict between 55−9, 221−2, 263−4
'pastoral curriculum' 263
pay dispute 261, 265, 270−8
'pedagogical harem' 192
perspective, defined 34−5
Peters, D. A. 91
Peterson, P. E. 258
Peterson, W. A. 63, 65, 66, 69
Pettigrew, A. M. 261
Pfeffer, J. 18
Phoenix Comprehensive xi, 44−6, 147, 178, 283
Plato 149
Pocock, J. G. A. 241
political affiliations 141−2
political behaviour 20−3
political efficacy 130
political motivation 142−3

political style of headship 87, 104−17
power: Duverger's definition of 28−9, 82; interactional and institutional 240; use of concept by author 25−6, 85
Pratt, S. 136, 141
Price, R. xi, 151, 160, 164
primary-schools data xii
primary schools 192, 271
Pring, R. 258
'privatizing ignorance' 22
Professional Association of Teachers (PAT) 274
professional communities 8−9
professionalism 135−6, 142, 186, 274
'proletarianization' of teachers 134, 267
promotion 73, 148, 166, 173; see also career
Promotion and Careers in Teaching 175
Promotion and the Woman Teacher 167−8, 193
pseudo-participation 124−9
public/grammar school traditions 42−3
public relations 253−8

qualifications of teachers 48

race 209−11
radicalism in student teachers 66
Radnor, H. 101, 103, 204
Ramazanoglu, C. 196
recruitment, and authoritarianism 114−15
redeployment 183−90
Redmond College 36, 64, 253, 255, 283
redundancy 186, 190
regulated autonomy 249, 259
Reid, M. 33
relative autonomy 247, 249
research, development and diffusion model of innovation (RD&D) 30

Reskin, B. F. 171, 215
restructuring of teaching 177–8
Reynolds, D. 43
rhetoric 33, 263
Richardson, E. xi, 4, 148, 206, 207, 216, 223–4
Rillie, I. 160–1
Riseborough, G. xi, 44–6, 147, 168, 171, 172, 174, 178, 203
Risinghill 250, 251
Riverton School 256–7
Rogers, E. M. 29
Rogers, R. 181, 200
role specialization 167
rolls, falling 139, 178, 183–90, 260
Roosevelt, Theodore 80
Rowan, B. 12
Roy, W. 166
rumour 219–20
'ruptural unity' 278

Sacks, H. 238
Sageton Comprehensive 239
St. John Brooks 232
Salaman, G. 2, 4, 102, 268
'Salieri phenomenon' 170
Saunders, P. 27, 128, 129, 130, 137
scale posts in primary and secondary schools by gender 193 (table)
Schegloff, E. A. 238
Schein, E. H. 30
school democracy 280
school management 5
schooling: redifinition of 265; role and purpose of 248
schools as organizations 3–9
Schutz, A. 41
scientific management 6, 102
secondary-modern school staff in comprehensives 42–55, 178–9
secondary schools data xii
Seeman, P. 42
self-interest 16–17, 21, 32, 36, 73
senior management team 100–3, 133
sexism 196
sexual division of labour 192

sexual stereotyping 195, 205
Shakespeare, William 60
Shapiro, H. Svi 15
Sharp, R. 2, 14, 23
Sharpe, S. 199
Shibutani, T. 219
Shoemaker, F. F. 29
Sikes, P. 61, 169
Silverman, D. 2, 5, 11, 28, 38
Simmel, G. 72
Simpson, I. H. 192
Simpson, R. L. 192
single-sex schools 200
sixth form appointments 181
small-group studies 30
Smetheram, D. 222
Smith, D. E. 73, 77, 78, 206, 208
Smith, F. 185
Smith, T. J. 116
social actors 26–7
'social dramas' 149, 150, 151
social psychology 30
sociology of education 1–2, 3
Spender, D. 77
sponsorship 170
stability 120
staff meetings 150, 238–43
staffroom, the 213–16
Start, K. R. 174, 175, 192
Statistics in Education 193
status quo 113–14, 144–5
strategic maintenance 50
Strauss, A. 10, 20, 66, 224, 227
Stray, C. 227–9
Strodbeck, F. L. 77
structural factors in social dynamics of institutions 23–4
'structural looseness' 11
Stubbs, M. 238
styles of headship 87–117
subject departments 222–30
subject hierarchy 42
subject specialization 41
subject status 230, 264
subject subcultures 41
subjects: and career opportunities 174–6; and gender as social arenas 76–7

sub-text 50
Sugarman, B. 4
Sullivan, M. 43
Summerhill 250, 251
Sussex University xi
Sutton Centre 250
Swann Report 211
Sweden 256
Swidler, A. 239
'symbolic bedazzlement' 130
systems analysis 3—4
systems theory 1, 25

Taafe, R. 127, 143, 158
talk: in decision-making 124;
    informal 214—15; male-
    dominated 20; political 237; in
    staff meetings 238, 240—1; and
    styles of headship 94, 104—6,
    110
Tarn, J. 162
Taylor, Frederick 'Speedy' 6, 95,
    101
'teacher appraisal' 135
teaching ideology 14
theory and data 26—7
Thompson, K. 4
trade-offs 32—3
Trask, A. E. 196
Turner, C. M. 4
Turner, G. 2
Turner, V. W. 149
TVEI 230, 263, 268
Twain, Mark 120
'two-person careers' 197—8
Tyack, D. 192

unemployment, effects of 263
unions 140, 186, 270—1, 274—5
United States: college
    administration in 206;
    organizational research in 6, 151
university organization 11

Van der Woerd, T. G. 178
vested interests: of activists 22;
    and change 32, 37; of teachers
    16—17; of women teachers 73—4

Victoria Road Comprehensive
    46—8, 182, 283
Voice, see 'Exit, Voice and
    Loyalty'

Wagstaff, C. 69, 70, 89, 90, 94,
    147, 148, 160, 162
Wallace, G. 186, 259, 260
Walker, R. 32, 33, 38
Watts, J. 126
Weber, M. 92, 95, 99, 101—3, 110
Weick, K. 12
West, C. 77
West Indian teachers 209—10
White, G. 16, 24
Whiteside, T. 170
Whitty, G. 279
Whyld, J. 196
Wildavsky, A. 221
Wildcat Strike 153
William Tyndale School 251—2,
    245—5, 256, 258
Williams, W. 250—2, 253, 258
Willis, P. 202
Wilkie, R. 15
Wilson, B. 4
Winkley, D. 162, 164
Wolcott, H. F. 79, 81, 88, 93, 159,
    160, 170
Wolin, S. 138
Women: and career in teaching
    192—3: experiences of as
    teachers 70—8, as a minority
    206—7; and policy-making
    205—6; and promotion 73,
    170—3; visibility of 207; 'who
    make it' 204—9
Woods, P. E. xi, 2, 15, 20, 23, 62,
    67—8, 162, 169, 197, 213, 220
work, control of 2
work group, sociological study of
    3
workloads 269
Wouterse, J. J. 178

Yeandle, S. 199

'zone of tolerance' 257